Syed Jaffer Hussain
Rm 3003 Conger

EECS Department
University of Michigan

 **MOTOROLA**

MC68000

16-BIT MICROPROCESSOR
User's Manual

" Was a required text for EECS 270 which
I first TAed in Winter 86 ".

MOTOROLA

MC68000

16-BIT MICROPROCESSOR
User's Manual

Third Edition

PRENTICE-HALL, Inc., Englewood Cliffs, N.J. 07632

Library of Congress Catalog Number 81-85502
ISBN 0-13-566695-3 (pbk.)
ISBN 0-13-566703-8 (case)
ISBN 0-13-566737-2 (limited ed.)
ISBN 0-13-566760-7 (special ed.)

Editorial/production supervision: Karen Skrable
Manufacturing buyer: Gordon Osbourne

This manual does not define a specific assembly programming language. The language and notation used within this manual is a register transfer language explained in Appendix B.

Printed in the United States of America

10   9   8   7   6   5

ISBN 0-13-566695-3 {PBK.}
ISBN 0-13-566703-8 {CASE}
ISBN 0-13-566737-2 {LIMITED ED.}
ISBN 0-13-566760-7 {SPECIAL ED.}

Prentice-Hall International, Inc., London
Prentice-Hall of Australia Pty. Limited, Sydney
Prentice-Hall of Canada, Ltd., Toronto
Prentice-Hall of India Private Limited, New Delhi
Prentice-Hall of Japan, Inc., Tokyo
Prentice-Hall of Southeast Asia Pte. Ltd., Singapore
Whitehall Books Limited, Wellington, New Zealand

TABLE OF CONTENTS

v

TABLE OF CONTENTS
(Continued)

TABLE OF CONTENTS
(Continued)

Section 5
Exception Processing

Section 6
Interface with M6800 Peripherals

Appendix A
Condition Codes Computation

TABLE OF CONTENTS
(Continued)

TABLE OF CONTENTS
(Continued)

TABLE OF CONTENTS
(Continued)

LIST OF ILLUSTRATIONS

LIST OF ILLUSTRATIONS
(Continued)

LIST OF TABLES

LIST OF TABLES
(Continued)

PREFACE

With the advent of 16-bit microprocessor technology, thorough, concise, and useful manuals must be provided to aid designers in development of their systems. This manual gives all the key information for design engineers, software architects, and computer designers to complete software systems using Motorola's M68000 Family of Microprocessors.

To facilitate design and for the fullest understanding, each instruction is described in detail in bit pattern format. Explicit examples are then shown to more thoroughly demonstrate how each instruction will operate.

This definitive information will allow the easiest and best designing possible. Additionally, the software in this manual will be upward compatible with all future M68000 family processors.

MC68000

16-BIT MICROPROCESSOR
User's Manual

SECTION 1
GENERAL DESCRIPTION

1.1 INTRODUCTION

This section contains a general description of the MC68000 Microprocessor.

1.2 OVERVIEW

Advances in semiconductor technology have provided the capability to place on a single silicon chip a microprocessor at least an order of magnitude higher in performance and circuit complexity than has been previously available. The MC68000 is the first of a family of such VLSI microprocessors from Motorola. It combines state-of-the-art technology and advanced circuit design techniques with computer sciences to achieve an architecturally advanced 16-bit microprocessor. The high density of active elements coupled with an order of magnitude increase in performance over the original MC6800 is the direct result of significant advances in semiconductor technology. Advances such as dry plasma etching, projection printing, and HMOS (high-density, short-channel MOS) circuit design techniques, shown in Figure 1-1, have provided a sound technological base that has allowed Motorola's system engineers, computer scientists, and marketing engineers a large degree of innovative freedom. The goals of applying this innovative freedom to microprocessors are to make the microprocessor easy to use, more reliable and more flexible for applications, while maximizing performance.

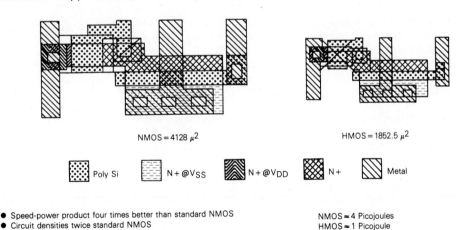

NMOS = 4128 μ^2 HMOS = 1852.5 μ^2

Poly Si	N+@V_{SS}	N+@V_{DD}	N+	Metal

- Speed-power product four times better than standard NMOS
- Circuit densities twice standard NMOS

NMOS ≈ 4 Picojoules
HMOS ≈ 1 Picojoule

Figure 1-1. HMOS Circuit Design Techniques

1

The resources available to the MC68000 user consist of the following:
- 32-Bit Data and Address Registers
- 16 Megabyte Direct Addressing Range
- 56 Powerful Instruction Types
- Operations on Five Main Data Types
- Memory Mapped I/O
- 14 Addressing Modes

Particular emphasis has been given to the architecture to make it regular with respect to the registers, instructions (including all addressing modes), and data types. A consistent structure makes the architecture easy to learn and program, and, in the process, reduces both the time required to write programs and the space required to store programs. The net result is a great reduction in the cost and risk of developing software.

High system throughput (up to an aggregate of two million instruction and data word transfers per second) is achieved even with readily available standard product memories with comparatively slow access times. The design flexibility of the data bus allows the mixing of slow and fast memories or peripherals, with the processor automatically optimizing the transfer rate on every access to keep the system operating at peak efficiency.

The hardware design of the CPU was heavily influenced by advances made in software technology. High-level language compilers as well as code produced from high-level languages must run efficiently on the new generation 16-bit and 32-bit microprocessors. The MC68000 supports high-level languages with its consistent architecture, multiple registers and stacks, large addressing range and high-level language oriented instructions (LINK, UNLK, CHK, etc.). Also, operating systems for controlling the software operating environment of the MC68000 are supported by privileged instructions, memory management, a powerful vectored multi-level interrupt and trap structure, and specific instructions (MOVEP, MOVEM, TRAP, etc.).

The processor also provides both hardware and software interlocks for multiprocessor systems. The MC68000 contains bus arbitration logic for a shared bus and shared memory environment (shared with other MC68000 processors, DMA devices, etc.). Multiprocessor systems are also supported with software instructions (TAS — test-and-set operand). The MC68000 offers the maximum flexibility for microprocessor-based multiprocessor systems.

Advanced architecture processors must not only offer efficient solutions to large complex problems but must be able to handle the small, simple problems with proportional efficiency. The MC68000 has been designed to offer the maximum in performance and versatility to solve simple and complex problems efficiently.

As shown in Figure 1-2, the MC68000 offers seventeen 32-bit registers in addition to the 32-bit program counter and 16-bit status register. The first eight registers (D0-D7) are used as data registers for byte (8-bit), word (16-bit), and long word (32-bit) data operations. The second set of seven registers (A0-A6) and the two system stack pointers (A7) may be used as software stack pointers and base address registers. In addition, these registers may be used for word and long word address operations. All of the seventeen registers may be used as index registers.

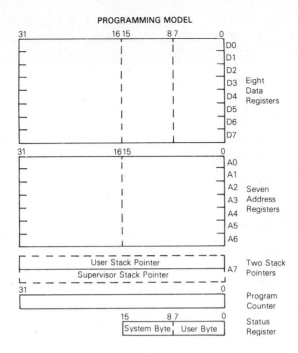

Figure 1-2. Programming Model

The 24-bit address bus provides a memory addressing range of more than 16 megabytes (actually 16,777,216 bytes). This large range of addressing capability, coupled with a memory management unit, allows large, modular programs to be developed and operated without resorting to cumbersome and time consuming software bookkeeping and paging techniques.

The status register, shown in Figure 1-3, contains the interrupt mask (8 levels available) as well as the condition codes: overflow (V), zero (Z), negative (N), carry (C), and extend (X). Additional status bits indicate that the processor is in a trace (T) mode and/or in a supervisor (S) state. Ample space remains in the status register for future extensions of the MC68000 family.

Five basic data types are supported. These data types are:
- Bits
- BCD Digits (4 Bits)
- Bytes (8 Bits)
- Words (16 Bits)
- Long Words (32 Bits)

In addition, operations on other data types such as memory addresses, status word data, etc. are provided for in the instruction set.

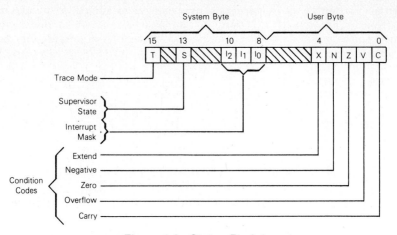

Figure 1-3. Status Register

The 14 flexible addressing modes, shown in Table 1-1, include six basic types:
- Register Direct
- Register Indirect
- Absolute
- Immediate
- Program Counter Relative
- Implied

Included in the register indirect addressing modes is the capability to do post-incrementing, predecrementing, offsetting, and indexing. Program counter relative mode can also be modified via indexing and offsetting.

Table 1-1. Data Addressing Modes

Mode	Generation
Register Direct Addressing	
Data Register Direct	EA = Dn
Address Register Direct	EA = An
Absolute Data Addressing	
Absolute Short	EA = (Next Word)
Absolute Long	EA = (Next Two Words)
Program Counter Relative Addressing	
Relative with Offset	EA = (PC) + d_{16}
Relative with Index and Offset	EA = (PC) + (Xn) + d_8
Register Indirect Addressing	
Register Indirect	EA = (An)
Postincrement Register Indirect	EA = (An), An $\leftarrow$ An + N
Predecrement Register Indirect	An $\leftarrow$ An − N, EA = (An)
Register Indirect with Offset	EA = (An) + d_{16}
Indexed Register Indirect with Offset	EA = (An) + (Xn) + d_8
Immediate Data Addressing	
Immediate	DATA = Next Word(s)
Quick Immediate	Inherent Data
Implied Addressing	
Implied Register	EA = SR, USP, SP, PC

NOTES:
EA = Effective Address
An = Address Register
Dn = Data Register
Xn = Address or Data Register used as Index Register
SR = Status Register
PC = Program Counter
d_8 = 8-bit Offset (displacement)
d_{16} = 16-bit Offset (displacement)
N = 1 for Byte, 2 for Words, and 4 for Long Words.
   If An is the stack pointer and the operand size is byte, N = 2 to keep the stack pointer on a word boundary.
( ) = Contents of
$\leftarrow$ = Replaces

4

The MC68000 instruction set is shown in Table 1-2. Some additional instructions are variations or subsets of these and they appear in Table 1-3. Special emphasis has been given to the instruction set's support of structured high-level languages to facilitate ease of programming. Each instruction, with few exceptions, operates on bytes, words, and long words and most instructions can use any of the 14 addressing modes. Combining instruction types, data types, and addressing modes, over 1000 useful instructions are provided. These instructions include signed and unsigned multiply and divide, "quick" arithmetic operations, BCD arithmetic, and expanded operations (through traps). Additionally, its high-symmetric, proprietary microcoded structure provides a sound, flexible base for the future.

1.3 SOFTWARE DEVELOPMENT

Many innovative features have been incorporated to make programming easier, faster, and more reliable.

1.3.1 CONSISTENT STRUCTURE. The highly regular structure of the MC68000 greatly simplifies the effort required to write programs in assembly language as well as high-level languages. Operations on integer data in registers and memory are independent of the data. Separate special instructions that operate on byte (8 bit), word (16 bit), and long word (32 bit) integers are not necessary. The programmer need only remember one mnemonic for each type of operation and then specify data size, source addressing mode, and destination addressing mode. This has helped keep the total number of instructions small.

The dual operand nature of many of the instructions significantly increases the flexibility and power of the MC68000. Consistency is again maintained since all data registers and memory locations may be either a source or destination for most operations on integer data.

The addressing modes have been kept simple without sacrificing efficiency. All fourteen addressing modes operate consistently and are independent of the instruction operation itself. Additionally, all address registers may be used for the direct, register indirect, and indexed addressing modes (immediate, program counter relative, and absolute addressing by definition do not use address registers). For increased flexiblity, any address or data register may be used as an index register. Address register consistency is maintained for stacking operations since any of the eight address registers may be utilized as user program stack pointers with the register indirect postincrement/predecrement addressing modes. Address register A7, however, is a special register that, in addition to its normal addressing capability, functions as the system stack pointer for stacking the program counter for subroutine calls as well as stacking the program counter and status register for traps and interrupts (while in the supervisor state).

1.3.2 STRUCTURED MODULAR PROGRAMMING. The art of programming microprocessors has evolved rapidly in the past few years. Numerous advanced techniques have been developed to allow easier, more consistent and reliable generation of software. In general, these techniques require that the programmer be more disciplined in observing a defined programming structure such as modular programming. Modular

Table 1-2. Instruction Set

Mnemonic	Description
ABCD	Add Decimal with Extend
ADD	Add
AND	Logical And
ASL	Arithmetic Shift Left
ASR	Arithmetic Shift Right
Bcc	Branch Conditionally
BCHG	Bit Test and Change
BCLR	Bit Test and Clear
BRA	Branch Always
BSET	Bit Test and Set
BSR	Branch to Subroutine
BTST	Bit Test
CHK	Check Register Against Bounds
CLR	Clear Operand
CMP	Compare
DBcc	Test Condition, Decrement and Branch
DIVS	Signed Divide
DIVU	Unsigned Divide
EOR	Exclusive Or
EXG	Exchange Registers
EXT	Sign Extend
JMP	Jump
JSR	Jump to Subroutine
LEA	Load Effective Address
LINK	Link Stack
LSL	Logical Shift Left
LSR	Logical Shift Right
MOVE	Move
MOVEM	Move Multiple Registers
MOVEP	Move Peripheral Data
MULS	Signed Multiply
MULU	Unsigned Multiply
NBCD	Negate Decimal with Extend
NEG	Negate
NOP	No Operation
NO	Ones Complement
OR	Logical Or
PEA	Push Effective Address
RESET	Reset External Devices
ROL	Rotate Left without Extend
ROR	Rotate Right without Extend
ROXL	Rotate Left with Extend
ROXR	Rotate Right with Extend
RTE	Return from Exception
RTR	Return and Restore
RTS	Return from Subroutine
SBCD	Subtract Decimal with Extend
Scc	Set Conditional
STOP	Stop
SUB	Subtract
SWAP	Swap Data Register Halves
TAS	Test and Set Operand
TRAP	Trap
TRAPV	Trap on Overflow
TST	Test
UNLK	Unlink

Table 1-3. Variations of Instruction Types

Instruction Type	Variation	Description
ADD	ADD ADDA ADDQ ADDI ADDX	Add Add Address Add Quick Add Immediate Add with Extend
AND	AND ANDI ANDI to CCR ANDI to SR	Logical AND AND Immediate AND Immediate to Condition Code AND Immediate to Status Register
CMP	CMP CMPA CMPM CMPI	Compare Compare Address Compare Memory Compare Immediate
EOR	EOR EORI EORI to CCR EORI to SR	Exclusive OR Exclusive OR Immediate Exclusive Immediate to Condition Codes Exclusive OR Immediate to Status Register
MOVE	MOVE MOVEA MOVEQ MOVE to CCR MOVE to SR MOVE from SR MOVE to USP	Move Move Address Move Quick Move to Condition Codes Move to Status Register Move from Status Register Move to User Stack Pointer
NEG	NEG NEGX	Negate Negate with Extend
OR	OR ORI ORI to CCR ORI to SR	Logical OR OR Immediate OR Immediate to Condition Codes OR Immediate to Status Register
SUB	SUB SUBA SUBI SUBQ SUBX	Subtract Subtract Address Subtract Immediate Subtract Quick Subtract with Extend

programming allows a required function or process to be broken down in short modules or subroutines that are concisely defined and easily programmed and tested. Such a technique is greatly simplified by the availability of advanced structured assemblers and block structured high-level languages such as Pascal. Such concepts are virtually useless, however, unless parameters are easily transferred between and within software modules that operate on a reentrant and recursive basis. (To be reentrant a routine must be usable by interrupt and non-interrupt driven programs without the loss of data. A recursive routine is one that may call or use itself.) The MC68000 provides the necessary architectural features to allow efficient reentrant modular programming. The LINK and UNLK instructions reduce subroutine call overhead in two complementary instructions by allowing the manipulation of linked lists of data areas on the stack. The MOVEM (Move Multiple Registers) instruction also reduces subroutine call programming overhead. This allows moving, via an effective address, multiple registers that are specified by the programmer. Sixteen software trap vectors are provided with the TRAP instruction and are useful in operating system call routines or user generated macro routines. Other instructions that support modern structured programming techniques are PEA (Push Effective Address), LEA (Load Effective Address), RTR (Return and Restore), RTE (Return from Exception) as well as JSR, BSR, and RTS.

The powerful vectored priority interrupt structure of the microprocessor allows straight-forward generation of reentrant modular input/output routines. Seven maskable levels of priority with 192 vector locations and seven autovector locations provide maximum flexibility for I/O control (a total of 255 vector locations are available for interrupts, hardware traps, and software traps).

1.3.3 IMPROVED SOFTWARE TESTABILITY. The MC68000 incorporates several features that reduce the chance for errors. Some of these features, such as consistent architecture and the structured modular programming capability, have already been discussed.

Of major importance to the systems programmer are features that have been incorporated specifically to detect the occurrence of programming errors or bugs. Several hardware traps, provided to indicate abnormal internal conditions, detect the following error conditions:
- Word Access with an Odd Address
- Illegal Instructions
- Unimplemented Instructions
- Illegal Memory Access (Bus Error)
- Divide by Zero
- Overflow Condition Code (Separate Instruction TRAPV)
- Register Out of Bounds (CHK Instruction)
- Spurious Interrupt

Additionally, the sixteen software TRAP instructions may be utilized by the programmer to provide applications oriented error detection or correction routines.

An additional error detection tool is the CHK (Check Register Against Bounds) instruction used for array bound checking by verifying that a data register contains a valid subscript. A trap occurs if the register contents are negative or greater than a limit.

Finally, the MC68000 includes a facility that allows instruction-by-instruction tracing of a program being debugged. This trace mode results in a trap being made to a tracing routine after each instruction executed. The trace mode is available to the programmer when the microprocessor is in the supervisor state as well as the user state but may only be entered while in the supervisor state. The supervisor/user states provide an additional degree of error protection for the microprocessor by allowing memory protection of selected areas of memory when an external memory management device is used.

1.3.4 FUTURE FLEXIBILITY. Microprocessor VLSI circuit technology is advancing at an ever increasing rate. For example, the Motorola MC6800 — originally introduced in 1974 — has evolved into a number of mode advanced products. This evolution has been along two paths, as shown in Figure 1-4: increased functionality, with the MC6802 and MC6801 microcomputers, and increased performance with the MC68A00, MC68B00, and MC6809 microprocessors. The sound, well planned, architectural base provided by the original MC6800 made it possible to develop these improved products while taking full advantage of the major speed and density enhancements to NMOS VLSI. This was accomplished while maintaining an unprecedented degree of compatibility and consistency with the original MC6800 microprocessor.

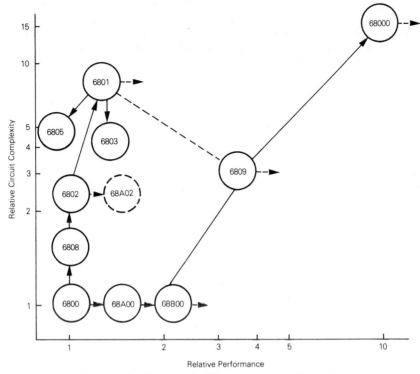

Figure 1-4. Motorola's Microprocessor Evolution

Similarly, a major consideration in the development of the MC68000 microprocessor has been to provide a good, solid, but flexible, base for future extendability. Several architectural concepts have been incorporated that will allow this advanced product to be enhanced as semiconductor technological advances are made. For example, the highly consistent structure of the processor allows operation on 8-bit, 16-bit, and 32-bit integers without the need for concatenation of registers or multiplexing of internal data buses. This regular structure of the processor lends itself to a more consistent, reliable design that can be easily expanded.

The MC68000 incorporates a proprietary multi-level microprogrammed structure that allows significant versatility in the implementation of instructions. In fact, more than one-eighth of the instruction op-code map has been set aside specifically for implementation of future instructions. In the interim, user implementation of instructions not currently in the instruction set is possible through the use of the trap instruction and the emulator traps.

1.3.5 MEMORY MANAGEMENT OF LARGE ADDRESSING SPACE. The ever decreasing costs of semiconductor memories in combination with the use of high-level languages and sophisticated disk operating systems allow Motorola's new generation of high performance microprocessors to be used in complex, memory intensive applications. In order to meet the needs of such applications, the MC68000 is capable of directly addressing more than 16 megabytes of memory. This large address space is directly accessed and managed very efficiently on a word or byte basis since operand size is specified by the instruction. The use of upper data strobe ($\overline{\text{UDS}}$) and lower data strobe ($\overline{\text{LDS}}$) signals allows easy access to high order bytes, low order bytes, or words.

Several additional useful features are provided that allow the programmer to efficiently manage memory usage. Powerful memory addressing modes such as register indirect, indexed, short and long absolute, and program counter relative allow well-ordered access to specific memory locations. These addressing modes allow easy address calculations (register indirect and indexed), direct access to memory location (short and long absolute), and position-independent or relocatable coding (program counter relative). Of course, the predecrement/postincrement register indirect addressing modes also allow efficient management of data in memory by permitting the programmer to generate as many as eight concurrent stacks or queues. Another feature that allows the programmer to manage the use of memory is the CHK (Check Register Against Bounds) instruction. This instruction permits the software implementation of a basic memory protection/management structure.

Still another significant feature provided in the MC68000 is the distinction between user and supervisor state. The supervisor state permits certain protected operations within the processor system. Of particular interest is that an external memory management unit may be used when the processor is in the user state to manage the large address space for the programmer. The memory management operations are transparent to the programmer when in the user state and can be changed or updated only in the supervisor state. The memory management unit provides both management of a variable number of variable size segments (memory segmentation) and dynamic management of multi-task memory relocation and protection. The memory management unit regulates access to storage segments that are dedicated to read only data, read/write data, program code, and protected data/code.

1.3.6 IMPROVED CODE DENSITY AND SPEED. With the advent of low cost, very high density VLSI RAMs and ROMs, it might incorrectly be assumed that the number of bytes of code needed to execute a given program is no longer important. Code density, however, is very critical, since microprocessor speed is highly dependent upon the number of executed instruction words. During the early development of the M68000, extensive studies were made of the use of instructions and sequences of instructions in many microprocessor applications. These studies identified not only statically frequent instructions but also dynamically frequent instructions. (The dynamic frequency of instructions is a measure of how often an instruction is executed while static frequency is a measure of how often it occurs in a program listing or is encountered by an assembler.) The result of these studies is that the major contributer to the increased efficiency is the highly regular structure of the architecture. The consistency of the architecture, instruction set, and addressing modes significantly reduces the number of instructions needed to accomplish a given task. Additionally, many instructions have been included to specifically improve code density and speed. For example, single word add and subtract instructions using quick immediate addressing allow fast, small value arithmetic operations on data registers and memory. A move quick (MOVEQ) provides the ability to load a small (8 bit) signed word into any register in a single word operation. In order to improve the speed of loop operations, a single instruction for test condition, decrement, and branch (DBcc) is included. Of course, the TRAP, move multiple registers (MOVEM), link stack (LINK), unlink stack (UNLK), and check limit (CHK) instructions significantly reduce code requirements for subroutines, operating system calls, and stacking operations.

Other instructions that help reduce coding requirements and improve performance of arithmetic operations are signed and unsigned multiply (MULS and MULU), signed and unsigned divide (DIVS and DIVU), BCD arithmetic (ABCD, SBCD), as well as the standard binary integer operations. In order to improve the efficiency of moving or transferring data, a powerful MOVE data instruction has been incorporated that allows the transfer of bytes, words and long words, and operates in all data addressing modes. Thus, register-to-register, register-to-memory, memory-to-register, and memory-to-memory transfers are permitted.

In addition to the powerful instructions that provide a substantial improvement in processor throughput, numerous architectural features significantly reduce the execution times for all instructions. The separate (non-multiplexed) address and data buses, instruction pre-fetch pipeline, and 32-bit internal registers are major contributors to the processor's unequaled performance.

1.3.7 SOFTWARE SUPPORT AND MC6800 COMPATIBILITY. The system designers and programmers using the MC68000 in an application have available a complete, compatible system of hardware and software. The microprocessor is supported by a full range of software development tools including disk operating systems, debug aids, assemblers, and high-level languages.

The careful planning of this new microprocessor provides a superset of the MC6800 instruction set enhanced by the addition of more and larger registers, powerful consistent structure and many flexible addressing modes. This allows efficient translation of existing MC6800 programs, which can then be further optimized by taking full advantage of the versatile and powerful features of the MC68000.

This careful planning of similarities between the MC68000 and the MC6800 does not stop at software compatibility (by translation) but also extends to peripheral controller interfacing. Motorola's extensive line of intelligent M6800 family peripherals (including MC6854 Advanced Data Link Controller and the MC68488 General Purpose Interface Adapter) can be directly and easily interfaced to the MC68000. Three signal lines: enable (E), valid memory address ($\overline{VMA}$), and valid peripheral address ($\overline{VPA}$) are provided to simplify the interface to Motorola's standard MC6800 peripherals.

SECTION 2
DATA ORGANIZATION AND
ADDRESSING CAPABILITIES

2.1 INTRODUCTION

This section describes the data organization and addressing capabilities of the MC68000.

2.2 OPERAND SIZE

Operand sizes are defined as follows: a byte equals 8 bits, a word equals 16 bits, and a long word equals 32 bits. The operand size for each instruction is either explicitly encoded in the instruction or implicitly defined by the instruction operation. All explicit instructions support byte, word, or long word operands. Implicit instructions support some subset of all three sizes.

2.3 DATA ORGANIZATION IN REGISTERS

The eight data registers support data operands of 1, 8, 16, or 32 bits. The seven address registers together with the active stack pointer support address operands of 32 bits.

2.3.1 DATA REGISTERS. Each data register is 32 bits wide. Byte operands occupy the low order 8 bits, word operands the low order 16 bits, and long word operands the entire 32 bits. The least significant bit is addressed as bit zero; the most significant bit is addressed as bit 31.

When a data register is used as either a source or destination operand, only the appropriate low order portion is changed; the remaining high-order portion is neither used nor changed.

2.3.2 ADDRESS REGISTERS. Each address register and the stack pointer is 32 bits wide and holds a full 32 bit address. Address registers do not support byte sized operands. Therefore, when an address register is used as a source operand, either the low order word or the entire long word operand is used depending upon the operation size. When an address register is used as the destination operand, the entire register is affected regardless of the operation size. If the operation size is word, any other operands are sign extended to 32 bits before the operation is performed.

13

2.4 DATA ORGANIZATION IN MEMORY

Bytes are individually addressable with the high order byte having an even address the same as the word as shown in Figure 2-1. The low order byte has an odd address that is one count higher than the word address. Instructions and multibyte data are accessed only on word (even byte) boundaries. If a long word datum is located at address n (n even), then the second word of that datum is located at address n + 2.

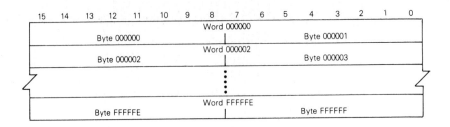

Figure 2-1. Word Organization In Memory

The data types supported by the MC68000 are: bit data, integer data of 8, 16, and 32 bits, 32-bit addresses, and binary coded decimal data. Each of these data types is put in memory as shown in Figure 2-2. The numbers indicate the order in which the data would be accessed from the processor.

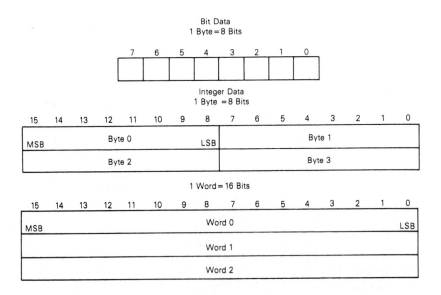

Figure 2-2. Data Organization In Memory (Sheet 1 of 2)

14

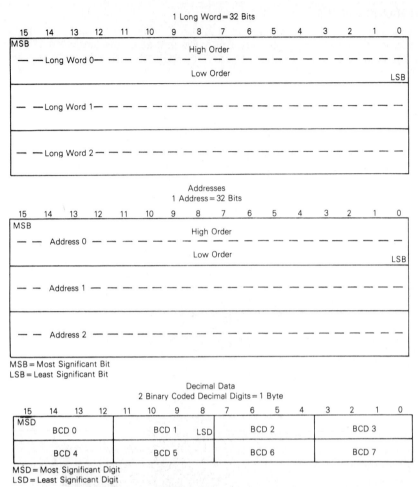

MSB = Most Significant Bit
LSB = Least Significant Bit

MSD = Most Significant Digit
LSD = Least Significant Digit

Figure 2-2. Data Organization In Memory (Sheet 2 of 2)

2.5 ADDRESSING

Instructions for the MC68000 contain two kinds of information: the type of function to be performed, and the location of the operand(s) on which to perform that function. The methods used to locate (address) the operand(s) are explained in the following paragraphs.

Instructions specify an operand location in one of three ways:
- Register Specification — the number of the register is given in the register field of the instruction.
- Effective Address — use of the different effective address modes.
- Implicit Reference — the definition of certain instructions implies the use of specific registers.

2.6 INSTRUCTION FORMAT

Instructions are from one to five words in length as shown in Figure 2-3. The length of the instruction and the operation to be performed is specified by the first word of the instruction which is called the operation word. The remaining words further specify the operands. These words are either immediate operands or extensions to the effective address mode specified in the operation word.

15	14	13	12	11	10	9	8	7	6	5	4	3	2	1	0
Operation Word (First Word Specifies Operation and Modes)															
Immediate Operand (If Any, One or Two Words)															
Source Effective Address Extension (If Any, One or Two Words)															
Destination Effective Address Extension (If Any, One or Two Words)															

Figure 2-3. Instruction Format

2.7 PROGRAM/DATA REFERENCES

The MC68000 separates memory references into two classes: program references and data references. Program references, as the name implies, are references to that section of memory that contains the program being executed. Data references refer to that section of memory that contains data. Generally, operand reads are from the data space. All operand writes are to the data space.

2.8 REGISTER NOTATION

Appendix B contains a definition of the register transfer language (RTL) used in describing instruction operations. The RTL description of registers identifies the registers as follows:

AN — Address Register (n specifies the register number)
Dn — Data Register (n specifies the register number)
Rn — Any Register, Address or Data (n specifies the register number)
PC — Program Counter
SR — Status Register
CCR — Condition Code Half of the Status Register
SP — The Active Stack Pointer (either user or supervisor)
USP — User Stack Pointer
SSP — Supervisor Stack Pointer
d — Displacement Value
N — Operand Size in Bytes (1, 2, 4)

2.9 ADDRESS REGISTER INDIRECT NOTATION

When an address register is used to point to a memory location, the addressing mode is called address register indirect. The term indirect is used because the operation of the instruction is not directed to the address register itself, but to the memory location pointed to by the address register. The RTL symbol for the indirect mode is an address register designation followed by an "at" symbol (@). The notation A4@ indicates that the content of address register four points to the memory location that will be used as the operand.

2.10 REGISTER SPECIFICATION

The register field within an instruction specifies the register to be used. Other fields within the instruction specify whether the register selected is an address or data register and how the register is to be used.

2.11 EFFECTIVE ADDRESS

Most instructions specify the location of an operand by using the effective address field in the operation word. For example, Figure 2-4 shows the general format of the single effective address instruction operation word. The effective address is composed of two 3-bit fields: the mode field, and the register field. The value in the mode field selects the different address modes. The register field contains the number of a register.

The effective address field may require additional information to fully specify the operand. This additional information, called the effective address extension, is contained in a following word or words and is considered part of the instruction as shown in Figure 2-3. The effective address modes are grouped into three categories: register direct, memory addressing, and special.

15	14	13	12	11	10	9	8	7	6	5	4	3	2	1	0
										\multicolumn{6}{c}{Effective Address}
X	X	X	X	X	X	X	X	X	X	\multicolumn{3}{c}{Mode}	\multicolumn{3}{c}{Register}

Figure 2-4. Single-Effective-Address-Instruction Operation Word — General Format

2.11.1 REGISTER DIRECT MODES. These effective addressing modes specify that the operand is in one of the 16 multifunction registers.

2.11.1.1 Data Register Direct. The operand is in the data register specified by the effective address register field.

    Generation: EA = Dn
    RTL Notation: Dn
    Mode: 000
    Register: n

Data Register Dn | Operand |

2.11.1.2 Address Register Direct. The operand is in the address register specified by the effective address register field.

    Generation: EA = An
    RTL Notation: An
    Mode: 001
    Register: n

Address Register An | Operand |

2.11.2 MEMORY ADDRESS MODES. These effective addressing modes specify that the operand is in memory and provide the specific address of the operand.

2.11.2.1 Address Register Indirect. The address of the operand is in the address register specified by the register field. The reference is classified as a data reference with the exception of the jump and jump to subroutine instructions.

Generation: EA = (An)
RTL Notation: An@
Mode: 010
Register: n

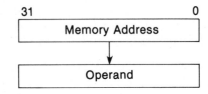

Address Register An

Memory Address

2.11.2.2 Address Register Indirect With Postincrement. The address of the operand is in the address register specified by the register field. After the operand address is used, it is incremented by one, two, or four depending upon whether the size of the operand is byte, word, or long word. If the address register is the stack pointer and the operand size is byte, the address is incremented by two rather than one to keep the stack pointer on a word boundary. The reference is classified as a data reference.

Generation: EA = (An)
                An = An + N
RTL Notation: An@ +
Mode: 011
Register: n

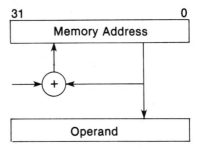

Address Register An

Operand Length (1, 2, or 4)

Memory Address

2.11.2.3 Address Register Indirect With Predecrement. The address of the operand is in the address register specified by the register field. Before the operand address is used, it is decremented by one, two, or four depending upon whether the operand size is byte, word, or long word. If the address register is the stack pointer and the operand size is byte, the address is decremented by two rather than one to keep the stack pointer on a word boundary. The reference is classified as a data reference.

Generation: An = An − N
                EA = (An)
RTL Notation: An@ −
Mode: 100
Register: n

Address Register An

Operand Length (1, 2, or 4)

Memory Address

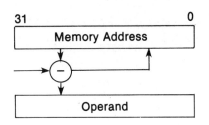

2.11.2.4 Address Register Indirect With Displacement.
This address mode requires one word of extension. The address of the operand is the sum of the address in the address register and the sign-extended 16-bit displacement integer in the extension word. The reference is classified as a data reference with the exception of the jump and jump to subroutine instructions.

Generation: EA = (An) + d
RTL Notation: An@(d)
Mode: 101
Register: n

Address Register An

Displacement

Memory Address

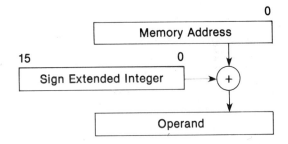

2.11.2.5 Address Register Indirect With Index.
This address mode requires one word of extension formatted as shown below.

15	14	13	12	11	10	9	8	7	6	5	4	3	2	1	0
D/A	Register			W/L	0	0	0	Displacement Integer							

Bit 15 — Index register indicator
  0 — data register
  1 — address register
Bits 14 through 12 — Index register number
Bit 11 — Index Size
  0 — sign-extended, low order integer in index register
  1 — long value in index register

The address of the operand is the sum of the address in the address register, the sign-extended displacement integer in the low order eight bits of the extension word, and the contents of the index register. The reference is classified as a data reference with the exception of the jump and jump to subroutine instructions. The size of the index register does not affect the execution time of the instructions.

Generation: EA = (An) + (Ri) + d   Mode: 110
RTL Notation: An@(d, Ri.W)   Register: n
               An@(d, Ri.L)

19

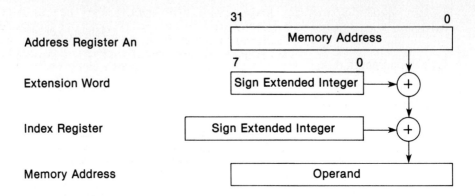

2.11.3 SPECIAL ADDRESS MODES.
The special address modes use the effective address register field to specify the special addressing mode instead of a register number.

2.11.3.1 Absolute Short Address.
This address mode requires one word of extension. The address of the operand is in the extension word. The 16-bit address is sign extended before it is used. The reference is classified as a data reference with the exception of the jump and jump to subroutine instructions.

Generation: EA given
RTL Notation: xxx.W
Mode: 111
Register: 000

2.11.3.2 Absolute Long Address.
This address mode requires two words of extension. The address of the operand is developed by the concatenation of the extension words. The high-order part of the address is the first extension word; the low order part of the address is the second extension word. The reference is classified as a data reference with the exception of the jump and jump to subroutine instructions.

Generation: EA given
RTL Notation: xxx.L
Mode: 111
Register: 001

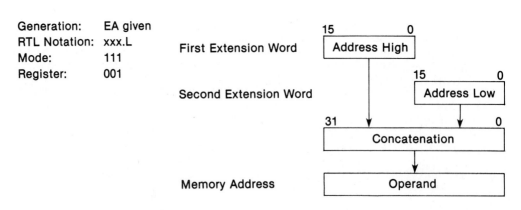

2.11.3.3 Program Counter With Displacement.

This address mode requires one word of extension. The address of the operand is the sum of the address in the program counter and the sign-extended 16-bit displacement integer in the extension word. The value in the program counter is the address of the extension word. The reference is classified as a program reference.

Generation: $EA = (PC) + d$
RTL Notation: PC@(d)
Mode: 111
Register: 010

Program Counter

Extension Word

Memory Address

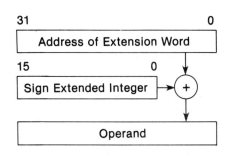

2.11.3.4 Program Counter With Index.

This address mode requires one word of extension formatted as shown below.

15	14	13	12	11	10	9	8	7	6	5	4	3	2	1	0
D/A	Register			W/L	0	0	0	Displacement Integer							

Bit 15 — Index register indicator
  0 — data register
  1 — address register
Bits 14 through 12 — Index register number
Bit 11 — Index size
  0 — sign-extended, low order word integer in index register
  1 — long value in index register

The address is the sum of the address in the program counter, the sign-extended displacement integer in the lower eight bits of the extension word, and the contents of the index register. The value in the program counter is the address of the extension word. This reference is classified as a program reference. The size of the index register does not affect the execution time of the instruction.

Generation: $EA = (PC) + (Ri) + d$
RTL Notation: PC@(d, Ri.W)
              PC@(d, Ri.L)
Mode: 111
Register: 011

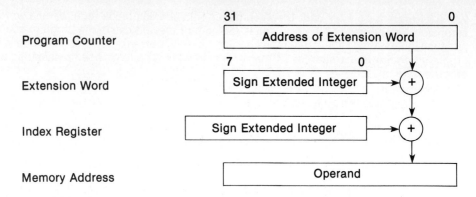

2.11.3.5 Immediate Data.
This address mode requires either one or two words of extension depending on the size of the operation.

Byte Operation — operand is low order byte of extension word

Word operation — operand is extension word

Long word operation — operand is in the two extension words, high order 16-bits are in the first extension word, low order 16 bits are in the second extension word.

Generation: Operand given
RTL Notation: #xxxx
Mode: 111
Register: 100

The extension word formats are shown below:

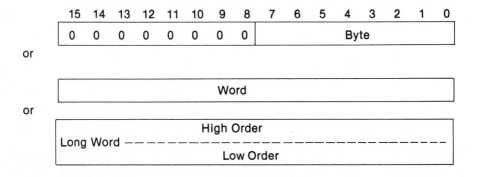

2.11.4 EFFECTIVE ADDRESS ENCODING SUMMARY.
Table 2-1 is a summary of the effective addressing modes discussed in the previous paragraphs.

2.12 IMPLICIT REFERENCE

Some instructions make implicit reference to the program counter (PC), the system stack pointer (SP), the supervisor stack pointer (SSP), the user stack pointer (USP), or the status register (SR). Table 2-2 provides a list of these instructions and the registers implied.

Table 2-1. Effective Address Encoding Summary

Addressing Mode	Mode	Register
Data Register Direct	000	register number
Address Register Direct	001	register number
Address Register Indirect	010	register number
Address Register Indirect with Postincrement	011	register number
Address Register Indirect with Predecrement	100	register number
Address Register Indirect with Displacement	101	register number
Address Register Indirect with Index	110	register number
Absolute Short	111	000
Absolute Long	111	001
Program Counter with Displacement	111	010
Program Counter with Index	111	011
Immediate	111	100

Table 2-2. Implicit Instruction Reference Summary

Instruction	Implied Register(s)
Branch Conditional (Bcc), Branch Always (BRA)	PC
Branch to Subroutine (BSR)	PC, SP
Check Register Against Bounds (CHK)	SSP, SR
Test Condition, Decrement and Branch (DBcc)	PC
Signed Divide (DIVS)	SSP, SR
Unsigned Divide (DIVU)	SSP, SR
Jump (JMP)	PC
Jump to Subroutine (JSR)	PC, SP
Link and Allocate (LINK)	SP
Move Condition Codes (MOVE CCR)	SR
Move Status Register (MOVE SR)	SR
Move User Stack Pointer (MOVE USP)	USP
Push Effective Address (PEA)	SP
Return from Exception (RTE)	PC, SP, SR
Return and Restore Condition Codes (RTR)	PC, SP, SR
Return from Subroutine (RTS)	PC, SP
Trap (TRAP)	SSP, SR
Trap on Overflow (TRAPV)	SSP, SR
Unlink (UNLK)	SP
Logical Immediate to CCR	SR
Logical Immediate to SR	SR

2.13 STACKS AND QUEUES

In addition to supporting the array data structure with the index addressing mode, the MC68000 also supports stack and queue data structures with the address register indirect postincrement and predecrement addressing modes. A stack is a last-in-first-out (LIFO) list, a queue is a first-in-first-out (FIFO) list. When data is added to a stack or queue, it is "pushed" onto the structure; when it is removed, it is "pulled" from the structure.

The system stack is used implicitly by many instructions; user stacks and queues may be created and maintained through the addressing modes.

2.13.1 SYSTEM STACK. Address register seven (A7) is the system stack pointer (SP). The system stack pointer is either the supervisor stack pointer (SSP) or the user stack pointer (USP), depending on the state of the S-bit in the status register. If the S-bit indicates

23

supervisor state the SSP is the active system stack pointer, and the USP cannot be referenced as an address register. If the S-bit indicates user state, the USP is the active system stack pointer, and the SSP cannot be referenced. Each system stack fills from high memory to low memory. The address mode SP@ − creates a new item on the active system stack, and the address mode SP@ + deletes an item from the active system stack.

The program counter is saved on the active system stack on subroutine calls, and restored from the active system stack on returns. On the other hand, both the program counter and the status register are saved on the supervisor stack during the processing of traps and interrupts. Thus, the correct execution of the supervisor state code is not dependent on the behavior of user code and user programs may use the user stack pointer arbitrarily.

In order to keep data on the system stack aligned properly, data entry on the stack is restricted so that data is always put in the stack on a word boundary. Thus byte data is pushed on or pulled from the system stack in the high order half of the word; the lower half is unchanged.

2.13.2 USER STACKS. User stacks can be implemented and manipulated by employing the address register indirect with postincrement and predecrement addressing modes. Using an address register (one of A0 through A6), the user may implement stacks which are filled either from high memory to low memory, or vice versa. The important things to remember are:

- using predecrement, the register is decremented before its contents are used as the pointer into the stack,
- using postincrement, the register is incremented after its contents are used as the pointer into the stack,
- byte data must be put on the stack in pairs when mixed with word or long data so that the stack will not get misaligned when the data is retrieved. Word and long accesses must be on word boundary (even) addresses.

Stack growth from high to low memory is implemented with

An@ − to push data on the stack,
An@ + to pull data from the stack.

After either a push or a pull operation, register An points to the last (top) item on the stack. This is illustrated as:

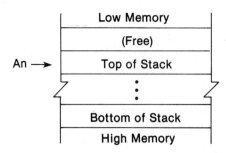

24

Stack growth from low to high memory is implemented with

An@ + to push data on the stack,

An@ − to pull data from the stack.

After either a push or a pull operation, register An points to the next available space on the stack. This is illustrated as:

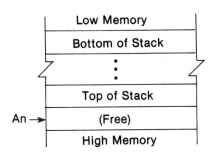

2.13.3 QUEUES. User queues can be implemented and manipulated with the address register indirect with postincrement or predecrement addressing modes. Using a pair of address registers (two of A0 through A6), the user may implement queues which are filled either from high memory to low memory, or vice versa. Because queues are pushed from one end and pulled from the other, two registers are used: the put and get pointers.

Queue growth from low to high memory is implemented with

Aput@ + to put data into the queue,

Aget@ + to get data from the queue.

After a put operation, the put address register points to the next available space in the queue and the unchanged get address register points to the next item to remove from the queue. After a get operation, the get address register points to the next item to remove from the queue and the unchanged put address register points to the next available space in the queue. This is illustrated as:

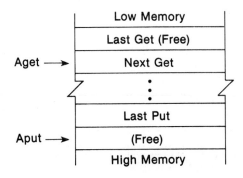

If the queue is to be implemented as a circular buffer, the address register should be checked and, if necessary, adjusted before the put or get operation is performed. The address register is adjusted by subtracting the buffer length (in bytes).

Queue growth from high to low memory is implemented with
    Aput@ – to put data into the queue,
    Aget@ – to get data from the queue.

After a put operation, the put address register points to the last item put in the queue, and the unchanged get address register points to the last item removed from the queue. After a get operation, the get address register points to the last item removed from the queue and the unchanged put address register points to the last item put in the queue. This is illustrated as:

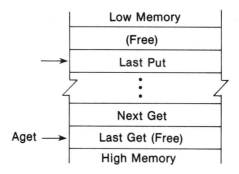

If the queue is to be implemented as a circular buffer, the get or put operation should be performed first, and then the address register should be checked and, if necessary, adjusted. The address register is adjusted by adding the buffer length (in bytes).

SECTION 3
INSTRUCTION SET SUMMARY

3.1 INTRODUCTION

This section contains an overview of the form and structure of the MC68000 instruction set. The instructions form a set of tools that include all the machine functions to perform the following operations:

- Data Movement
- Integer Arithmetic
- Logical
- Shift and Rotate
- Bit Manipulation
- Binary Coded Decimal
- Program Control
- System Control

The complete range of instruction capabilities combined with the flexible addressing modes described in Section 2 provide a very flexible base for program development. Detailed information about each instruction is given in Appendix B.

3.2 DATA MOVEMENT OPERATIONS

The basic method of data acquisition (transfer and storage) is provided by the move (MOVE) instruction. The move instruction and the effective addressing modes allow both address and data manipulation. Data move instructions allow byte, word, and long word operands to be transferred from memory to memory, memory to register, register to memory, and register to register. Address move instructions allow word and long word operand transfers and ensure that only legal address manipulations are executed. In addition to the general move instruction, there are several special data movement instructions: move multiple registers (MOVEM), move peripheral data (MOVEP), exchange registers (EXG), load effective address (LEA), push effective address (PEA), link stack (LINK), unlink stack (UNLK), and move quick (MOVEQ). Table 3-1 is a summary of the data movement operations.

3.3 INTEGER ARITHMETIC OPERATIONS

The arithmetic operations include the four basic operations of add (ADD), subtract (SUB), multiply (MUL), and divide (DIV) as well as arithmetic compare (CMP), clear (CLR), and negate (NEG). The add and subtract instructions are available for both address and data operations, with data operations accepting all operand sizes. Address operations are

27

Table 3-1. Data Movement Operations

Instruction	Operand Size	Operation
EXG	32	Rx ↔ Ry
LEA	32	EA → An
LINK	—	An → SP@ − SP → An SP + d → SP
MOVE	8, 16, 32	(EA)s → EAd
MOVEM	16, 32	(EA) → An, Dn An, Dn → EA
MOVEP	16, 32	(EA) → Dn Dn → EA
MOVEQ	8	#xxx → Dn
PEA	32	EA → SP@ −
SWAP	32	Dn [31:16] ↔ Dn [15:0]
UNLK	—	An → SP SP@ + → An

NOTES:
s = source
d = destination
[ ] = bit numbers

limited to legal address size operands (16 or 32 bits). Data, address, and memory compare operations are also available. The clear and negate instructions may be used on all sizes of data operands.

The multiply and divide operations are available for signed and unsigned operands using word multiply to produce a long product, and a long word dividend with word divisor to produce a word quotient with a word remainder.

Multiprecision and mixed size arithmetic can be accomplished using a set of extended instructions. These instructions are: add extended (ADDX), subtract extended (SUBX), sign extend (EXT), and negate binary with extend (NEGX).

A test operand (TST) instruction that will set the condition codes as a result of a compare of the operand with zero is also available. Test and set (TAS) is a synchronization instruction useful in multiprocessor systems. Table 3-2 is a summary of the integer arithmetic operations.

3.4 LOGICAL OPERATIONS

Logical operation instructions AND, OR, EOR, and NOT are available for all sizes of integer data operands. A similar set of immediate instructions (ANDI, ORI, and EORI) provide these logical operations with all sizes of immediate data. Table 3-3 is a summary of the logical operations.

3.5 SHIFT AND ROTATE OPERATIONS

Shift operations in both directions are provided by the arithmetic instructions ASR and ASL and logical shift instructions LSR and LSL. The rotate instructions (with and without extend) available are ROXR, ROXL, ROR, and ROL. All shift and rotate operations can be performed in either registers or memory. Register shifts and rotates support all operand

Table 3-2. Integer Arithmetic Operations

Instruction	Operand Size	Operation
ADD	8, 16, 32 16, 32	Dn + (EA) → Dn (EA) + Dn → EA (EA) + #xxx → EA An + (EA) → An
ADDX	8, 16, 32 16, 32	Dx + Dy + X → Dx Ax@ − Ay@ − + X → Ax@
CLR	8, 16, 32	0 → EA
CMP	8, 16, 32 16, 32	Dn − (EA) (EA) − #xxx Ax@ + − Ay@ + An − (EA)
DIVS	32 ÷ 16	Dn/(EA) → Dn
DIVU	32 ÷ 16	Dn/(EA) → Dn
EXT	8 → 16 16 → 32	(Dn)$_8$ → Dn$_{16}$ (Dn)$_{16}$ → Dn$_{32}$
MULS	16 * 16 → 32	Dn * (EA) → 32 Dn
MULU	16 * 16 → 32	Dn * (EA) → Dn
NEG	8, 16, 32	0 − (EA) → EA
NEGX	8, 16, 32	0 − (EA) − X → EA
SUB	8, 16, 32 16, 32	Dn − (EA) → Dn (EA) − Dn → EA (EA) − #xxx → EA An − (EA) → An
SUBX	8, 16, 32	Dx − Dy − X → Dx Ax@ − − Λy@ − − X → Ax@
TAS	8	(EA) − 0, 1 → EA [7]
TST	8, 16, 32	(EA) − 0

NOTE:

[ ] = bit number

sizes and allow a shift count specified in the instruction of one or eight bits, or 0 to 63 bits specified in a data register.

Memory shifts and rotates are for word operands only and allow only single-bit shifts or rotates.

Table 3-4 is a summary of the shift and rotate operations.

Table 3-3. Logical Operations

Instruction	Operand Size	Operation
AND	8, 16, 32	Dn Λ (EA) → Dn (EA) Λ Dn → EA (EA) Λ #xxx → EA
OR	8, 16, 32	Dn v (EA) → Dn (EA) v Dn → EA (EA) v #xxx → EA
EOR	8, 16, 32	(Ea) ⊕ Dy → EA (EA) ⊕ #xxx → EA
NOT	8, 16, 32	~ (EA) → EA

NOTE:

~ = invert

Table 3-4. Shift and Rotate Operations

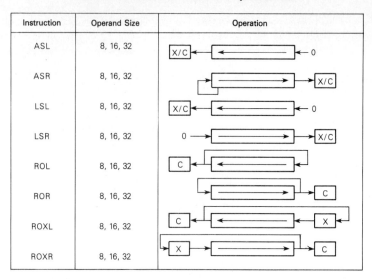

Instruction	Operand Size	Operation
ASL	8, 16, 32	
ASR	8, 16, 32	
LSL	8, 16, 32	
LSR	8, 16, 32	
ROL	8, 16, 32	
ROR	8, 16, 32	
ROXL	8, 16, 32	
ROXR	8, 16, 32	

3.6 BIT MANIPULATION OPERATIONS

Bit manipulation operations are accomplished using the following instructions: bit test (BTST), bit test and set (BSET), bit test and clear (BCLR), and bit test and change (BCHG). Table 3-5 is a summary of the bit manipulation operations.

Table 3-5. Bit Manipulation Operations

Instruction	Operand Size	Operation
BTST	8, 32	$\sim$ bit of (EA) $\rightarrow$ Z
BSET	8, 32	$\sim$ bit of (EA) $\rightarrow$ Z $1 \rightarrow$ bit of EA
BCLR	8, 32	$\sim$ bit of (EA) $\rightarrow$ Z $0 \rightarrow$ bit of EA
BCHG	8, 32	$\sim$ bit of (EA) $\rightarrow$ Z $\sim$ bit of (EA) $\rightarrow$ bit of EA

3.7 BINARY CODED DECIMAL OPERATIONS

Multiprecision arithmetic operations on binary coded decimal numbers are accomplished using the following instructions: add decimal with extend (ABCD), subtract decimal with extend (SBCD), and negate decimal with extend (NBCD). Table 3-6 is a summary of the binary coded decimal operations.

Table 3-6. Binary Coded Decimal Operations

Instruction	Operand Size	Operation
ABCD	8	$Dx_{10} + Dy_{10} + X \rightarrow Dx$ $Ax@ - _{10} + Ay@ - _{10} + X \rightarrow Ax@$
SBCD	8	$Dy_{10} - Dy_{10} - X \rightarrow Dx$ $Ax@ - _{10} - Ay@ - _{10} - X \rightarrow Ax@$
NBCD	8	$0 - (EA)_{10} - X \rightarrow EA$

3.8 PROGRAM CONTROL OPERATIONS

Program control operations are accomplished using a series of conditional and unconditional branch instructions and return instructions. These instructions are summarized in Table 3-7.

The conditional instructions provide setting and branching for the following conditions:

CC	— Carry Clear	LS	— Low or Same
CS	— Carry Set	LT	— Less Than
EQ	— Equal	MI	— Minus
F	— Never True	NE	— Not Equal
GE	— Greater or Equal	PL	— Plus
GT	— Greater Than	T	— Always True
HI	— High	VC	— No Overflow
LE	— Less or Equal	VS	— Overflow

Table 3-7. Program Control Operations

Instruction	Operation
Conditional	
Bcc	Branch conditionally (14 conditions), 8- and 16-bit displacement
DBcc	Test condition, decrement and branch. 16-bit displacement
Scc	Set byte conditionally (16 conditions)
Unconditional	
BRA	Branch always, 8- and 16-bit displacement
BSR	Branch to subroutine, 8- and 16-bit displacement
JMP	Jump
JSR	Jump to subroutine
Returns	
RTR	Return and restore condition codes
RTS	Return from subroutine

3.9 SYSTEM CONTROL OPERATIONS

System control operations are accomplished by using privileged instructions, trap generating instructions, and instructions that use or modify the status register. These instructions are summarized in Table 3-8.

Table 3-8. System Control Operations

Instruction	Operation
Privileged	
ANDI to SR	Logical AND to status register
EORI to SR	Logical EOR to status register
MOVE EA to SR	Load new status register
MOVE USP	Move user stack pointer
ORI to SR	Logical OR to status register
RESET	Reset external devices
RTE	Return from exception
STOP	Stop program execution
Trap Generating	
CHK	Check register against bounds
TRAP	Trap
TRAPV	Trap on overflow
Status Register	
ANDI to CCR	Logical AND to condition codes
EORI to CCR	Logical EOR to condition codes
MOVE EA to CCR	Load new condition codes
MOVE SR to EA	Store status register
ORI to CCR	Logical OR to condition codes

SECTION 4
SIGNAL AND BUS OPERATION DESCRIPTION

4.1 INTRODUCTION

This section contains a brief description of the input and output signals. A discussion of bus operation during the various machine cycles and operations is also given.

4.2 SIGNAL DESCRIPTION

The input and output signals can be functionally organized into the groups shown in Figure 4-1. The following paragraphs provide a brief description of the signals and also a reference (if applicable) to other chapters that contain more detail about the function being performed.

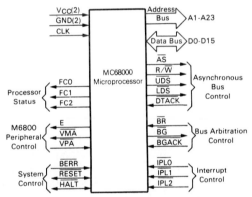

Figure 4-1. Input and Output Signals

4.2.1 ADDRESS BUS (A1 THROUGH A23).
This 23-bit, unidirectional, three-state bus is capable of addressing eight megawords of data. It provides the address for bus operation during all cycles except interrupt cycles. During interrupt cycles, address lines A1, A2, and A3 provide information about what level interrupt is being serviced while address lines A4 through A23 are all set to a logic high.

4.2.2 DATA BUS (D0 THROUGH D15).
This 16-bit, bidirectional, three-state bus is the general purpose data path. It can transfer and accept data in either word or byte length. During an interrupt acknowledge cycle, the external device supplies the vector number on data lines D0 through D7.

4.2.3 ASYNCHRONOUS BUS CONTROL. Asynchronous data transfers are handled using the following control signals: address strobe, read/write, upper and lower data strobes, and data transfer acknowledge. These signals are explained in the following paragraphs.

4.2.3.1 Address Strobe ($\overline{\text{AS}}$). This signal indicates that there is a valid address on the address bus.

4.2.3.2 Read/Write (R/$\overline{\text{W}}$). This signal defines the data bus transfer as a read or write cycle. The R/$\overline{\text{W}}$ signal also works in conjunction with the upper and lower data strobes as explained in the following paragraph.

4.2.3.3 Upper and Lower Data Strobes ($\overline{\text{UDS}}$, $\overline{\text{LDS}}$). These signals control the data on the data bus as shown in Table 4-1. When the R/$\overline{\text{W}}$ line is high, the processor will read from the data bus as indicated. When the R/$\overline{\text{W}}$ line is low, the processor will write to the data bus as shown.

Table 4-1. Data Strobe Control of Data Bus

$\overline{\text{UDS}}$	$\overline{\text{LDS}}$	R/$\overline{\text{W}}$	D8-D15	D0-D17
High	High	—	No Valid Data	No Valid Data
Low	Low	High	Valid Data Bits 8-15	Valid Data Bits 0-7
High	Low	High	No Valid Data	Valid Data Bits 0-7
Low	High	High	Valid Data Bits 8-15	No Valid Data
Low	Low	Low	Valid Data Bits 8-15	Valid Data Bits 0-7
High	Low	Low	Valid Data Bits 0-7*	Valid Data Bits 0-7
Low	High	Low	Valid Data Bits 8-15	Valid Data Bits 8-15*

*These conditions are a result of current implementation and may not appear on future devices.

4.2.3.4 Data Transfer Acknowledge ($\overline{\text{DTACK}}$). This input indicates that the data transfer is completed. When the processor recognizes $\overline{\text{DTACK}}$ during a read cycle, data is latched and the bus cycle terminated. When $\overline{\text{DTACK}}$ is recognized during a write cycle, the bus cycle is terminated. Refer to paragraphs 4.3.4 and 4.3.5 for additional information about $\overline{\text{DTACK}}$.

4.2.4 BUS ARBITRATION CONTROL. These three signals form a bus arbitration circuit to determine which device will be the bus master device. Refer to paragraph 4.3.2 for a detailed description.

4.2.4.1 Bus Request ($\overline{\text{BR}}$). This input is wire ORed with all other devices that could be bus masters. This input indicates to the processor that some other device desires to become the bus master.

4.2.4.2 Bus Grant ($\overline{\text{BG}}$). This output indicates to all other potential bus master devices that the processor will release bus control at the end of the current bus cycle.

4.2.4.3 Bus Grant Acknowledge ($\overline{\text{BGACK}}$). This input indicates that some other device has become the bus master. This signal cannot be asserted until the following four conditions are met:

1. a bus grant has been received
2. address strobe is inactive which indicates that the microprocessor is not using the bus
3. data transfer acknowledge is inactive which indicates that either memory or the peripherals are not using the bus
4. bus grant acknowledge is inactive which indicates that no other device is still claiming bus mastership.

4.2.5 INTERRUPT CONTROL ($\overline{\text{IPL0}}$, $\overline{\text{IPL1}}$, $\overline{\text{IPL2}}$). These input pins indicate the encoded priority level of the device requesting an interrupt. Level seven is the highest priority while level zero indicates that no interrupts are requested. The least significant bit is contained in $\overline{\text{IPL0}}$ and the most significant bit is contained in $\overline{\text{IPL2}}$. Refer to Section 5 for details on interrupt operation.

4.2.6 SYSTEM CONTROL. The system control inputs are used to either reset or halt the processor and to indicate to the processor that bus errors have occurred. The three system control inputs are explained in the following paragraphs.

4.2.6.1 Bus Error ($\overline{\text{BERR}}$). This input informs the processor that there is a problem with the cycle currently being executed. Problems may be a result of:

1. nonresponding devices
2. interrupt vector number acquisition failure
3. illegal access request as determined by a memory management unit
4. other application dependent errors.

The bus error signal interacts with the halt signal to determine if exception processing should be performed or the current bus cycle should be retried.

Refer to paragraph 4.3.3 for additional information about the interaction of the bus error and halt signals.

4.2.6.2 Reset ($\overline{\text{RESET}}$). This bidirectional signal line acts to reset (initiate a system initialization sequence) the processor in response to an external reset signal. An internally generated reset (result of a RESET instruction) causes all external devices to be reset and the internal state of the processor is not affected. A total system reset (processor and external devices) is the result of external halt and reset signals applied at the same time. Refer to paragraph 4.3.6 for additional information about reset operation.

4.2.6.3 Halt ($\overline{\text{HALT}}$). When this bidirectional line is driven by an external device, it will cause the processor to stop at the completion of the current bus cycle. When the processor has been halted using this input, all control signals are inactive and all three-state lines are put in their high-impedance state. Refer to paragraphs 4.3.3 and 4.3.4 for additional information about the interaction between the halt and bus error signals.

When the processor has stopped executing instructions, such as in a double bus fault condition, the halt line is driven by the processor to indicate to external devices that the processor has stopped.

4.2.7 M6800 PERIPHERAL CONTROL. These control signals are used to allow the interfacing of synchronous M6800 peripheral devices with the asynchronous MC68000. These signals are explained in the following paragraphs.

4.2.7.1 Enable (E). This signal is the standard enable signal common to all M6800 type peripheral devices. The period for this output is ten MC68000 clock periods (six clocks low; four clocks high).

4.2.7.2 Valid Peripheral Address ($\overline{VPA}$). This input indicates that the device or region addressed is an M6800 family device and that data transfer should coincide with the enable (E) signal. This input also indicates that the processor should use automatic vectoring for an interrupt. Refer to Section 6.

4.2.7.3 Valid Memory Address ($\overline{VMA}$). This output is used to indicate to M6800 peripheral devices that there is a valid address on the address bus and the processor is synchronized to enable. This signal only responds to a valid peripheral address ($\overline{VPA}$) input which indicates that the peripheral is an M6800 family device.

4.2.8 PROCESSOR STATUS (FC0, FC1, FC2). These function code outputs indicate the mode (user or supervisor) and the cycle type currently being executed as shown in Table 4-2. The information indicated by the function code outputs is valid whenever address strobe ($\overline{AS}$) is active.

Table 4-2. Function Code Outputs

FC2	FC1	FC0	Cycle Type
Low	Low	Low	(Undefined, Reserved)
Low	Low	High	User Data
Low	High	Low	User Program
Low	High	High	(Undefined, Reserved)
High	Low	Low	(Undefined, Reserved)
High	Low	High	Supervisor Data
High	High	Low	Supervisor Program
High	High	High	Interrupt Acknowledge

4.2.9 CLOCK (CLK). The clock input is a TTL compatible signal that is internally buffered for development of the internal clocks needed by the processor. The clock input shall be a constant frequency.

4.2.10 SIGNAL SUMMARY. Table 4-3 is a summary of all the signals discussed in the previous paragraphs.

Table 4-3. Signal Summary

Signal Name	Mnemonic	Input/Output	Active State	Three State
Address Bus	A1-A23	Output	High	Yes
Data Bus	D0-D15	Input/Output	High	Yes
Address Strobe	$\overline{AS}$	Output	Low	Yes
Read/Write	R/$\overline{W}$	Output	Read-High Write-Low	Yes
Upper and Lower Data Strobes	$\overline{UDS}$, $\overline{LDS}$	Output	Low	Yes
Data Transfer Acknowledge	$\overline{DTACK}$	Input	Low	No
Bus Request	$\overline{BR}$	Input	Low	No
Bus Grant	$\overline{BG}$	Output	Low	No
Bus Grant Acknowledge	$\overline{BGACK}$	Input	Low	No
Interrupt Priority Level	$\overline{IPL0}$, $\overline{IPL1}$, $\overline{IPL2}$	Input	Low	No
Bus Error	$\overline{BERR}$	Input	Low	No
Reset	$\overline{RESET}$	Input/Output	Low	No*
Halt	$\overline{HALT}$	Input/Output	Low	No*
Enable	E	Output	High	No
Valid Memory Address	$\overline{VMA}$	Output	Low	Yes
Valid Peripheral Address	$\overline{VPA}$	Input	Low	No
Function Code Output	FC0, FC1, FC2	Output	High	Yes
Clock	CLK	Input	High	No
Power Input	V$_{CC}$	Input	—	—
Ground	GND	Input	—	—

*Open Drain

4.3 BUS OPERATION

The following paragraphs explain control signal and bus operation during data transfer operations, bus arbitration, bus error and halt conditions, and reset operation.

4.3.1 DATA TRANSFER OPERATIONS. Transfer of data between devices involves the following leads:
- Address Bus A1 through A23
- Data Bus D0 through D15
- Control Signals

The address and data buses are separate parallel buses used to transfer data using an asynchronous bus structure. In all cycles, the bus master assumes responsibility for deskewing all signals it issues at both the start and end of a cycle. In addition, the bus master is responsible for deskewing the acknowledge and data signals from the slave device.

The following paragraphs explain the read, write, and read-modify-write cycles. The indivisible read-modify-write cycle is the method used by the MC68000 for interlocked multiprocessor communications.

NOTE

The terms **assertion** and **negation** will be used extensively. This is done to avoid confusion when dealing with a mixture of "active-low" and "active-high" signals. The term assert or assertion is used to indicate that a signal is active independent of whether that voltage is low or high. The term negation is used to indicate that a signal is inactive.

Each of the bus cycle operations is defined in terms of a succession of states. These states are described for reference purposes only, and do not necessarily correspond to any implemented machine states.

4.3.1.1 Read Cycle. During a read cycle, the processor receives data from memory or a peripheral device. The processor reads bytes of data in all cases. If the instruction specifies a word (or long word) operation, the processor reads both bytes. When the instruction specifies byte operation, the processor uses the internal A0 bit to determine which byte to read and then issues the data strobe required for that byte. For byte operations, when the A0 bit equals zero, the upper data strobe is issued. When the A0 bit equals one, the lower data strobe is issued. When the data is received, the processor correctly positions it internally.

A word read cycle flow chart is given in Figure 4-2. A byte read cycle flow chart is given in Figure 4-3. Read cycle timing is given in Figure 4-4 and Figure 4-5 details word and byte read cycle operation. Refer to these illustrations during the following detailed discussion.

At state zero (S0) in the read cycle, the address bus (A1 through A23) is in the high-impedance state. A function code is asserted on function code output lines FC0, FC1, and FC2 to indicate which address space this cycle will operate on. The read/write (R/$\overline{W}$) signal is switched high to indicate a read cycle. One-half clock cycle later, at state 1, the address bus is released from the high-impedance state.

In state 2, the address strobe ($\overline{AS}$) is asserted to indicate that there is a valid address on the address bus and the upper and lower data strobe ($\overline{UDS}$, $\overline{LDS}$) is asserted as required. The memory or peripheral device uses the address bus and the address strobe to determine if it has been selected. The selected device uses the read/write signal and the data strobe to place its information on the data bus. Concurrent with placing data on the data bus, the selected device asserts data transfer acknowledge ($\overline{DTACK}$). No new control signals are issued during states 3 and 4.

Data transfer acknowledge must be present at the processor a setup time before the end of state 4 or the processor will substitute wait states for states 5 and 6. State 5 starts the synchronization of the returning data transfer acknowledge. The bus interface circuitry issues requests for subsequent internal cycles during state 6. At the end of state 6 (beginning of state 7) incoming data is latched into an internal data bus holding register.

During state 7, address strobe and the upper and/or lower data strobes are negated. The address bus is held valid through state 7 to allow for static memory operation and signal skew. The read/write signal and the function code outputs also remain valid through state 7 to ensure a correct transfer operation. The slave device keeps its data asserted until it detects the negation of either the address strobe or the upper and/or lower data strobe. The slave device must remove its data and data transfer acknowledge within one clock period of recognizing the negation of the address or data strobes. Note that the data bus might not become free and data transfer acknowledge might not be removed until state 0 or 1.

When address strobe is negated, the slave device is released. Note that a slave device must remain selected as long as address strobe is asserted to ensure the correct functioning of the read-modify-write cycle as explained in paragraph 4.3.1.3.

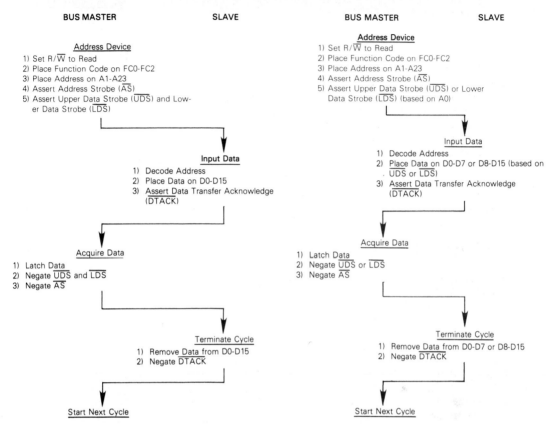

Figure 4-2. Word Read Cycle Flow Chart   Figure 4-3. Byte Read Cycle Flow Chart

4.3.1.2 Write Cycle. During a write cycle, the processor sends data to memory or a peripheral device. The processor writes bytes of data in all cases. If the instruction specifies a word operation, the processor writes both bytes. When the instruction specifies a byte operation, the processor uses the internal A0 bit to determine which byte to write and then issues the data strobe required for that byte. For byte operations, when the A0 bit equals zero, the upper data strobe is issued. When the A0 bit equals one, the lower data strobe is issued. A word write cycle flow chart is given in Figure 4-6. A byte write cycle flow chart is given in Figure 4-7. Write cycle timing is given in Figure 4-4 and Figure 4-8 details word and byte write cycle operation. Refer to these illustrations during the following detailed discussion.

At state zero (S0) in the write cycle, the address bus (A1 through A23) is in the high-impedance state. A function code is asserted on function code output lines FC0, FC1, and FC2 to indicate which address space this cycle will operate on.

39

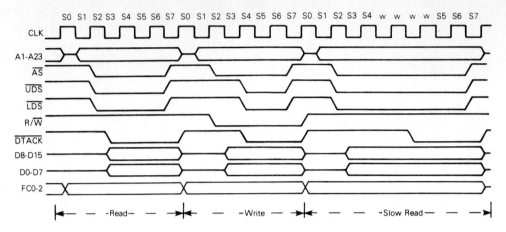

Figure 4-4. Read and Write Cycle Timing Diagram

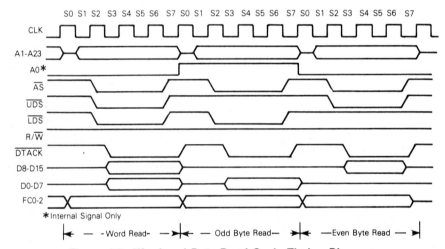

*Internal Signal Only

Figure 4-5. Word and Byte Read Cycle Timing Diagram

NOTE

The read/write (R/W̄) signal remains high until state 2 to prevent bus conflicts with preceding read cycles. The data bus is not driven until state 3.

One-half clock cycle later, at state 1, the address bus is released from the high-impedance state.

In state 2, the address strobe (A̅S̅) is asserted to indicate that there is a valid address on the address bus. The memory or peripheral device uses the address bus and the address strobe to determine if it has been selected. During state 2, the read/write signal is switched low to indicate a write cycle. When external processor data bus buffers are required,

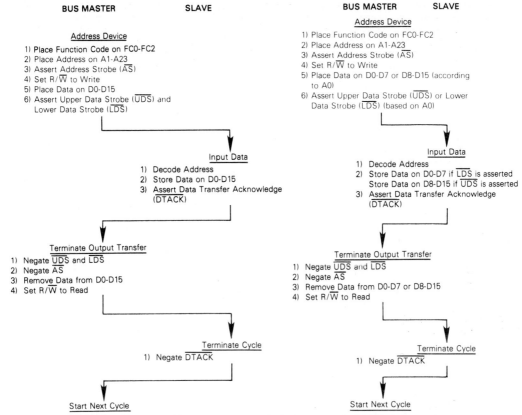

BUS MASTER   **SLAVE**

Address Device

1) Place Function Code on FC0-FC2
2) Place Address on A1-A23
3) Assert Address Strobe ($\overline{AS}$)
4) Set R/$\overline{W}$ to Write
5) Place Data on D0-D15
6) Assert Upper Data Strobe ($\overline{UDS}$) and Lower Data Strobe ($\overline{LDS}$)

Input Data

1) Decode Address
2) Store Data on D0-D15
3) Assert Data Transfer Acknowledge ($\overline{DTACK}$)

Terminate Output Transfer

1) Negate $\overline{UDS}$ and $\overline{LDS}$
2) Negate $\overline{AS}$
3) Remove Data from D0-D15
4) Set R/$\overline{W}$ to Read

Terminate Cycle

1) Negate $\overline{DTACK}$

Start Next Cycle

Figure 4-6. Word Write Cycle Flow Chart

BUS MASTER   **SLAVE**

Address Device

1) Place Function Code on FC0-FC2
2) Place Address on A1-A23
3) Assert Address Strobe ($\overline{AS}$)
4) Set R/$\overline{W}$ to Write
5) Place Data on D0-D7 or D8-D15 (according to A0)
6) Assert Upper Data Strobe ($\overline{UDS}$) or Lower Data Strobe ($\overline{LDS}$) (based on A0)

Input Data

1) Decode Address
2) Store Data on D0-D7 if $\overline{LDS}$ is asserted
   Store Data on D8-D15 if $\overline{UDS}$ is asserted
3) Assert Data Transfer Acknowledge ($\overline{DTACK}$)

Terminate Output Transfer

1) Negate $\overline{UDS}$ and $\overline{LDS}$
2) Negate $\overline{AS}$
3) Remove Data from D0-D7 or D8-D15
4) Set R/$\overline{W}$ to Read

Terminate Cycle

1) Negate $\overline{DTACK}$

Start Next Cycle

Figure 4-7. Byte Write Cycle Flow Chart

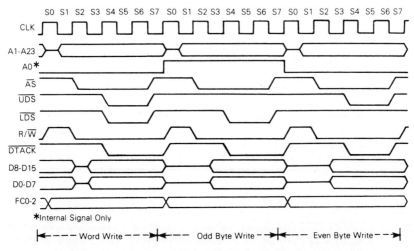

*Internal Signal Only

Word Write — Odd Byte Write — Even Byte Write

Figure 4-8. Word and Byte Write Cycle Timing Diagram

41

the read/write line provides sufficient directional control. Data is not asserted during this state to allow sufficient turnaround time for external data buffers (if used). Data is asserted onto the data bus during state 3.

In state 4, the data strobes are asserted as required to indicate that the data bus is stable. The selected device uses the read/write signal and the data strobes to take its information from the data bus.The selected device asserts data transfer acknowledge (DTACK) when it has successfully stored the data.

Data transfer acknowledge must be present at the processor a setup time before the end of state 4 or the processor will substitute wait states for states 5 and 6. State 5 starts the synchronization of the returning data transfer acknowledge. The bus interface circuitry issues requests for subsequent internal cycles during state 6.

During state 7, address strobe and the upper and/or lower data strobes are negated. The address and data buses are held valid through state 7 to allow for static memory operation and signal skew. The read/write signal and the function code outputs also remain valid through state 7 to ensure a correct transfer operation. The slave device keeps its data transfer acknowledge asserted until it detects the negation of either the address strobe or the upper and/or lower data strobe. The slave device must remove its data transfer acknowledge within one clock period after recognizing the negation of the address or data strobes. Note that the processor releases the data bus at the end of state 7 but that data transfer acknowledge might not be removed until state 0 or 1. When address strobe is negated, the slave device is released.

4.3.1.3 Read-Modify-Write Cycle. The read-modify-write cycle performs a read, modifies the data in the arithmetic-logic unit, and writes the data back to the same address. In the MC68000 this cycle is indivisible in that the address strobe is asserted throughout the entire cycle. The test and set (TAS) instruction uses this cycle to provide meaningful communication between processors in a multiple processor environment. This instruction is the only instruction that uses the read-modify-write cycle and since the test and set instruction only operates on bytes, all read-modify-write cycles are byte operations. A read-modify-write cycle flow chart is given in Figure 4-9 and a timing diagram is given in Figure 4-10. Refer to these illustrations during the following detailed discussions.

At state zero (S0) in the read-modify-write cycle, the address bus (A1 through A23) is in the high-impedance state. A function code is asserted on function code output lines FC0, FC1, and FC2 to indicate which address space this cycle will operate on. The read/write (R/W) signal is switched high to indicate a read cycle. One-half clock cycle later, at state 1, the address bus is released from the high-impedance state.

In state 2, the address strobe (AS) is asserted to indicate that there is a valid address on the address bus and the upper or lower data strobe (UDS, LDS) is asserted as required. The memory or peripheral device uses the address bus and the address strobe to determine if it has been selected. The selected device uses the read/write signal and the data strobe to place its information on the data bus. Concurrent with placing data on the data bus, the selected device asserts data transfer acknowledge (DTACK). No new control signals are issued during states 3 and 4.

Data transfer acknowledge must be present at the processor a setup time before the end of state 4 or the processor will substitute wait states for states 5 and 6. State 5 starts the synchronization of the returning data transfer acknowledge. The bus interface circuitry issues requests for subsequent internal cycles during state 6. At the end of state 6 (beginning of state 7) incoming data is latched into an internal data bus holding register.

During state 7, the upper or lower data strobe is negated. The address bus, address strobe, read/write signal, and function code outputs remain as they were in preparation for the write portion of the cycle. The slave device keeps its data asserted until it detects the negation of the upper or lower data strobe. The slave device must remove its data and data transfer acknowledge within one clock period of recognizing the negation of the data strobes. No new control signals are issued during state 8. Internal modification of data may occur at this time.

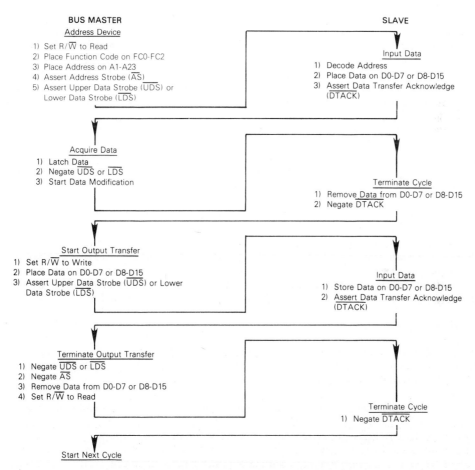

Figure 4-9. Read-Modify-Write Cycle Flow Chart

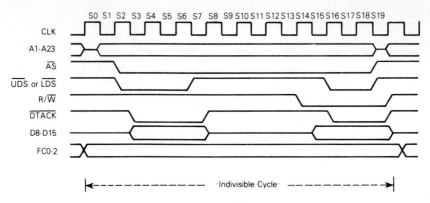

Figure 4-10. Read-Modify-Write Cycle Timing Diagram

NOTE

The read/write signal remains high until state 14 to prevent bus conflicts with the preceding read portion of the cycle and the data bus is not asserted by the processor until state 15.

No new control signals are issued in state 9.

In state 14, the read/write signal is switched low to indicate a write cycle. When external processor data bus buffers are required, the read/write line provides sufficient directional control. Data is not asserted during this state to allow sufficient turnaround time for external data buffers (if used). Data is asserted onto the data bus during state 15.

In state 16, the data strobe is asserted as required to indicate that the data bus is stable. The selected device uses the read/write signal and the data strobe to take its information from the data bus. The selected device asserts data transfer acknowledge (DTACK) when it has successfully stored its data. No new control signals are issued during states 17 and 18.

Data transfer acknowledge must be present at the processor a setup time before the end of state 16 or the processor will substitute wait states for states 17 and 18. State 17 starts the synchronization of the returning data transfer acknowledge for the write portion of the cycle. The bus interface circuitry issues requests for subsequent internal cycles during state 18.

During state 19, address strobe and the upper or lower data strobe is negated. The address and data buses are held valid through state 19 to allow for static memory operation and signal skew. The read/write signal and the function code outputs also remain valid through state 19 to ensure a correct transfer operation. The slave device keeps its data transfer acknowledge asserted until it detects the negation of either the address strobe or the upper or lower data strobe. The slave device must remove its data transfer acknowledge within one clock period after recognizing the negation of the address or data strobes. Note that the processor releases the data bus at the end of state 19 but that data transfer acknowledge might not be removed until state 0 or 1. When address strobe is negated the slave device is released.

4.3.2 BUS ARBITRATION. Bus arbitration is a technique used by master-type devices to request, be granted, and acknowledge bus mastership. In it simplest form, it consists of:

1. Asserting a bus mastership request
2. Receiving a grant that the bus is available at the end of the current cycle
3. Acknowledging that mastership has been assumed.

Figure 4-11 is a flow chart showing the detail involved in a request from a single device. Figure 4-12 is a timing diagram for the same operations. This technique allows processing of bus requests during data transfer cycles.

The timing diagram shows that the bus request is negated at the time that an acknowledge is asserted. This type of operation would be true for a system consisting of the processor and one device capable of bus mastership. In systems having a number of devices capable of bus mastership, the bus request line from each device is wire ORed to the processor. In this system, it is easy to see that there could be more than one bus request being made. The timing diagram shows that the bus grant signal is negated a few clock cycles after the transition of the acknowledge ($\overline{\text{BGACK}}$) signal.

However, if the bus requests are still pending, the processor will assert another bus grant within a few clock cycles after it was negated. This additional assertion of bus grant allows external arbitration circuitry to select the next bus master before the current bus master has completed its requirements. The following paragraphs provide additional information about the three steps in the arbitration process.

4.3.2.1 Requesting the Bus. External devices capable of becoming bus masters request the bus by asserting the bus request ($\overline{\text{BR}}$) signal. This is a wire ORed signal (although it need not be constructed from open collector devices) that indicates to the processor that some external device requires control of the external bus. The processor is effectively at a lower bus priority level than the external device and will relinquish the bus after it has completed the last bus cycle it has started.

When no acknowledge is received before the bus request signal goes inactive, the processor will continue processing when it detects that the bus request is inactive. This allows ordinary processing to continue if the arbitration circuitry responded to noise inadvertently.

4.3.2.2 Receiving the Bus Grant. The processor asserts bus grant ($\overline{\text{BG}}$) as soon as possible. Normally, this is immediately after internal synchronization. The only exception to this occurs when the processor has made an internal decision to execute the next bus cycle but has not progressed far enough into the cycle to have asserted the address strobe ($\overline{\text{AS}}$) signal. In this case, bus grant will not be asserted until one clock after address strobe is asserted to indicate to external devices that a bus cycle is being executed.

The bus grant signal may be routed through a daisy-chained network or through a specific priority-encoded network. The processor is not affected by the external method of arbitration as long as the protocol is obeyed.

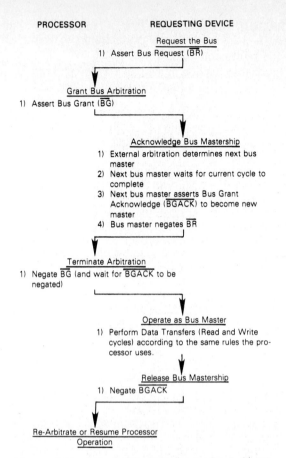

PROCESSOR   REQUESTING DEVICE

Request the Bus
1) Assert Bus Request (BR)

Grant Bus Arbitration
1) Assert Bus Grant (BG)

Acknowledge Bus Mastership
1) External arbitration determines next bus master
2) Next bus master waits for current cycle to complete
3) Next bus master asserts Bus Grant Acknowledge (BGACK) to become new master
4) Bus master negates BR

Terminate Arbitration
1) Negate BG (and wait for BGACK to be negated)

Operate as Bus Master
1) Perform Data Transfers (Read and Write cycles) according to the same rules the processor uses.

Release Bus Mastership
1) Negate BGACK

Re-Arbitrate or Resume Processor Operation

Figure 4-11. Bus Arbitration Cycle Flow-Chart

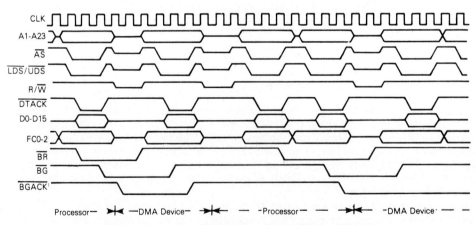

Figure 4-12. Bus Arbitration Cycle Timing Diagram

4.3.2.3 Acknowledgement of Mastership. Upon receiving a bus grant, the requesting device waits until address strobe, data transfer acknowledge, and bus grant acknowledge are negated before issuing its own $\overline{\text{BGACK}}$. The negation of the address strobe indicates that the previous master has completed its cycle, the negation of bus grant acknowledge indicates that the previous master has released the bus. (While address strobe is asserted no device is allowed to "break into" a cycle.) The negation of data transfer acknowledge indicates the previous slave has terminated its connection to the previous master. Note that in some applications data transfer acknowledge might not enter into this function. General purpose devices would then be connected such that they were only dependent on address strobe. When bus grant acknowledge is issued, the device is bus master until it negates bus grant acknowledge. Bus grant acknowledge should not be negated until after the bus cycle(s) is (are) completed. Bus mastership is terminated at the negation of bus grant acknowledge.

The bus request from the granted device should be dropped after bus grant acknowledge is asserted. If bus request is still pending, another bus grant will be asserted within a few cycles of the negation of bus grant. Refer to paragraph 4.3.2.4 for information on bus arbitration control within the processor.

4.3.2.4 Bus Arbitration Control. The bus arbitration control unit in the MC68000 is implemented with a finite state machine. A state diagram of this machine is shown in Figure 4-13. All asynchronous signals to the MC68000 are synchronized before being used internally. This synchronization is accomplished in a maximum of one cycle of the system clock, assuming that the asynchronous input setup time (No. 47 in the data sheet) has been met. The input signal is sampled on the falling edge of the clock and is valid internally after the next falling edge.

As shown in Figure 4-13, input signals labeled R and A are internally synchronized on the bus request and bus grant acknowledge pins, respectively. The bus grant output is labeled G and the internal three-state control signal G. If T is true, the address, data, and control buses are placed in a high-impedance state when address strobe is negated. All signals are shown in positive logic (active high) regardless of their true active voltage level. State changes (valid outputs) occur on the next rising edge after the internal signal is valid.

A timing diagram of the bus arbitration sequence during a processor bus cycle is shown in Figure 4-14. The bus arbitration sequence while the bus is inactive (i.e., executing internal operations such as a multiply instruction) is shown in Figure 4-15.

4.3.3 BUS ERROR AND HALT OPERATION. In a bus architecture that requires a handshake from an external device, the possibility exists that the handshake might not occur. Since different systems will require different maximum response time, a bus error input is provided. External circuitry must be used to determine the duration between address strobe and data transfer acknowledge before issuing a bus error signal. When a bus error signal is received, the processor has two options: initiate a bus error exception sequence or try running the bus cycle again.

47

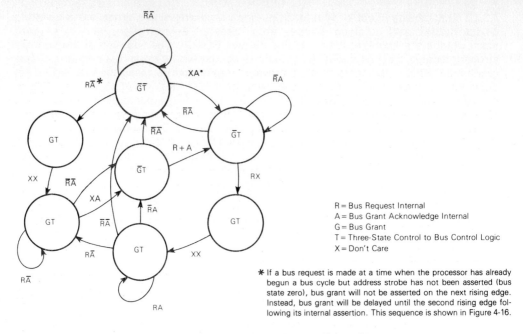

R = Bus Request Internal
A = Bus Grant Acknowledge Internal
G = Bus Grant
T = Three-State Control to Bus Control Logic
X = Don't Care

✱ If a bus request is made at a time when the processor has already
   begun a bus cycle but address strobe has not been asserted (bus
   state zero), bus grant will not be asserted on the next rising edge.
   Instead, bus grant will be delayed until the second rising edge following its internal assertion. This sequence is shown in Figure 4-16.

Figure 4-13. Bus Arbitration Control-State Diagram

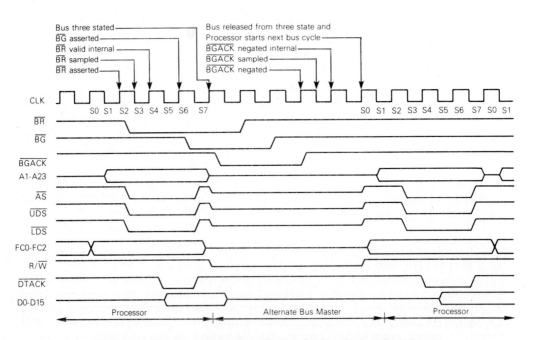

Figure 4-14. Bus Arbitration Timing During Active Bus Cycle

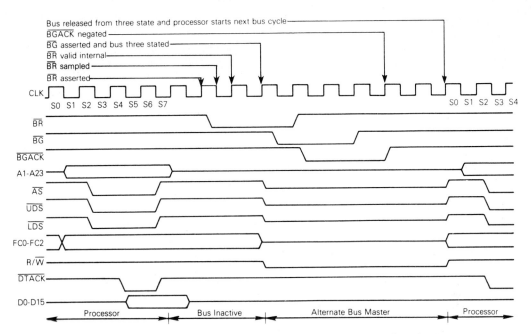

Figure 4-15. Bus Arbitration Timing During Inactive Bus Cycle

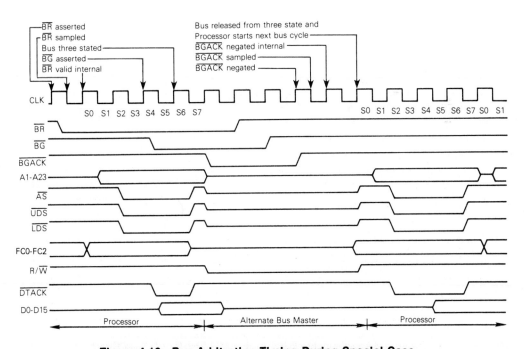

Figure 4-16. Bus Arbitration Timing During Special Case

4.3.3.1 Exception Sequence. When a bus error signal is asserted, the current bus cycle is terminated. If bus error is asserted before the falling edge of S4, address strobe will be negated in S7 in either a read or write cycle. As long as bus error remains asserted, the data and address buses will be in the high-impedance state. When bus error is negated, the processor will begin stacking for exception processing. Figure 4-17 is a timing diagram for the exception sequence. The sequence is composed of the following elements:

1. Stacking the program counter and status register
2. Stacking the error information
3. Reading the bus error vector table entry
4. Executing the bus error handler routine

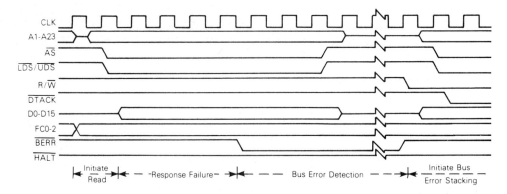

Figure 4-17. Bus Error Timing Diagram

The stacking of the program counter and the status register is the same as if an interrupt had occurred. Several additional items are stacked when a bus error occurs. These items are used to determine the nature of the error and to correct it, if possible. The bus error vector is vector number two located at address $000008. The processor loads the new program counter from this location. A software bus error handler routine is then executed by the processor. Refer to Section 5 for additional information.

4.3.3.2 Re-Running the Bus Cycle. When, during a bus-cycle, the processor receives a bus error signal and the halt pin is being driven by an external device, the processor enters the re-run sequence. Figure 4-18 is a timing diagram for re-running of the bus cycle.

The processor terminates the bus cycle, then puts the address and data output lines in the high-impedance state. The processor remains "halted," and will not run another bus cycle until the halt signal is removed by external logic. Then the processor will re-run the previous bus cycle, using the same address, the same function codes, the same data (for a write operation), and the same controls. The bus error signal should be removed at least one clock cycle before the halt signal is removed.

The processor will not re-run a read-modify-write cycle. This restriction is made to guarantee that the entire cycle runs correctly and that the write operation of a Test-and-Set operation is performed without ever releasing address strobe. If bus error and halt are asserted during a read-modify-write bus cycle, a bus error operation results.

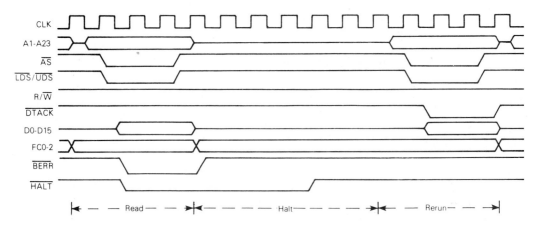

Figure 4-18. Re-Run Bus Cycle Timing Information

4.3.3.3 Halt Operation with No Bus Error. The halt input signal to the MC68000 performs a halt/run/single-step function in a similar fashion to the M6800 halt function. The halt and run modes are somewhat self explanatory in that when the halt signal is constantly active the processor "halts" (does nothing) and when the halt signal is constantly inactive the processor "runs" (does something).

The single-step mode is derived from correctly timed transitions on the halt signal input. It forces the processor to execute a single bus cycle by entering the "run" mode until the processor starts a bus cycle then changing to the "halt" mode. Thus, the single step mode allows the user to proceed through (and therefore debug) processor operations one bus cycle at a time.

Figure 4-19 details the timing required for correct single-step operation and Figure 4-20 shows a simple circuit for providing the single-step function. Some care must be exercised to avoid harmful interactions between the bus error signal and the halt pin when using the single cycle mode as a debugging tool. This is also true of interactions between the halt and reset lines since these can reset the machine.

When the processor completes a bus cycle after recognizing that the halt signal is active, the address and data lines are put in the high-impedance state. This is required for correct performance of the re-run bus cycle operation described in paragraph 4.3.3.2.

While the processor is honoring the halt request, bus arbitration performs as usual. That is, halting has no effect on bus arbitration. It is the bus arbitration function that removes the control signals from the bus.

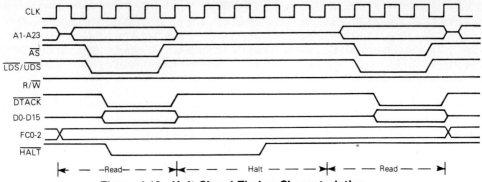

Figure 4-19. Halt Signal Timing Characteristics

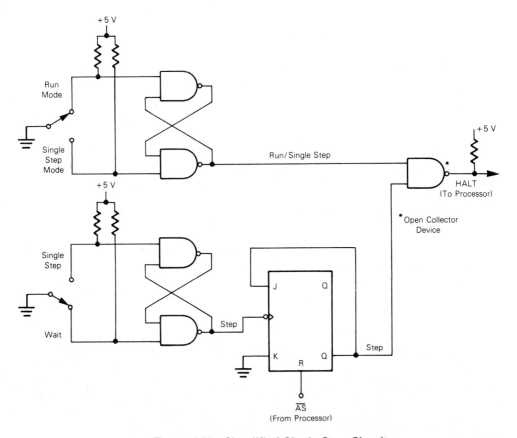

Figure 4-20. Simplified Single-Step Circuit

The halt function and the hardware trace capability allow the hardware debugger to trace single bus cycles or single instructions at a time. These processor capabilities, along with a software debugging package, give total debugging flexibility.

52

4.3.3.4 Double Bus Faults. When a bus error exception occurs, the processor will attempt to stack several words containing information about the state of the machine. If a bus error exception occurs during the stacking operation, there have been two bus errors in a row. This is commonly referred to as a double bus fault. When a double bus fault occurs, the processor will halt. Once a bus error exception has occurred, any bus error exception occurring before the execution of the next instruction constitutes a double bus fault.

Note that a bus cycle which is re-run does not constitute a bus error exception, and does not contribute to a double bus fault. Note also that this means that as long as the external hardware requests it, the processor will continue to re-run the same bus cycle.

The bus error pin also has an effect on processor operation after the processor receives an external reset input. The processor reads the vector table after a reset to determine the address to start program execution. If a bus error occurs while reading the vector table (or at any time before the first instruction is executed), the processor reacts as if a double bus fault has occurred and it halts. Only an external reset will start a halted processor.

4.3.4 $\overline{\text{DTACK}}$, $\overline{\text{BERR}}$, $\overline{\text{HALT}}$ RELATIONSHIP. In order to reliably control termination of a bus cycle for re-run or bus error conditions, $\overline{\text{DTACK}}$, $\overline{\text{BERR}}$, and $\overline{\text{HALT}}$ should be asserted and negated on the rising edge of the clock input to the MC68000. This will ensure that when $\overline{\text{BERR}}$ and $\overline{\text{DTACK}}$ are asserted simultaneously, the asynchronous setup time for both of them will be met during the same bus state. The $\overline{\text{BERR}}$-to-$\overline{\text{DTACK}}$-low parameter (No. 48 on the data sheet) is intended to ensure performance in a totally asynchronous system, and may be ignored if the above conditions are met.

The preferred methods for terminating a bus cycle may be summarized as follows.

Normal Termination — $\overline{\text{DTACK}}$ occurs first (case 1, Table 4-4).

Halt Termination — $\overline{\text{HALT}}$ is asserted at same time as $\overline{\text{DTACK}}$ or precedes $\overline{\text{DTACK}}$ (no $\overline{\text{BERR}}$) (cases 2 and 3, Table 4-4).

Bus Error Termination — $\overline{\text{BERR}}$ is asserted in lieu of, at same time, or precedes $\overline{\text{DTACK}}$ (case 4, Table 4-4); $\overline{\text{BERR}}$ is negated at same time, or after $\overline{\text{DTACK}}$.

Re-Run Termination — $\overline{\text{HALT}}$ and $\overline{\text{BERR}}$ asserted at same time as, or before $\overline{\text{DTACK}}$ (cases 6 and 7, Table 4-4); $\overline{\text{HALT}}$ must be negated at least one cycle after $\overline{\text{BERR}}$. Case 5 indicates that $\overline{\text{BERR}}$ may precede $\overline{\text{HALT}}$ on all except R9M, T6E, and BF4 mask sets, allowing fully asynchronous assertion.

Table A and B detail the resulting bus cycle termination due to the assertion and negation of various combinations of control signal sequences. These tables assume that the asynchronous setup time requirement for both $\overline{\text{BERR}}$ and $\overline{\text{DTACK}}$ is met in the same bus state. Also, $\overline{\text{DTACK}}$ is assumed to be negated normally in all cases; for best results, both $\overline{\text{BERR}}$ and $\overline{\text{DTACK}}$ should be negated when address strobe is negated. The following examples illustrate how these control signals might be used.

Example A:

A system uses a watch-dog timer to terminate accesses to unpopulated address space. The timer asserts $\overline{\text{BERR}}$ and $\overline{\text{DTACK}}$ simultaneously after timeout (case 4, Table 4-4).

Example B:

A system uses error detection on RAM content. The designer may:
   a. Delay $\overline{\text{DTACK}}$ until data is verified; if valid, return $\overline{\text{DTACK}}$. If invalid, return $\overline{\text{BERR}}$ and $\overline{\text{HALT}}$ simultaneously to re-run the bus cycle (case 6, Table 4-4).
   b. Delay $\overline{\text{DTACK}}$ until data is verified; if valid, return $\overline{\text{DTACK}}$. If invalid, return $\overline{\text{BERR}}$ and $\overline{\text{DTACK}}$ simultaneously (case 4, Table 4-4).
   c. Return $\overline{\text{DTACK}}$ before data is verified; if data is invalid, assert $\overline{\text{BERR}}$ in *next* bus cycle. Error-handling software must know how to recover error cycle.

Table 4-4. $\overline{\text{DTACK}}$, $\overline{\text{BERR}}$, $\overline{\text{HALT}}$ Assertion Results

Case No.	Control Signal	Asserted on Rising Edge of State N	Asserted on Rising Edge of State N+2	Result
1	$\overline{\text{DTACK}}$	A	S	Normal cycle terminate and continue.
	$\overline{\text{BERR}}$	NA	X	
	$\overline{\text{HALT}}$	NA	X	
2	$\overline{\text{DTACK}}$	A	S	Normal cycle terminate and halt. Continue when HALT removed.
	$\overline{\text{BERR}}$	NA	X	
	$\overline{\text{HALT}}$	A	S	
3	$\overline{\text{DTACK}}$	NA	A	Normal cycle terminate and halt. Continue when HALT removed.
	$\overline{\text{BERR}}$	NA	NA	
	$\overline{\text{HALT}}$	A	S	
4	$\overline{\text{DTACK}}$	X	X	Terminate and take bus error trap.
	$\overline{\text{BERR}}$	A	S	
	$\overline{\text{HALT}}$	NA	NA	
5	$\overline{\text{DTACK}}$	X	X	R9M, T6E, BF4: Unpredictable results, no re-run, no error trap; usually traps to vector number 0. All others: terminate and re-run.
	$\overline{\text{BERR}}$	A	S	
	$\overline{\text{HALT}}$	NA	A	
6	$\overline{\text{DTACK}}$	X	X	Terminate and re-run.
	$\overline{\text{BERR}}$	A	S	
	$\overline{\text{HALT}}$	A	S	
7	$\overline{\text{DTACK}}$	NA	X	Terminate and re-run when HALT removed.
	$\overline{\text{BERR}}$	NA	A	
	$\overline{\text{HALT}}$	A	S	

Legend:
N = the number of the current even bus state (e.g., S2, S4, etc.)
A = signal is asserted in this bus state
NA = signal is not asserted in this state
X = don't care
S = signal was asserted in previous state and remains asserted in this state

Table 4-5. $\overline{\text{BERR}}$ and $\overline{\text{HALT}}$ Negation Results

Conditions of Termination in Table A	Control Signal	Negated on Rising Edge of State N		N+2	Results — Next Cycle
Bus Error	$\overline{\text{BERR}}$	X	or	X	Takes bus error trap.
	$\overline{\text{HALT}}$	X	or	X	
Re-run	$\overline{\text{BERR}}$	X	or	X	Illegal sequence; usually traps to vector number 0.
	$\overline{\text{HALT}}$	X			
Re-run	$\overline{\text{BERR}}$	X			Re-runs the bus cycle.
	$\overline{\text{HALT}}$			X	
Normal	$\overline{\text{BERR}}$	X			May lengthen next cycle.
	$\overline{\text{HALT}}$	X	or	X	
Normal	$\overline{\text{BERR}}$			X	If next cycle is started, it will be terminated as a bus error.
	$\overline{\text{HALT}}$	X	or	none	

X = signal is negated in this bus state

4.3.5 RESET OPERATION. The reset signal is a bidirectional signal that allows either the processor or an external signal to reset the system. Figure 4-21 is a timing diagram for the reset operation. Both the halt and the reset lines must be applied to ensure total reset of the processor.

When the reset and halt lines are driven by an external device, it is recognized as an entire system reset, including the processor. The processor responds by reading the reset vector table entry (vector number zero, address $000000) and loads it into the supervisor stack pointer (SSP). Vector table entry number one at address $000004 is read next and loaded into the program counter. The processor initializes the status register to an interrupt level of seven. No other registers are affected by the reset sequence.

When a RESET instruction is executed, the processor drives the reset pin for 124 clock pulses. In this case, the processor is trying to reset the rest of the system. Therefore, there is no effect on the internal state of the processor. All of the processor's internal registers and the status register are unaffected by the execution of a RESET instruction.

All external devices connected to the reset line should be reset at the completion of the RESET instruction.

Asserting the reset and halt lines for ten clock cycles will cause a processor reset, except when V$_{CC}$ is initially applied to the processor. In this case, an external reset must be applied to the reset pin for at least 100 milliseconds.

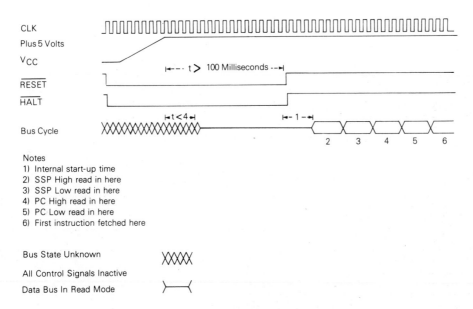

Figure 4-21. Reset Operation Timing Diagram

SECTION 5
EXCEPTION PROCESSING

5.1 INTRODUCTION

This section describes the actions of the MC68000 which are outside the normal processing associated with the execution of instructions. The functions of the bits in the supervisor portion of the status register are covered: the supervisor/user bit, the trace enable bit, and the processor priority mask. Finally, the sequence of memory references and actions taken by the processor on exception conditions is detailed.

5.2 PROCESSING STATES

The MC68000 is always in one of three processing states: normal, exception, or halted. The normal processing state is that associated with instruction execution; the memory references are to fetch instructions and operands, and to store results. A special case of the normal state is the stopped state which the processor enters when a STOP instruction is executed. In this state, no further memory references are made.

The exception processing state is associated with interrupts, trap instructions, tracing and other exceptional conditions. The exception may be internally generated by an instruction or by an unusual condition arising during the execution of an instruction. Externally, exception processing can be forced by an interrupt, by a bus error, or by a reset. Exception processing is designed to provide an efficient context switch so that the processor may handle unusual conditions.

The halted processing state is an indication of catastrophic hardware failure. For example, if during the exception processing of a bus error another bus error occurs, the processor assumes that the system is unusable and halts. Only an external reset can restart a halted processor. Note that a processor in the stopped state is not in the halted state, nor vice versa.

5.3 PRIVILEGE STATES

The processor operates in one of two states of privilege: the "user" state or the "supervisor" state. The privilege state determines which operations are legal, is used by the external memory management device to control and translate accesses, and is used to choose between the supervisor stack pointer and the user stack pointer in instruction references.

The privilege state is a mechanism for providing security in a computer system. Programs should access only their own code and data areas, and ought to be restricted from accessing information which they do not need and must not modify.

The privilege mechanism provides security by allowing most programs to execute in user state. In this state, the accesses are controlled and the effects on other parts of the system are limited. The operating system executes in the supervisor state, has access to all resources, and performs the overhead tasks for the user state programs.

5.3.1 SUPERVISOR STATE. The supervisor state is the higher state of privilege. For instruction execution, the supervisor state is determined by the S-bit of the status register; if the S-bit is asserted (high), the processor is in the supervisor state. All instructions can be executed in the supervisor state. The bus cycles generated by instructions executed in the supervisor state are classified as supervisor references. While the processor is in the supervisor privilege state, those instructions which use either the system stack pointer implicitly or address register seven explicitly access the supervisor stack pointer.

All exception processing is done in the supervisor state, regardless of the setting of the S-bit. The bus cycles generated during exception processing are classified as supervisor references. All stacking operations during exception processing use the supervisor stack pointer.

5.3.2 USER STATE. The user state is the lower state of privilege. For instruction execution, the user state is determined by the S-bit of the status register; if the S-bit is negated (low), the processor is executing instructions in the user state.

Most instructions execute the same in user state as in the supervisor state. However, some instructions which have important system effects are made privileged. User programs are not permitted to execute the STOP instruction, or the RESET instruction. To ensure that a user program cannot enter the supervisor state except in a controlled manner, the instructions which modify the whole status register are privileged. To aid in debugging programs which are to be used as operating systems, the move to user stack pointer (MOVE to USP) and move from user stack pointer (MOVE from USP) instructions are also privileged.

The bus cycles generated by an instruction executed in user state are classified as user state references. This allows an external memory management device to translate the address and to control access to protected portions of the address space. While the processor is in the user privilege state, those instructions which use either the system stack pointer implicitly, or address register seven explicitly, access the user stack pointer.

5.3.3 PRIVILEGE STATE CHANGES. Once the processor is in the user state and executing instructions, only exception processing can change the privilege state. During exception processing, the current setting of the S-bit of the status register is saved and the S-bit is asserted, putting the processing in the supervisor state. Therefore, when instruction execution resumes at the address specified to process the exception, the processor is in the supervisor privilege state.

The transition from supervisor to user state can be accomplished by any of four instructions: return from exception (RTE), move to status register (MOVE word to SR), AND immediate to status register (ANDI to SR), and exclusive OR immediate to status register (EORI to SR). The RTE instruction fetches the new status register and program counter from the supervisor stack, loads each into its respective register, and then begins the instruction fetch at the new program counter address in the privilege state determined by the S-bit of the new contents of the status register. The MOVE, ANDI, and EORI to Status Register instructions each fetch all operands in the supervisor state, perform the appropriate update to the status register, and then fetch the next instruction at the next sequential program counter address in the privilege state determined by the new S-bit.

5.3.4 REFERENCE CLASSIFICATION. When the processor makes a reference, it classifies the kind of reference being made, using the encoding of the three function code output lines. This allows external translation of addresses, control of access, and differentiation of special processor states, such as interrupt acknowledge. Table 5-1 lists the classification of references.

Table 5-1. Reference Classification

Function Code Output			Reference Class
FC2	FC1	FC0	
0	0	0	(Unassigned)
0	0	1	User Data
0	1	0	User Program
0	1	1	(Unassigned)
1	0	0	(Unassigned)
1	0	1	Supervisor Data
1	1	0	Supervisor Program
1	1	1	Interrupt Acknowledge

If the four address spaces, user program, user data, supervisor program, and supervisor data, are externally separated, the processor can address up to 64 megabytes of memory.

5.4 EXCEPTION PROCESSING

Before discussing the details of interrupts, traps, and tracing, a general description of exception processing is in order. The processing of an exception occurs in four steps, with variations for different exception causes. During the first step, a temporary copy of the status register is made, and the status register is set for exception processing. In the second step the exception vector is determined, and the third step is the saving of the current processor context. In the fourth step a new context is obtained, and the processor switches to instruction processing.

5.4.1 EXCEPTION VECTORS. Exception vectors are memory locations from which the processor fetches the address of a routine which will handle the exception.

NOTE
All exception vectors are two words in length as shown in Figure 5-1, except for the reset vector which is four words. All exception vectors lie in the supervisor data space, except for the reset vector which is in the supervisor program space.

A vector number is an 8-bit number which, when multiplied by four, gives the address of an exception vector. Vector numbers are generated internally or externally, depending on the cause of the exception. In the case of interrupts a peripheral provides an 8-bit vector number (Figure 5-2) to the processor on data bus lines D0 through D7 during the interrupt acknowledge bus cycle. The processor translates the vector number into a full 24-bit address as shown in Figure 5-3. The memory map for exception vectors is given in Table 5-2.

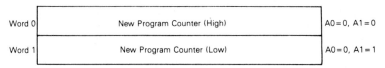

Figure 5-1. Exception Vector Format

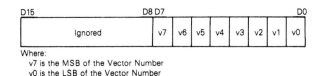

Where:
v7 is the MSB of the Vector Number
v0 is the LSB of the Vector Number

Figure 5-2. Peripheral Vector Number Format

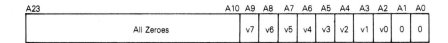

Figure 5-3. Address Translated from 8-Bit Vector Number

As shown in Table 5-2, the memory layout is 512 words long (1024 bytes). It starts at address 0 (decimal) and proceeds through address 1023 (decimal). This provides 255 unique vectors; some of these are reserved for TRAPS and other system functions. Of the 255, there are 192 reserved for user interrupt vectors. However, there is no protection on the first 64 entries, so user interrupt vectors may overlap at the discretion of the systems designer.

5.4.2 KINDS OF EXCEPTIONS. Exceptions can be generated by either internal or external causes. The externally generated exceptions are the interrupts and the bus error and reset requests. The interrupts are requests from peripheral devices for processor action while the bus error and reset inputs are used for access control and processor restart. The internally generated exceptions come from instructions, or from address errors or tracing. The trap (TRAP), trap on overflow (TRAPV), check register against bounds (CHK), and divide (DIV) instructions all can generate exceptions as part of their instruction execution. In addition, illegal instructions, word fetches from odd addresses, and privilege violations cause exceptions. Tracing behaves like a very high priority, internally generated interrupt after each instruction execution.

Table 5-2. Exception Vector Assignment

Vector Number(s)	Dec	Address Hex	Space	Assignment
0	0	000	SP	Reset: Initial SSP[2]
	4	004	SP	Reset: Initial PC[2]
2	8	008	SD	Bus Error
3	12	00C	SD	Address Error
4	16	010	SD	Illegal Instruction
5	20	014	SD	Zero Divide
6	24	018	SD	CHK Instruction
7	28	01C	SD	TRAPV Instruction
8	32	020	SD	Privilege Violation
9	36	024	SD	Trace
10	40	028	SD	Line 1010 Emulator
11	44	02C	SD	Line 1111 Emulator
12[1]	48	030	SD	(Unassigned, Reserved)
13[1]	52	034	SD	(Unassigned, Reserved)
14[1]	56	038	SD	(Unassigned, Reserved)
15	60	03C	SD	Uninitialized Interrupt Vector
16-23[1]	64	040	SD	(Unassigned, Reserved)
	95	05F		—
24	96	060	SD	Spurious Interrupt[3]
25	100	064	SD	Level 1 Interrupt Autovector
26	104	068	SD	Level 2 Interrupt Autovector
27	108	06C	SD	Level 3 Interrupt Autovector
28	112	070	SD	Level 4 Interrupt Autovector
29	116	074	SD	Level 5 Interrupt Autovector
30	120	078	SD	Level 6 Interrupt Autovector
31	124	07C	SD	Level 7 Interrupt Autovector
32-47	128	080	SD	TRAP Instruction Vectors[4]
	191	0BF		
48-63[1]	192	0C0	SD	(Unassigned, Reserved)
	255	0FF		—
64-255	256	100	SD	User Interrupt Vectors
	1023	3FF		—

NOTES:
1. Vector numbers 12, 13, 14, 16 through 23, and 48 through 63 are reserved for future enhancements by Motorola. No user peripheral devices should be assigned these numbers.
2. Reset vector (0) requires four words, unlike the other vectors which only require two words, and is located in the supervisor program space.
3. The spurious interrupt vector is taken when there is a bus error indication during interrupt processing. Refer to Paragraph 5.5.2.
4. TRAP #n uses vector number 32 + n.

5.4.3 EXCEPTION PROCESSING SEQUENCE. Exception processing occurs in four identifiable steps. In the first step, an internal copy is made of the status register. After the copy is made, the S-bit is asserted, putting the processor into the supervisor privilege state. Also, the T-bit is negated which will allow the exception handler to execute unhindered by tracing. For the reset and interrupt exceptions, the interrupt priority mask is also updated.

In the second step, the vector number of the exception is determined. For interrupts, the vector number is obtained by a processor fetch, classified as an interrupt acknowledge. For all other exceptions, internal logic provides the vector number. This vector number is then used to generate the address of the exception vector.

The third step is to save the current processor status, except for the reset exception. The current program counter value and the saved copy of the status register are stacked using the supervisor stack pointer. The program counter value stacked usually points to the next unexecuted instruction, however for bus error and address error, the value stacked for the program counter is unpredictable and may be incremented from the address of the instruction which caused the error. Additional information defining the current context is stacked for the bus error and address error exceptions.

The last step is the same for all exceptions. The new program counter value is fetched from the exception vector. The processor then resumes instruction execution. The instruction at the address given in the exception vector is fetched and normal instruction decoding and execution is started.

5.4.4 MULTIPLE EXCEPTIONS. These paragraphs describe the processing which occurs when multiple exceptions arise simultaneously. Exceptions can be grouped according to their occurrence and priority. The Group 0 exceptions are reset, bus error, and address error. These exceptions cause the instruction currently being executed to be aborted, and the exception processing to commence at the next minor cycle of the processor. The Group 1 exceptions are trace and interrupt, as well as the privilege violations and illegal instructions. These exceptions allow the current instruction to execute to completion, but preempt the execution of the next instruction by forcing exception processing to occur (privilege violations and illegal instructions are detected when they are the next instruction to be executed). The Group 2 exceptions occur as part of the normal processing of instructions. The TRAP, TRAPV, CHK, and zero divide exceptions are in this group. For these exceptions, the normal execution of an instruction may lead to exception processing.

Group 0 exceptions have highest priority, while Group 2 exceptions have lowest priority. Within Group 0, reset has highest priority, followed by bus error and then address error. Within Group 1, trace has priority over external interrupts, which in turn takes priority over illegal instruction and privilege violation. Since only one instruction can be executed at a time, there is no priority relation within Group 2.

The priority relation between two exceptions determines which is taken, or taken first, if the conditions for both arise simultaneously. Therefore, if a bus error occurs during a TRAP instruction, the bus error takes precedence, and the TRAP instruction processing is aborted. In another example, if an interrupt request occurs during the execution of an instruction while the T-bit is asserted, the trace exception has priority, and is processed first. Before instruction execution resumes, however, the interrupt exception is also processed and instruction processing commences finally in the interrupt handler routine. A summary of exception grouping and priority is given in Table 5-3.

Table 5-3. Exception Grouping and Priority

Group	Exception	Processing
0	Reset Bus Error Address Error	Exception processing begins at the next minor cycle
1	Trace Interrupt Illegal Privilege	Exception processing begins before the next instruction
2	TRAP, TRAPV, CHK Zero Divide	Exception processing is started by normal instruction execution

5.5 EXCEPTION PROCESSING DETAILED DISCUSSION

Exceptions have a number of sources and each exception has processing which is peculiar to it. The following paragraphs detail the sources of exceptions, how each arises, and how each is processed.

5.5.1 RESET. The reset input provides the highest exception level. The processing of the reset signal is designed for system initiation, and recovery from catastrophic failure. Any processing in progress at the time of the reset is aborted and cannot be recovered. The processor is forced into the supervisor state and the trace state is forced off. The processor interrupt priority mask is set at level seven. The vector number is internally generated to reference the reset exception vector at location 0 in the supervisor program space. Because no assumptions can be made about the validity of register contents, in particular the supervisor stack pointer, neither the program counter nor the status register is saved. The address contained in the first two words of the reset exception vector is fetched as the initial supervisor stack pointer, and the address in the last two words of the reset exception vector is fetched as the initial program counter. Finally, instruction execution is started at the address in the program counter. The power-up/restart code should be pointed to by the initial program counter.

The RESET instruction does not cause loading of the reset vector, but does assert the reset line to reset external devices. This allows the software to reset the system to a known state and then continue processing with the next instruction.

5.5.2 INTERRUPTS. Seven levels of interrupt priorities are provided. Devices may be chained externally within interrupt priority levels, allowing an unlimited number of peripheral devices to interrupt the processor. Interrupt priority levels are numbered from one to seven, level seven being the highest priority. The status register contains a three-bit mask which indicates the current processor priority, and interrupts are inhibited for all priority levels less than or equal to the current processor priority.

An interrupt request is made to the processor by encoding the interrupt request level on the interrupt request lines; a zero indicates no interrupt request. Interrupt requests arriving at the processor do not force immediate exception processing, but are made pending. Pending interrupts are detected between instruction executions. If the priority of the pending interrupt is lower than or equal to the current processor priority, execution continues with the next instruction and the interrupt exception processing is postponed. (The recognition of level seven is slightly different, as explained in the following paragraph.)

If the priority of the pending interrupt is greater than the current processor priority, the exception processing sequence is started. First a copy of the status register is saved, and the privilege state is set to supervisor, tracing is suppressed, and the processor priority level is set to the level of the interrupt being acknowledged. The processor fetches the vector number from the interrupting device, classifying the reference as an interrupt acknowledge and displaying the level number of the interrupt being acknowledged on the address bus. If external logic requests an automatic vectoring, the processor internally generates a vector number which is determined by the interrupt level number (see paragraph 6.3). If external logic indicates a bus error, the interrupt is taken to be spurious and the generated vector number references the spurious interrupt vector. The processor then proceeds with the usual exception processing, saving the program counter and status register on the supervisor stack. The saved value of the program counter is the address of the instruction which would have been executed had the interrupt not been present. The content of the interrupt vector whose vector number was previously obtained is fetched and loaded into the program counter and normal instruction execution commences in the interrupt handling routine. A flow chart for the interrupt acknowledge sequence is given in Figure 5-4; a timing diagram is given in Figure 5-5.

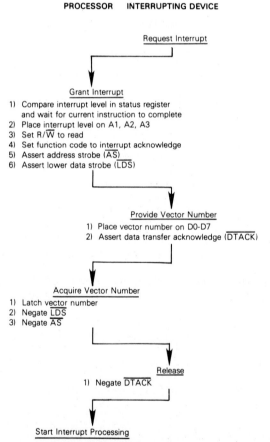

Figure 5-4. Interrupt Acknowledge Sequence Flow Chart

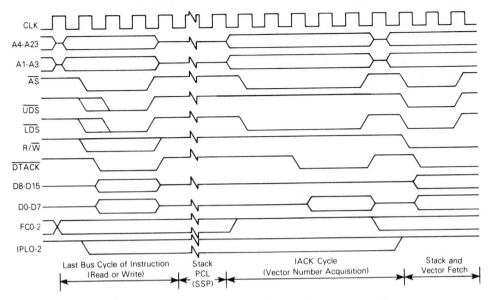

Figure 5-5. Interrupt Acknowledge Sequence Timing Diagram

Priority level seven is a special case. Level seven interrupts cannot be inhibited by the interrupt priority mask, thus providing a "non-maskable interrupt" capability. An interrupt is generated each time the interrupt request level changes from some lower level to level seven. Note that a level seven interrupt may still be caused by the level comparison if the request level is a seven and the processor priority is set to a lower level by an instruction.

5.5.3 INSTRUCTION TRAPS. Traps are exceptions caused by instructions. They arise either from processor recognition of abornomal conditions during instruction, execution, or from use of instructions whose normal behavior is trapping.

Exception processing for traps is straightforward. The status register is copied, the supervisor state is entered, and the trace state is turned off. The vector number is internally generated; for the TRAP instruction, part of the vector number comes from the instruction itself. The program counter and the copy of the status register are saved on the supervisor stack. The saved value of the program counter is the address of the instruction after the instruction which generated the trap. Finally, instruction execution commences at the address contained in the exception vector.

Some instructions are used specifically to generate traps. The TRAP instruction always forces an exception and is useful for implementing system calls for user programs. The TRAPV and CHK instructions force an exception if the user program detects a runtime error, which may be an arithmetic overflow or a subscript out of bounds.

The signed divide (DIVS) and unsigned divide (DIVU) instructions will force an exception if a division operation is attempted with a divisor of zero.

5.5.4 ILLEGAL AND UNIMPLEMENTED INSTRUCTIONS.

Illegal instruction is the term used to refer to any word bit patterns which are not the bit pattern of the first word of a legal instruction. During instruction execution, if such an instruction is fetched, an illegal instruction exception occurs. Motorola reserves the right to define instructions whose opcodes may be any of the illegal instructions. Three bit patterns are reserved as permanently illegal; they are: $4AFA, $4AFB, and $4AFC. Two of the patterns, $4AFA and $4AFB, are reserved for Motorola system products. The third pattern, $4AFC, is reserved for customer use and will always force an illegal instruction trap.

Word patterns with bits 15 through 12 equaling 1010 or 1111 are distinguished as unimplemented instructions and separate exception vectors are given to these patterns to permit efficient emulation. This facility allows the operating system to detect program errors, or to emulate unimplemented instructions in software.

Exception processing for illegal instructions is similar to that for traps. After the instruction is fetched and decoding is attempted, the processor determines that execution of an illegal instruction is being attempted and starts exception processing. The status register is copied, the supervisor state is entered, and the trace state is turned off. The vector number is generated to refer to the illegal instruction vector, or in the case of unimplemented instructions, to the corresponding emulation vector. The current program counter and copy of the status register are saved on the supervisor stack, with the saved value of the program counter being the address of the illegal instruction. Finally, instruction commences at the address contained in the exception vector.

5.5.5 PRIVILEGE VIOLATIONS.

In order to provide system security, various instructions are privileged. An attempt to execute one of the privileged instructions while in the user state will cause an exception. The privileged instructions are:

STOP	AND Immediate to SR
RESET	EOR Immediate to SR
RTE	OR Immediate to SR
MOVE to SR	MOVE USP

Exception processing for privilege violations is nearly identical to that for illegal instructions. After the instruction is fetched and decoded, and the processor determines that a privilege violation is being attempted, the processor starts exception processing. The status register is copied, the supervisor state is entered, and the trace state is turned off. The vector number is generated to reference the privilege violation vector, and the current program counter and the copy of the status register are saved on the supervisor stack. The saved value of the program counter is the address of the first word of the instruction which caused the privilege violation. Finally, instruction execution commences at the address contained in the privilege violation exception vector.

5.5.6 TRACING.

To aid in program development, the MC68000 includes a facility to allow instruction by instruction tracing. In the trace state, after each instruction is executed, an exception is forced, allowing a debugging program to monitor the execution of the program under test.

The trace facility uses the T-bit in the supervisor portion of the status register. If the T-bit is negated (off), tracing is disabled and instruction execution proceeds from instruction to instruction as normal. If the T-bit is asserted (on) at the beginning of the execution of an instruction, a trace exception will be generated after the execution of that instruction is completed. If the instruction is not executed, either because an interrupt is taken or the instruction is illegal or privileged, the trace exception does not occur. The trace exception also does not occur if the instruction is aborted by a reset, bus error, or address error exception. If the instruction is indeed executed and an interrupt is pending on completion, the trace exception is processed before the interrupt exception. If, during the execution of the instruction, an exception is forced by that instruction, the forced exception is processed before the trace exception.

As an extreme illustration of the above rules, consider the arrival of an interrupt during the exception of a TRAP instruction while tracing is enabled. First the trap exception is processed, then the trace exception, and finally the interrupt exception. Instruction execution resumes in the interrupt handler routine.

The exception processing for trace is quite simple. After the execution of the instruction is completed and before the start of the next instruction, exception processing begins. A copy is made of the status register. The transition to supervisor privilege state is made and, as usual, the T-bit of the status register is turned off, disabling further tracing. The vector number is generated to reference the trace exception vector, and the current program counter and the copy of the status register are saved on the supervisor stack. The saved value of the program counter is the address of the next instruction. Instruction execution commences at the address contained in the trace exception vector.

5.5.7 BUS ERROR. Bus error exceptions occur when the external logic requests that a bus error be processed by an exception. The current bus cycle which the processor is making is then aborted. Whether the processor was doing instruction or exception processing, that processing is terminated, and the processor immediately begins exception processing.

Exception processing for bus error follows the usual sequence of steps. The status register is copied, the supervisor state is entered, and the trace state is turned off. The vector number is generated to refer to the bus error vector. Since the processor was not between instructions when the bus error exception request was made, the context of the processor is more detailed. To save more of this context, additional information is saved on the supervisor stack. The program counter and the copy of the status register are of course saved. The value saved for the program counter is advanced by some amount, two to ten bytes beyond the address of the first word of the instruction which made the reference causing the bus error. If the bus error occurred during the fetch of the next instruction, the saved program counter has a value in the vicinity of the current instruction, even if the current instruction is a branch, a jump, or a return instruction. Besides the usual information, the processor saves its internal copy of the first word of the instruction being processed and the address which was being accessed by the aborted bus cycle. Specific information about the access is also saved: whether it was a read or a write, whether the processor was processing an instruction or not, and the classification displayed on the function code outputs when the bus error occurred. The processor is processing an instruction if it is in the normal state or processing a Group 2 exception; the processor is not processing an instruction if it is processing a Group 0 or a Group 1 exception. Figure 5-6 illustrates how this information is organized on the supervisor stack. If a bus error occurs during the last step of exception processing, while either reading the exception vector or fetching the instruction, the value of the program counter is the address of the exception vector. Although this information is not sufficient in general to effect full recovery from the bus error, it does allow software diagnosis. Finally, the processor commences instruction processing at the address contained in the vector. It is the responsibility of the error handler routine to clean up the stack and determine where to continue execution.

If a bus error occurs during the exception processing for a bus error, address error, or reset, the processor is halted, and all processing ceases. This simplifies the detection of a catastrophic system failure, since the processor removes itself from the system rather than destroy all memory contents. Only the RESET pin can restart a halted processor.

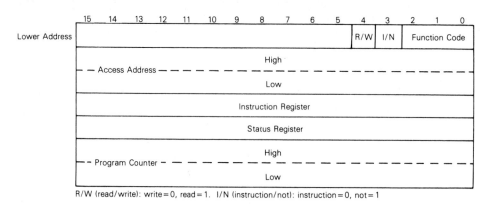

R/W (read/write): write = 0, read = 1. I/N (instruction/not): instruction = 0, not = 1

Figure 5-6. Supervisor Stack Order for Bus or Address Error Exception

5.5.8 ADDRESS ERROR. Address error exceptions occur when the processor attempts to access a word or a long word operand or an instruction at an odd address. The effect is much like an internally generated bus error, so that the bus cycle is aborted, and the processor ceases whatever processing it is currently doing and begins exception processing. After exception processing commences, the sequence is the same as that for bus error including the information that is stacked, except that the vector number refers to the address error vector instead. Likewise, if an address error occurs during the exception processing for a bus error, address error, or reset, the processor is halted. As shown in Figure 5-7, an address error will execute a short bus cycle followed by exception processing.

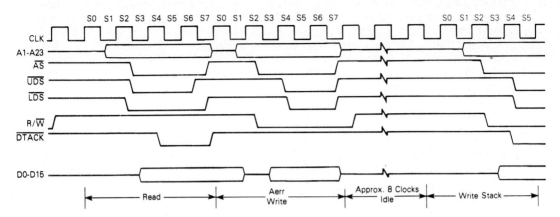

Figure 5-7. Address Error Timing Diagram

SECTION 6
INTERFACE WITH M6800 PERIPHERALS

6.1 INTRODUCTION

Motorola's extensive line of M6800 peripherals are directly compatible with the MC68000. Some of these devices that are particularly useful are:

- MC6821 Peripheral Interface Adapter
- MC6840 Programmable Timer Module
- MC6843 Floppy Disk Controller
- MC6845 CRT Controller
- MC6849 Dual Density Floppy Disk Controller
- MC6850 Asynchronous Communication Interface Adapter
- MC6852 Synchronous Serial Data Adapter
- MC6854 Advanced Data Link Controller
- MC68488 General Purpose Interface Adapter

To interface the synchronous M6800 peripherals with the asynchronous MC68000, the processor modifies its bus cycle to meet the M6800 cycle requirements whenever an M6800 device address is detected. This is possible since both processors use memory mapped I/O. Figure 6-1 is a flow chart of the interface operations between the processor and M6800 devices.

6.2 DATA TRANSFER OPERATION

Three signals on the processor provide the M6800 interface. They are: enable (E), valid memory address ($\overline{\text{VMA}}$), and valid peripheral address ($\overline{\text{VPA}}$). Enable corresponds to the E or φ2 signal in existing M6800 systems. It is the bus clock used by the M6800 peripherals to synchronize data transfer. Enable is a constant frequency clock that is one-tenth of the incoming MC68000 clock frequency. The timing of E allows 1 MHz peripherals to be used with an 8 MHz MC68000. Enable has a 60/40 duty cycle; that is, it is low for six input clocks and high for four input clocks. This duty cycle allows the processor to do two successive $\overline{\text{VPA}}$ accesses on successive E pulses.

M6800 cycle timing is given in Figure 6-2. At state zero (S0) in the cycle, the address bus is in the high-impedance state. A function code is asserted on the function code output lines. One-half clock cycle later, in state 1, the address bus is released from the high-impedance state.

During state 2, the address strobe ($\overline{\text{AS}}$) is asserted to indicate that there is a valid address on the address bus. If the bus cycle is a read cycle, the upper and/or lower data strobes are also asserted in state 2. If the bus cycle is a write cycle, the read/write ($\text{R}/\overline{\text{W}}$) signal is

71

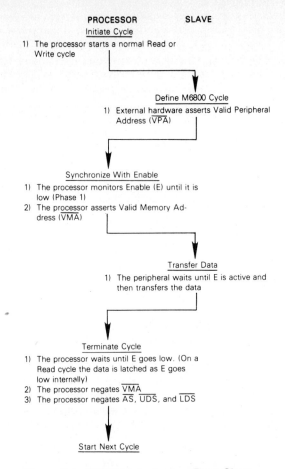

PROCESSOR   SLAVE

Initiate Cycle

1) The processor starts a normal Read or
   Write cycle

Define M6800 Cycle

1) External hardware asserts Valid Peripheral
   Address ($\overline{\text{VPA}}$)

Synchronize With Enable

1) The processor monitors Enable (E) until it is
   low (Phase 1)
2) The processor asserts Valid Memory Address ($\overline{\text{VMA}}$)

Transfer Data

1) The peripheral waits until E is active and
   then transfers the data

Terminate Cycle

1) The processor waits until E goes low. (On a
   Read cycle the data is latched as E goes
   low internally)
2) The processor negates $\overline{\text{VMA}}$
3) The processor negates $\overline{\text{AS}}$, $\overline{\text{UDS}}$, and $\overline{\text{LDS}}$

Start Next Cycle

Figure 6-1. M6800 Interfacing Flow Chart

switched to low (write) during state 2. One-half clock later, in state 3, the write data is placed on the data bus; and in state 4, the data strobes are issued to indicate valid data on the bus. The processor now inserts wait states until it recognizes the assertion of $\overline{\text{VPA}}$.

The $\overline{\text{VPA}}$ input signals the processor that the address on the bus is the address of an M6800 device (or an area reserved for M6800 devices) and that the bus should conform to the $\phi 2$ transfer characteristics of the M6800 bus. Valid peripheral address is derived by decoding the address bus, conditioned by address strobe.

After the recognition of $\overline{\text{VPA}}$, the processor assures that the Enable (E) is low, by waiting if necessary, and subsequently asserts $\overline{\text{VMA}}$. Valid memory address is then used as part of the chip select equation of the peripheral. This ensures that the M6800 peripherals are selected and deselected at the correct time. The peripheral now runs its cycle during the high portion of the E signal.

72

During a read cycle, the processor latches the peripheral data in state 6. For all cycles, the processor negates the address and data strobes one-half clock cycle later in state 7, and the enable signal goes low at this time. Another half clock later, the address bus is put in the high-impedance state. During a write cycle, the data bus is put in the high-impedance state and the read/write signal is switched high at this time. The peripheral logic must remove $\overline{VPA}$ within one clock after address strobe is negated.

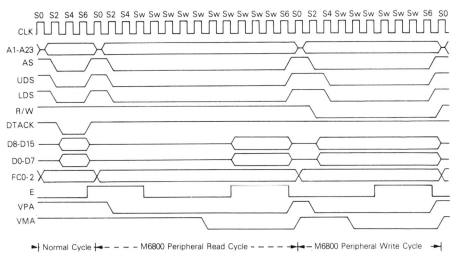

Figure 6-2. M6800 Cycle Operation

Timing information for interfacing with M6800 peripheral devices is contained in the data sheet for the MC68000. Always refer to the latest revision of the MC68000 and desired M6800 peripheral device data sheet when interfacing these devices.

A number of application notes have been published detailing the use of the MC68000 with M6800 Family peripheral devices. The following listing of application notes is current through September 1981. They are available from the Motorola Literature Distribution Center in Phoenix, Arizona.

Title	No.
Interfacing M6800 Peripheral Devices to the MC68000 Asynchronously	808
Interfacing the MC68000 to the MC6846 RIOT	809
Dual 16-Bit Ports for the MC68000 Using Two MC6821s	810
Color Graphics for the MC68000 Using the MC6847	815
A Software Refreshed Memory Card for the MC68000	816
Asynchronous Communications for the MC68000 Using the MC6850	817
Synchronous I/O for the MC68000 Using the MC6852	818
Prioritized Individually Vectored Interrupts for Multiple Peripheral Systems with the MC68000	819
MC68000 DMA Using the MC6844 DMA Controller	824
Using the MC68000 and the MC6845 for a Color Graphics System	834

6.3 INTERRUPT INTERFACE OPERATION

During an interrupt acknowledge cycle while the processor is fetching the vector, if $\overline{VPA}$ is asserted, the MC68000 will assert $\overline{VMA}$ and complete a normal M6800 read cycle, as shown in Figure 6-3. The processor will then use an internally generated vector that is a function of the interrupt being serviced. This process is known as autovectoring. The seven autovectors are vector numbers 25 through 31 (decimal).

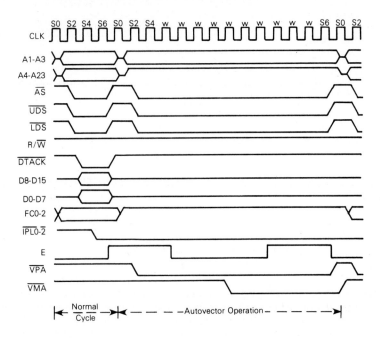

Figure 6-3. Autovector Operation Timing Diagram

This operates in the same fashion (but is not restricted to) the M6800 interrupt sequence. The basic difference is that there are six normal interrupt vectors and one NMI-type vector. As with both the M6800 and the MC68000's normal vectored interrupt, the interrupt service routine can be located anywhere in the address space. This is due to the fact that while the vector numbers are fixed, the contents of the vector table entries are assigned by the user.

Since $\overline{VMA}$ is asserted during autovectoring, the M6800 peripheral address decoding should prevent unintended accesses.

APPENDIX A
CONDITION CODES COMPUTATION

A.1 INTRODUCTION

This appendix provides a discussion of how the condition codes were developed, the meanings of each bit, how they are computed, and how they are represented in the instruction set details.

Two criteria were used in developing the condition codes:
- Consistency — across instruction, uses, and instances
- Meaningful Results — no change unless it provides useful information

The consistency across instructions means that instructions which are special cases of more general instructions affect the condition codes in the same way. Consistency across instances means that if an instruction ever affects a condition code, it will always affect that condition code. Consistency across uses means that whether the condition codes were set by a compare, test, or move instruction, the conditional instructions test the same situation. The tests used for the conditional instructions and the code computations are given in paragraph A.5.

A.2 CONDITION CODE REGISTER

The condition code register portion of the status register contains five bits:

N — Negative
Z — Zero
V — Overflow
C — Carry
X — Extend

The first four bits are true condition code bits in that they reflect the condition of the result of a processor operation. The X bit is an operand for multiprecision computations. The carry bit (C) and the multiprecision operand extend bit (X) are separate in the MC68000 to simplify the programming model.

A.3 CONDITION CODE REGISTER NOTATION

In the instruction set details given in Appendix B, the description of the effect on the condition codes is given in the following form:

Condition Codes:

	X	N	Z	V	C

where:

N (negative) Set if the most significant bit of the result is set. Cleared otherwise.

Z (zero) Set if the result equals zero. Cleared otherwise.

V (overflow) Set if there was an arithmetic overflow. This implies that the result is not representable in the operand size. Cleared otherwise.

C (carry) Set if a carry is generated out of the most significant bit of the operands for an addition. Also set if a borrow is generated in a subtraction. Cleared otherwise.

X (extend) Transparent to data movement. When affected, it is set the same as the C bit.

The notational convention that appears in the representation of the condition code register is:

*   set according to the result of the operation
—   not affected by the operation
0   cleared
1   set
U   undefined after the operation

A.4 CONDITION CODE COMPUTATION

Most operations take a source operand and a destination operand, compute, and store the result in the destination location. Unary operations take a destination operand, compute, and store the result in the destination location. Table A-1 details how each instruction sets the condition codes.

Table A-1. Condition Code Computations

Operations	X	N	Z	V	C	Special Definition
ABCD	*	U	?	U	?	$C =$ Decimal Carry $Z = Z \cdot \overline{Rm} \cdot \ldots \cdot \overline{R0}$
ADD, ADDI, ADDQ	*	*	*	?	?	$V = Sm \cdot Dm \cdot \overline{Rm} + \overline{Sm} \cdot \overline{Dm} \cdot Rm$ $C = Sm \cdot Dm + \overline{Rm} \cdot Dm + Sm \cdot \overline{Rm}$
ADDX	*	*	?	?	?	$V = Sm \cdot Dm \cdot \overline{Rm} + \overline{Sm} \cdot \overline{Dm} \cdot Rm$ $C = Sm \cdot Dm + Rm \cdot \overline{Dm} + Sm \cdot \overline{Rm}$ $Z = Z \cdot \overline{Rm} \cdot \ldots \cdot \overline{R0}$
AND, ANDI, EOR, EORI, MOVEQ, MOVE, OR, ORI, CLR, EXT, NOT, TAS, TST	−	*	*	0	0	
CHK	−	*	U	U	U	
SUB, SUBI, SUBQ	*	*	*	?	?	$V = \overline{Sm} \cdot Dm \cdot \overline{Rm} + Sm \cdot \overline{Dm} \cdot Rm$ $C = Sm \cdot \overline{Dm} + Rm \cdot \overline{Dm} + Sm \cdot Rm$
SUBX	*	*	?	?	?	$V = \overline{Sm} \cdot Dm \cdot \overline{Rm} + Sm \cdot \overline{Dm} \cdot Rm$ $C = Sm \cdot \overline{Dm} + Rm \cdot \overline{Dm} + Sm \cdot Rm$ $Z = Z \cdot \overline{Rm} \cdot \ldots \cdot R0$
CMP, CMPI, CMPM	−	*	*	?	?	$V = \overline{Sm} \cdot Dm \cdot \overline{Rm} + Sm \cdot \overline{Dm} \cdot Rm$ $C = Sm \cdot \overline{Dm} + Rm \cdot \overline{Dm} + Sm \cdot Rm$
DIVS, DIVU	−	*	*	?	0	$V =$ Division Overflow
MULS, MULU	−	*	*	0	0	
SBCD, NBCD	*	U	?	U	?	$C =$ Decimal Borrow $Z = Z \cdot \overline{Rm} \cdot \ldots \cdot \overline{R0}$
NEG	*	*	*	?	?	$V = Dm \cdot Rm,\ C = Dm + Rm$
NEGX	*	*	?	?	?	$V = Dm \cdot Rm,\ C = Dm + Rm$ $Z = Z \cdot \overline{Rm} \cdot \ldots \cdot \overline{R0}$
BTST, BCHG, BSET, BCLR	−	−	?	−	−	$Z = \overline{Dn}$
ASL	*	*	*	?	?	$V = Dm \cdot (\overline{D_{m-1}} + \ldots + \overline{D_{m-r}})$ $\quad + \overline{Dm} \cdot (D_{m-1} + \ldots + D_{m-r})$ $C = D_{m-r+1}$
ASL (r=0)	−	*	*	0	0	
LSL, ROXL	*	*	*	0	?	$C = D_{m-r+1}$
LSR (r=0)	−	*	*	0	0	
ROXL (r=0)	−	*	*	0	?	$C = X$
ROL	−	*	*	0	?	$C = D_{m-r+1}$
ROL (r=0)	−	*	*	0	0	
ASR, LSR, ROXR	*	*	*	0	?	$C = D_{r-1}$
ASR, LSR (r=0)	−	*	*	0	0	
ROXR (r=0)	−	*	*	0	?	$C = X$
ROR	−	*	*	0	?	$C = D_{r-1}$
ROR (r=0)	−	*	*	0	0	

− Not affected
U Undefined
? Other — see Special Definition

*General Case:
$X = C$
$N = Rm$
$Z = Rm \cdot \ldots \cdot R0$

Sm   Source Operand — most significant bit
Dm   Destination operand — most significant bit
Rm   Result operand — most significant bit
n   bit number
r   shift count

A.5 CONDITIONAL TESTS

Table A-2 lists the condition names, encodings, and tests for the conditional branch and set instructions. The test associated with each condition is a logical formula based on the current state of the condition codes. If this formula evaluates to 1, the condition succeeds, or is true. If the formula evaluates to 0, the condition is unsuccessful, or false. For example, the T condition always succeeds, while the EQ condition succeeds only if the Z bit is currently set in the condition codes.

Table A-2. Conditional Tests

Mnemonic	Condition	Encoding	Test
T	true	0000	1
F	false	0001	0
HI	high	0010	$\overline{C} \cdot \overline{Z}$
LS	low or same	0011	$C + Z$
CC (HS)	carry clear	0100	$\overline{C}$
CS (LO)	carry set	0101	C
NE	not equal	0110	$\overline{Z}$
EQ	equal	0111	Z
VC	overflow clear	1000	$\overline{V}$
VS	overflow set	1001	V
PL	plus	1010	$\overline{N}$
MI	minus	1011	N
GE	greater or equal	1100	$N \cdot V + \overline{N} \cdot \overline{V}$
LT	less than	1101	$N \cdot \overline{V} + \overline{N} \cdot V$
GT	greater than	1110	$N \cdot V \cdot \overline{Z} + \overline{N} \cdot \overline{V} \cdot \overline{Z}$
LE	less or equal	1111	$Z + N \cdot \overline{V} + \overline{N} \cdot V$

APPENDIX B
INSTRUCTION SET DETAILS

B.1 INTRODUCTION

This appendix contains detailed information about each instruction in the MC68000 instruction set. They are arranged in alphabetical order with the mnemonic heading set in large bold type for easy reference.

B.2 ADDRESSING CATEGORIES

Effective address modes may be categorized by the ways in which they may be used. The following classifications will be used in the instruction definitions.

Data If an effective address mode may be used to refer to data operands, it is considered a data addressing effective address mode.

Memory If an effective address mode may be used to refer to memory operands, it is considered a memory addressing effective address mode.

Alterable If an effective address mode may be used to refer to alterable (writable) operands, it is considered an alterable addressing effective address mode.

Control If an effective address mode may be used to refer to memory operands without an associated size, it is considered a control addressing effective address mode.

Table B-1 shows the various categories to which each of the effective address modes belong.

Table B-1. Effective Addressing Mode Categories

Addressing Mode	Mode	Register	Addressing Categories				Assembler Syntax
			Data	Mem	Cont	Alter	
Data Reg Dir	000	reg no.	X	—	—	X	Dn
Addr Reg Dir	001	reg no.	—	—	—	X	An
Addr Reg Ind	010	reg no.	X	X	X	X	(An)
Addr Reg Ind w/Postinc	011	reg no.	X	X	—	X	(An) +
Addr Reg Ind w/Predec	100	reg no.	X	X	—	X	– (An)
Addr Reg Ind w/Disp	101	reg no.	X	X	X	X	d(An)
Addr Reg Ind w/Index	110	reg no.	X	X	X	X	d(An, Ri)
Absolute Short	111	000	X	X	X	X	XXX
Absolute Long	111	001	X	X	X	X	XXXXXX
Prog Ctr w/Disp	111	010	X	X	X	—	d(PC)
Prog Ctr w/Index	111	011	X	X	X	—	d(PC, Ri)
Immediate	111	100	X	X	—	—	#XXX

The status register addressing mode is not permitted unless it is explicitly mentioned as a legal addressing mode.

These categories may be combined so that additional, more restrictive, classifications may be defined. For example, the instruction descriptions use such classifications as alterable memory or data alterable. The former refers to those addressing modes which are both alterable and memory addresses, and the latter refers to addressing modes which are both data and alterable.

B.3 INSTRUCTION DESCRIPTION

The formats of each instruction are given in the following pages. Figure B-1 illustrates what information is given.

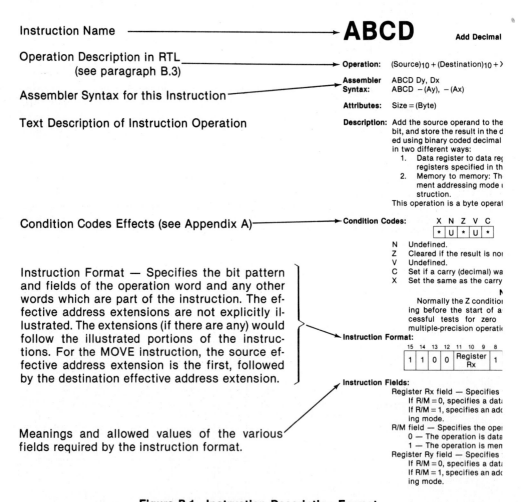

Figure B-1. Instruction Description Format

B.4 REGISTER TRANSFER LANGUAGE DEFINITIONS

The following register transfer language definitions are used for the operation description in the details of the instruction set.

OPERANDS:

An	— address register	**SSP**	— supervisor stack pointer
Dn	— data register	**USP**	— user stack pointer
Rn	— any data or address register	**SP**	— active stack pointer (equivalent to A7)
PC	— program counter	**X**	— extend operand (from condition codes)
SR	— status register		
CCR	— condition codes (low order byte of status register)	**Z**	— zero condition code
		V	— overflow condition code

Immediate Data — immediate data from the instruction
d — address displacement **Destination** — destination location
Source — source location **Vector** — location of exception vector

SUBFIELDS AND QUALIFIERS:

<bit>OF<operand> selects a single bit of the operand
<operand>[<bit number>:<bit number>] selects a subfield of an operand
(<operand>) the contents of the referenced location
<operand>10 the operand is binary coded decimal; operations are to be performed in decimal.
<operand>@<mode> the register indirect operator which indicates that the operand register points to the memory location of the instruction operand. The optional mode qualifiers are −, +, (d) and (d, ix); these are explained in Chapter 2.

OPERATIONS: Operations are grouped into binary, unary, and other.

Binary — These operations are written <operand><op><operand> where <op> is one of the following:

→ the left operand is moved to the location specified by the right operand
↔ the contents of the two operands are exchanged
+ the operands are added
− the right operand is subtracted from the left operand
* the operands are multiplied
/ the first operand is divided by the second operand
Λ the operands are logically ANDed
v the operands are logically ORed
⊕ the operands are logically exclusively ORed
< relational test, true if left operand is less than right operand
> relational test, true if left operand is not equal to right operand
shifted by the left operand is shifted or rotated by the number of positions specified by the
rotated by right operand

Unary:

~<operand> the operand is logically complemented
<operand>sign-extended the operand is sign extended, all bits of the upper half are made equal to high order bit of the lower half
<operand>tested the operand is compared to 0, the results are used to set the condition codes

Other:

TRAP equivalent to PC→SSP@ −; SR→SSP@ −; (vector)→PC
STOP enter the stopped state, waiting for interrupts

If <condition> then <operations> else <operations> The condition is tested. If true, the operations after the "then" are performed. If the condition is false and the optional "else" clause is present, the operations after the "else" are performed. If the condition is false and the optional "else" clause is absent, the instruction performs no operation.

ABCD   Add Decimal with Extend   ABCD

Operation: $(Source)_{10} + (Destination)_{10} + X \rightarrow$ Destination

Assembler   ABCD Dy, Dx
Syntax: ABCD $-(Ay), -(Ax)$

Attributes: Size = (Byte)

Description: Add the source operand to the destination operand along with the extend bit, and store the result in the destination location. The addition is performed using binary coded decimal arithmetic. The operands may be addressed in two different ways:

1. Data register to data register: The operands are contained in the data registers specified in the instruction.
2. Memory to memory: The operands are addressed with the predecrement addressing mode using the address registers specified in the instruction.

This operation is a byte operation only.

Condition Codes:

X	N	Z	V	C
*	U	*	U	*

N   Undefined.
Z   Cleared if the result is non-zero. Unchanged otherwise.
V   Undefined.
C   Set if a carry (decimal) was generated. Cleared otherwise.
X   Set the same as the carry bit.

NOTE

Normally the Z condition code bit is set via programming before the start of an operation. This allows successful tests for zero results upon completion of multiple-precision operations.

Instruction Format:

15	14	13	12	11	10	9	8	7	6	5	4	3	2	1	0
1	1	0	0	Register Rx			1	0	0	0	0	R/M	Register Ry		

Instruction Fields:

Register Rx field — Specifies the destination register:
If R/M = 0, specifies a data register.
If R/M = 1, specifies an address register for the predecrement addressing mode.

R/M field — Specifies the operand addressing mode:
0 — The operation is data register to data register.
1 — The operation is memory to memory.

Register Ry field — Specifies the source register:
If R/M = 0, specifies a data register.
If R/M = 1, specifies an address register for the predecrement addressing mode.

ADD

Add Binary

ADD

Operation: (Source) + (Destination) → Destination

Assembler ADD <ea>, Dn
Syntax: ADD Dn, <ea>

Attributes: Size = (Byte, Word, Long)

Description: Add the source operand to the destination operand, and store the result in the destination location. The size of the operation may be specified to be byte, word, or long. The mode of the instruction indicates which operand is the source and which is the destination as well as the operand size.

Condition Codes:

X	N	Z	V	C
*	*	*	*	*

N   Set if the result is negative. Cleared otherwise.
Z   Set if the result is zero. Cleared otherwise.
V   Set if an overflow is generated. Cleared otherwise.
C   Set if a carry is generated. Cleared otherwise.
X   Set the same as the carry bit.

Instruction Format:

15	14	13	12	11 10 9	8 7 6	5 4 3	2 1 0
1	1	0	1	Register	Op-Mode	Effective Address Mode	Register

Instruction Fields:

Register field — Specifies any of the eight data registers.
Op-Mode field —

Byte	Word	Long	Operation
000	001	010	(<Dn>)+(<ea>)→ <Dn>
100	101	110	(<ea>)+(<Dn>)→ <ea>

Effective Address field — Determines addressing mode:
a. If the location specified is a source operand, then all addressing modes are allowed as shown:

Addressing Mode	Mode	Register	Addressing Mode	Mode	Register
Dn	000	register number	d(An, Xi)	110	register number
An*	001	register number	Abs.W	111	000
(An)	010	register number	Abs.L	111	001
(An)+	011	register number	d(PC)	111	010
-(An)	100	register number	d(PC, Xi)	111	011
d(An)	101	register number	Imm	111	100

*Word and Long only.

— Continued —

Add Binary

Effective Address field (Continued)

b. If the location specified is a destination operand, then only alterable memory addressing modes are allowed as shown:

Addressing Mode	Mode	Register	Addressing Mode	Mode	Register
Dn	—	—	d(An, Xi)	110	register number
An	—	—	Abs.W	111	000
(An)	010	register number	Abs.L	111	001
(An)+	011	register number	d(PC)	—	—
−(An)	100	register number	d(PC, Xi)	—	—
d(An)	101	register number	Imm	—	—

Notes:
1. If the destination is a data register, then it cannot be specified by using the destination <ea> mode, but must use the destination Dn mode instead.
2. ADDA is used when the destination is an address register. ADDI and ADDQ are used when the source is immediate data. Most assemblers automatically make this distinction.

ADDA

Add Address

ADDA

Operation: (Source) + (Destination) → Destination

**Assembler
Syntax:**   ADD < ea >, An

Attributes: Size = (Word, Long)

Description: Add the source operand to the destination address register, and store the
result in the address register. The size of the operation may be specified to
be word or long. The entire destination address register is used regardless
of the operation size.

Condition Codes: Not affected.

Instruction Format:

15	14	13	12	11 10 9	8 7 6	5 4 3	2 1 0
1	1	0	1	Register	Op-Mode	Effective Address Mode	Register

Instruction Fields:

Register field — Specifies any of the eight address registers. This is always
the destination.

Op-Mode field — Specifies the size of the operation:

011 — word operation. The source operand is sign-extended to a long
operand and the operation is performed on the address register using
all 32 bits.

111 — long operation.

Effective Address field — Specifies the source operand. All addressing
modes are allowed as shown:

Addressing Mode	Mode	Register	Addressing Mode	Mode	Register
Dn	000	register number	d(An, Xi)	110	register number
An	001	register number	Abs.W	111	000
(An)	010	register number	Abs.L	111	001
(An) +	011	register number	d(PC)	111	010
− (An)	100	register number	d(PC, Xi)	111	011
d(An)	101	register number	Imm	111	100

ADDI

Add Immediate

ADDI

Operation: Immediate Data + (Destination) → Destination

Assembler Syntax: ADDI #<data>,<ea>

Attributes: Size = (Byte, Word, Long)

Description: Add the immediate data to the destination operand, and store the result in the destination location. The size of the operation may be specified to be byte, word, or long. The size of the immediate data matches the operation size.

Condition Codes:

X	N	Z	V	C
*	*	*	*	*

N   Set if the result is negative. Cleared otherwise.
Z   Set if the result is zero. Cleared otherwise.
V   Set if an overflow is generated. Cleared otherwise.
C   Set if a carry is generated. Cleared otherwise.
X   Set the same as the carry bit.

Instruction Format:

15	14	13	12	11	10	9	8	7	6	5	4	3	2	1	0
0	0	0	0	0	1	1	0	Size		Effective Address Mode | Register					
Word Data (16 bits)								Byte Data (8 bits)							
Long Data (32 bits, including previous word)															

Instruction Fields:

Size field — Specifies the size of the operation:
  00 — byte operation.
  01 — word operation.
  10 — long operation.

Effective Address field — Specifies the destination operand. Only data alterable addressing modes are allowed as shown:

Addressing Mode	Mode	Register	Addressing Mode	Mode	Register
Dn	000	register number	d(An, Xi)	110	register number
An	—	—	Abs.W	111	000
(An)	010	register number	Abs.L	111	001
(An)+	011	register number	d(PC)	—	—
−(An)	100	register number	d(PC, Xi)	—	—
d(An)	101	register number	Imm	—	—

Immediate field — (Data immediately following the instruction):
  If size = 00, then the data is the low order byte of the immediate word.
  If size = 01, then the data is the entire immediate word.
  If size = 10, then the data is the next two immediate words.

86

ADDQ

Add Quick

ADDQ

Operation: Immediate Data + (Destination) → Destination

**Assembler
Syntax:** ADDQ #<data>, <ea>

Attributes: Size = (Byte, Word, Long)

Description: Add the immediate data to the operand at the destination location. The data range is from 1 to 8. The size of the operation may be specified to be byte, word, or long. Word and long operations are also allowed on the address registers and the condition codes are not affected. The entire destination address register is used regardless of the operation size.

Condition Codes:

X	N	Z	V	C
*	*	*	*	*

N   Set if the result is negative. Cleared otherwise.
Z   Set if the result is zero. Cleared otherwise.
V   Set if an overflow is generated. Cleared otherwise.
C   Set if a carry is generated. Cleared otherwise.
X   Set the same as the carry bit.

The condition codes are not affected if an addition to an address register is made.

Instruction Format:

15	14	13	12	11 10 9	8	7 6	5 4 3	2 1 0
0	1	0	1	Data	0	Size	Effective Address Mode	Register

Instruction Fields:

Data field — Three bits of immediate data, 0, 1-7 representing a range of 8, 1 to 7 respectively.

Size field — Specifies the size of the operation:
  00 — byte operation.
  01 — word operation.
  10 — long operation.

Effective Address field — Specifies the destination location. Only alterable addressing modes are allowed as shown:

Addressing Mode	Mode	Register	Addressing Mode	Mode	Register
Dn	000	register number	d(An, Xi)	110	register number
An*	001	register number	Abs.W	111	000
(An)	010	register number	Abs.L	111	001
(An)+	011	register number	d(PC)	—	—
−(An)	100	register number	d(PC, Xi)	—	—
d(An)	101	register number	Imm	—	—

*Word and Long only.

ADDX

Add Extended

ADDX

Operation: (Source) + (Destination) + X → Destination

Assembler ADDX Dy, Dx
Syntax: ADDX − (Ay), − (Ax)

Attributes: Size = (Byte, Word, Long)

Description: Add the source operand to the destination operand along with the extend bit and store the result in the destination location. The operands may be addressed in two different ways:

1. Data register to data register: the operands are contained in data registers specified in the instruction.
2. Memory to memory: the operands are addressed with the predecrement addressing mode using the address registers specified in the instruction.

The size of the operation may be specified to be byte, word, or long.

Condition Codes:

X	N	Z	V	C
*	*	*	*	*

N   Set if the result is negative. Cleared otherwise.
Z   Cleared if the result is non-zero. Unchanged otherwise.
V   Set if an overflow is generated. Cleared otherwise.
C   Set if a carry is generated. Cleared otherwise.
X   Set the same as the carry bit.

NOTE

Normally the Z condition code bit is set via programming before the start of an operation. This allows successful tests for zero results upon completion of multiple-precision operations.

Instruction Format:

15	14	13	12	11 10 9	8	7 6 5	4	3	2 1 0
1	1	0	1	Register Rx	1	Size	0 0	R/M	Register Ry

Instruction Fields:

Register Rx field — Specifies the destination register:
  If R/M = 0, specifies a data register.
  If R/M = 1, specifies an address register for the predecrement addressing mode.
Size field — Specifies the size of the operation:
  00 — byte operation.
  01 — word operation.
  10 — long operation.

— Continued —

ADDX

Add Extended

ADDX

Instruction Fields: (Continued)

R/M field — Specifies the operand addressing mode:
0 — The operation is data register to data register.
1 — The operation is memory to memory.
Register Ry field — Specifies the source register:
If R/M = 0, specifies a data register.
If R/M = 1, specifies an address register for the predecrement addressing mode.

AND

AND Logical

AND

Operation: (Source)Λ(Destination)$\rightarrow$ Destination

Assembler   AND <ea>, Dn
Syntax: AND Dn, <ea>

Attributes: Size = (Byte, Word, Long)

Description: AND the source operand to the destination operand and store the result in the destination location. The size of the operation may be specified to be byte, word, or long. The contents of an address register may not be used as an operand.

Condition Codes:

X	N	Z	V	C
—	*	*	0	0

N   Set if the most significant bit of the result is set. Cleared otherwise.
Z   Set if the result is zero. Cleared otherwise.
V   Always cleared.
C   Always cleared.
X   Not affected.

Instruction Format:

15	14	13	12	11 10 9	8 7 6	5 4 3	2 1 0
1	1	0	0	Register	Op-Mode	Effective Address Mode	Register

Instruction Fields:

Register field — Specifies any of the eight data registers.
Op-Mode field —

Byte	Word	Long	Operation
000	001	010	(<Dn>) Λ (<ea>)$\rightarrow$ <Dn>
100	101	110	(<ea>) Λ (<Dn>)$\rightarrow$ <ea>

Effective Address field — Determines addressing mode:
If the location specified is a source operand then only data addressing modes are allowed as shown:

Addressing Mode	Mode	Register	Addressing Mode	Mode	Register
Dn	000	register number	d(An, Xi)	110	register number
An	—	—	Abs.W	111	000
(An)	010	register number	Abs.L	111	001
(An)+	011	register number	d(PC)	111	010
−(An)	100	register number	d(PC, Xi)	111	011
d(An)	101	register number	Imm	111	100

— Continued —

AND

AND Logical

AND

Effective Address field (Continued)

If the location specified is a destination operand then only alterable memory addressing modes are allowed as shown:

Addressing Mode	Mode	Register	Addressing Mode	Mode	Register
Dn	—	—	d(An, Xi)	110	register number
An	—	—	Abs.W	111	000
(An)	010	register number	Abs.L	111	001
(An)+	011	register number	d(PC)	—	—
−(An)	100	register number	d(PC, Xi)	—	—
d(An)	101	register number	Imm	—	—

Notes:

1. If the destination is a data register, then it cannot be specified by using the destination <ea> mode, but must use the destination Dn mode instead.

2. ANDI is used when the source is immediate data. Most assemblers automatically make this distinction.

ANDI

AND Immediate

Operation: Immediate Data Λ (Destination)→ Destination

**Assembler
Syntax:** ANDI #<data>, <ea>

Attributes: Size = (Byte, Word, Long)

Description: AND the immediate data to the destination operand and store the result in the destination location. The size of the operation may be specified to be byte, word, or long. The size of the immediate data matches the operation size.

Condition Codes:

X	N	Z	V	C
—	*	*	0	0

N   Set if the most significant bit of the result is set. Cleared otherwise.
Z   Set if the result is zero. Cleared otherwise.
V   Always cleared.
C   Always cleared.
X   Not affected.

Instruction Format:

15	14	13	12	11	10	9	8	7	6	5	4	3	2	1	0
0	0	0	0	0	0	1	0		Size		Effective Address Mode | Register				

Word Data (16 bits)	Byte Data (8 bits)

Long Data (32 bits, including previous word)

Instruction Fields:

Size field — Specifies the size of the operation:
00 — byte operation.
01 — word operation.
10 — long operation.

Effective Address field — Specifies the destination operand. Only data alterable addressing modes are allowed as shown:

Addressing Mode	Mode	Register	Addressing Mode	Mode	Register
Dn	000	register number	d(An, Xi)	110	register number
An	—	—	Abs.W	111	000
(An)	010	register number	Abs.L	111	001
(An) +	011	register number	d(PC)	—	—
− (An)	100	register number	d(PC, Xi)	—	—
d(An)	101	register number	Imm	—	—

Immediate field — (Data immediately following the instruction):
If size = 00, then the data is the low order byte of the immediate word.
If size = 01, then the data is the entire immediate word.
If size = 10, then the data is the next two immediate words.

ANDI
to CCR

ANDI
to CCR

Operation: (Source)$\wedge$CCR$\rightarrow$CCR

**Assembler
Syntax:**   ANDI #xxx, CCR

Attributes: Size = (Byte)

Description: AND the immediate operand with the condition codes and store the result in the low-order byte of the status register.

Condition Codes:

X	N	Z	V	C
*	*	*	*	*

N   Cleared if bit 3 of immediate operand is zero. Unchanged otherwise.
Z   Cleared if bit 2 of immediate operand is zero. Unchanged otherwise.
V   Cleared if bit 1 of immediate operand is zero. Unchanged otherwise.
C   Cleared if bit 0 of immediate operand is zero. Unchanged otherwise.
X   Cleared if bit 4 of immediate operand is zero. Unchanged otherwise.

Instruction Format:

15	14	13	12	11	10	9	8	7	6	5	4	3	2	1	0
0	0	0	0	0	0	1	0	0	0	1	1	1	1	0	0
0	0	0	0	0	0	0	0	Byte Data (8 bits)							

ANDI to SR

ANDI to SR

AND Immediate to the Status Register
(Privileged Instruction)

Operation: If supervisor state
then (Source)∧SR → SR
else TRAP

**Assembler
Syntax:** ANDI #xxx, SR

Attributes: Size = (Word)

Description: AND the immediate operand with the contents of the status register and store the result in the status register. All bits of the status register are affected.

Condition Codes:

X	N	Z	V	C
*	*	*	*	*

N Cleared if bit 3 of immediate operand is zero. Unchanged otherwise.
Z Cleared if bit 2 of immediate operand is zero. Unchanged otherwise.
V Cleared if bit 1 of immediate operand is zero. Unchanged otherwise.
C Cleared if bit 0 of immediate operand is zero. Unchanged otherwise.
X Cleared if bit 4 of immediate operand is zero. Unchanged otherwise.

Instruction Format:

15	14	13	12	11	10	9	8	7	6	5	4	3	2	1	0
0	0	0	0	0	0	1	0	0	1	1	1	1	1	0	0
Word Data (16 bits)															

ASL, ASR   Arithmetic Shift   ASL, ASR

Operation: (Destination) Shifted by <count> → Destination

Assembler
Syntax:
ASd Dx, Dy
ASd #<data>, Dy
ASd <ea>

Attributes: Size = (Byte, Word, Long)

Description: Arithmetically shift the bits of the operand in the direction specified. The carry bit receives the last bit shifted out of the operand. The shift count for the shifting of a register may be specified in two different ways:
1. Immediate: the shift count is specified in the instruction (shift range, 1-8).
2. Register: the shift count is contained in a data register specified in the instruction.

The size of the operation may be specified to be byte, word, or long. The content of memory may be shifted one bit only and the operand size is restricted to a word.

For ASL, the operand is shifted left; the number of positions shifted is the shift count. Bits shifted out of the high order bit go to both the carry and the extend bits; zeroes are shifted into the low order bit. The overflow bit indicates if any sign changes occur during the shift.

ASL:

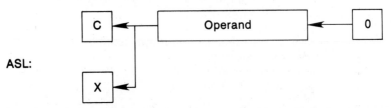

For ASR, the operand is shifted right; the number of positions shifted is the shift count. Bits shifted out of the low order bit go to both the carry and the extend bits; the sign bit is replicated into the high order bit.

ASR:

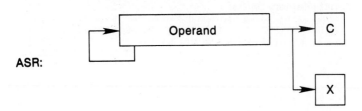

— Continued —

ASL, ASR Arithmetic Shift ASL, ASR

Condition Codes:

X	N	Z	V	C
*	*	*	*	*

N   Set if the most significant bit of the result is set. Cleared otherwise.
Z   Set if the result is zero. Cleared otherwise.
V   Set if the most significant bit is changed at any time during the shift operation. Cleared otherwise.
C   Set according to the last bit shifted out of the operand. Cleared for a shift count of zero.
X   Set according to the last bit shifted out of the operand. Unaffected for a shift count of zero.

Instruction Format (Register Shifts):

15	14	13	12	11	10	9	8	7	6	5	4	3	2	1	0
1	1	1	0	Count/Register			dr	Size		i/r	0	0	Register		

Instruction Fields (Register Shifts):

Count/Register field — Specifies shift count or register where count is located:

If i/r = 0, the shift count is specified in this field. The values 0, 1-7 represent a range of 8, 1 to 7 respectively.

If i/r = 1, the shift count (modulo 64) is contained in the data register specified in this field.

dr field — Specifies the direction of the shift:
0 — shift right.
1 — shift left.

Size field — Specifies the size of the operation:
00 — byte operation.
01 — word operation.
10 — long operation.

i/r field —
If i/r = 0, specifies immediate shift count.
if i/r = 1, specifies register shift count.

Register field — Specifies a data register whose content is to be shifted.

Instruction Format (Memory Shifts):

15	14	13	12	11	10	9	8	7	6	5	4	3	2	1	0
1	1	1	0	0	0	0	dr	1	1	Effective Address Mode			Register		

— Continued —

ASL, ASR Arithmetic Shift ASL, ASR

Instruction Fields (Memory Shifts):

dr field — Specifies the direction of the shift:

0 — shift right.

1 — shift left.

Effective Address field — Specifies the operand to be shifted. Only memory alterable addressing modes are allowed as shown:

Addressing Mode	Mode	Register	Addressing Mode	Mode	Register
Dn	—	—	d(An, Xi)	110	register number
An	—	—	Abs.W	111	000
(An)	010	register number	Abs.L	111	001
(An)+	011	register number	d(PC)	—	—
−(An)	100	register number	d(PC, Xi)	—	—
d(An)	101	register number	Imm	—	—

Bcc

Bcc

Operation: If (condition true) then PC + d → PC

**Assembler
Syntax:** Bcc <label>

Attributes: Size = (Byte, Word)

Description: If the specified condition is met, program execution continues at location (PC) + displacement. Displacement is a twos complement integer which counts the relative distance in bytes. The value in PC is the current instruction location plus two. If the 8-bit displacement in the instruction word is zero, then the 16-bit displacement (word immediately following the instruction) is used. "cc" may specify the following conditions:

CC	carry clear	0100	$\overline{C}$	LS	low or same	0011	$C + Z$
CC	carry set	0101	C	LT	less than	1101	$N \cdot \overline{V} + \overline{N} \cdot V$
EQ	equal	0111	Z	MI	minus	1011	N
GE	greater or equal	1100	$N \cdot V + \overline{N} \cdot \overline{V}$	NE	not equal	0110	$\overline{Z}$
GT	greater than	1110	$N \cdot V \cdot \overline{Z} + \overline{N} \cdot \overline{V} \cdot \overline{Z}$	PL	plus	1010	$\overline{N}$
HI	high	0010	$\overline{C} \cdot \overline{Z}$	VC	overflow clear	1000	$\overline{V}$
LE	less or equal	1111	$Z + N \cdot \overline{V} + \overline{N} \cdot V$	VS	overflow set	1001	V

Condition Codes: Not affected.

Instruction Format:

15	14	13	12	11	10	9	8	7	6	5	4	3	2	1	0
0	1	1	0	Condition				8-bit Displacement							
16-bit Displacement if 8-bit Displacement = 0															

Instruction Fields:

Condition field — One of fourteen conditions discussed in description.

8-bit Displacement field — Twos complement integer specifying the relative distance (in bytes) between the branch instruction and the next instruction to be executed if the condition is met.

16-bit Displacement field — Allows a larger displacement than 8 bits. Used only if the 8-bit displacement is equal to zero.

Note: A short branch to the immediately following instruction cannot be done because it would result in a zero offset which forces a word branch instruction definition.

BCHG

Test a Bit and Change

BCHG

Operation: ~(<bit number> OF Destination)→Z;
~(<bit number> OF Destination)→ <bit number> OF Destination

Assembler BCHG Dn, <ea>
Syntax: BCHG #<data>, <ea>

Attributes: Size = (Byte, Long)

Description: A bit in the destination operand is tested and the state of the specified bit is reflected in the Z condition code. After the test, the state of the specified bit is changed in the destination. If a data register is the destination, then the bit numbering is modulo 32 allowing bit manipulation on all bits in a data register. If a memory location is the destination, a byte is read from that location, the bit operation performed using the bit number modulo 8, and the byte written back to the location with zero referring to the least-significant bit. The bit number for this operation may be specified in two different ways:

1. Immediate — the bit number is specified in a second word of the instruction.
2. Register — the bit number is contained in a data register specified in the instruction.

Condition Codes:

X	N	Z	V	C
—	—	*	—	—

N   Not affected.
Z   Set if the bit tested is zero. Cleared otherwise.
V   Not affected.
C   Not affected.
X   Not affected.

Instruction Format (Bit Number Dynamic):

15	14	13	12	11	10	9	8	7	6	5	4	3	2	1	0
0	0	0	0	Register			1	0	1	Effective Address Mode			Register		

Instruction Fields (Bit Number Dynamic):

Register field — Specifies the data register whose content is the bit number.

Effective Address field — Specifies the destination location. Only data alterable addressing modes are allowed as shown:

Addressing Mode	Mode	Register	Addressing Mode	Mode	Register
Dn*	000	register number	d(An, Xi)	110	register number
An	—	—	Abs.W	111	000
(An)	010	register number	Abs.L	111	001
(An) +	011	register number	d(PC)	—	—
− (An)	100	register number	d(PC, Xi)	—	—
d(An)	101	register number	Imm	—	—

*Long only; all others are byte only.   — Continued —

BCHG

Test a Bit and Change

BCHG

Instruction Format (Bit Number Static):

	15	14	13	12	11	10	9	8	7	6	5 4 3	2 1 0
	0	0	0	0	1	0	0	0	0	1	Effective Address Mode | Register	
	0	0	0	0	0	0	0	0			bit number	

Instruction Fields (Bit Number Static):

Effective Address field — Specifies the destination location. Only data alterable addressing modes are allowed as shown:

Addressing Mode	Mode	Register	Addressing Mode	Mode	Register
Dn	000	register number	d(An, Xi)	110	register number
An	—	—	Abs.W	111	000
(An)	010	register number	Abs.L	111	001
(An) +	011	register number	d(PC)	—	—
– (An)	100	register number	d(PC, Xi)	—	—
d(An)	101	register number	Imm	—	—

*Long only; all others are byte only.

bit number field — Specifies the bit numbers.

BCLR

Test a Bit and Clear

BCLR

Operation: ~(<bit number>) OF Destination)→Z;
0→<bit number> OF Destination

Assembler BLCR Dn, <ea>
Syntax: BCLR #<data>, <ea>

Attributes: Size = (Byte, Long)

Description: A bit in the destination operand is tested and the state of the specified bit is reflected in the Z condition code. After the test, the specified bit is cleared in the destination. If a data register is the destination, then the bit numbering is modulo 32 allowing bit manipulation on all bits in a data register. If a memory location is the destination, a byte is read from that location, the bit operation performed using the bit number modulo 8, and the byte written back to the location with zero referring to the least-significant bit. The bit number for this operation may be specified in two different ways:

1. Immediate — the bit number is specified in a second word of the instruction.
2. Register — the bit number is contained in a data register specified in the instruction.

Condition Codes:

X	N	Z	V	C
—	—	*	—	—

N   Not affected.
Z   Set if the bit tested is zero. Cleared otherwise.
V   Not affected.
C   Not affected.
X   Not affected.

Instruction Format (Bit Number Dynamic):

15	14	13	12	11	10	9	8	7	6	5 4 3	2 1 0
0	0	0	0	Register			1	1	0	Effective Address Mode	Register

Instruction Fields (Bit Number Dynamic):

Register field — Specifies the data register whose content is the bit number.

Effective Address field — Specifies the destination location. Only data alterable addressing modes are allowed as shown:

Addressing Mode	Mode	Register	Addressing Mode	Mode	Register
Dn*	000	register number	d(An, Xi)	110	register number
An	—	—	Abs.W	111	000
(An)	010	register number	Abs.L	111	001
(An) +	011	register number	d(PC)	—	—
– (An)	100	register number	d(PC, Xi)	—	—
d(An)	101	register number	Imm	—	—

*Long only; all others are byte only.

— Continued —

BCLR

Test a Bit and Clear

BCLR

Instruction Format (Bit Number Static):

15	14	13	12	11	10	9	8	7	6	5	4	3	2	1	0
0	0	0	0	1	0	0	0	1	0	\multicolumn{6}{Effective Address}

15	14	13	12	11	10	9	8	7	6	5	4	3	2	1	0
0	0	0	0	1	0	0	0	1	0	Effective Address Mode			Register		
						bit number									

Instruction Fields (Bit Number Static):

Effective Address field — Specifies the destination location. Only data alterable addressing modes are allowed as shown:

Addressing Mode	Mode	Register	Addressing Mode	Mode	Register
Dn*	000	register only	d(An, Xi)	110	register number
An	—	—	Abs.W	111	000
(An)	010	register number	Abs.L	111	001
(An)+	011	register number	d(PC)	—	—
−(An)	100	register number	d(PC, Xi)	—	—
d(An)	101	register number	Imm	—	—

*Long only; all others are byte only.

bit number field — Specifies the bit number.

BRA

Branch Always

BRA

Operation: PC + d → PC

**Assembler
Syntax:**   BRA <label>

Attributes: Size = (Byte, Word)

Description: Program execution continues at location (PC) + displacement. Displacement is a twos complement integer which counts the relative distance in bytes. The value in PC is the current instruction location plus two. If the 8-bit displacement in the instruction word is zero, then the 16-bit displacement (word immediately following the instruction) is used.

Condition Codes: Not affected.

Instruction Format:

15	14	13	12	11	10	9	8	7	6	5	4	3	2	1	0
0	1	1	0	0	0	0	0	8-bit Displacement							
16-bit Displacement if 8-bit Displacement = 0															

Instruction Fields:

8-bit Displacement field — Twos complement integer specifying the relative distance (in bytes) between the branch instruction and the next instruction to be executed if the condition is met.

16-bit Displacement field — Allows a larger displacement than 8 bits. Used only if the 8-bit displacement is equal to zero.

Note: A short branch to the immediately following instruction cannot be done because it would result in a zero offset which forces a word branch instruction definition.

BSET

Test a Bit and Set

BSET

Operation: ~(<bit number>) OF Destination→Z
1→<bit number> OF Destination

Assembler BSET Dn, <ea>
Syntax: BSET #<data>, <ea>

Attributes: Size = (Byte, Long)

Description: A bit in the destination operand is tested and the state of the specified bit is reflected in the Z condition code. After the test, the specified bit is set in the destination. If a data register is the destination, then the bit numbering is modulo 32, allowing bit manipulation on all bits in a data register. If a memory location is the destination, a byte is read from that location, the bit operation performed using the bit number modulo 8, and the byte written back to the location with zero referring to the least-significant bit. The bit number for this operation may be specified in two different ways:
1. Immediate — the bit number is specified in a second word of the instruction.
2. Register — the bit number is contained in a data register specified in the instruction.

Condition Codes:

X	N	Z	V	C
—	—	*	—	—

N   Not affected.
Z   Set if the bit tested is zero. Cleared otherwise.
V   Not affected.
C   Not affected.
X   Not affected.

Instruction Format (Bit Number Dynamic):

15	14	13	12	11	10	9	8	7	6	5	4	3	2	1	0
0	0	0	0	Register			1	1	1	Effective Address Mode			Register		

Instruction Fields (Bit Number Dynamic):

Register field — Specifies the data register whose content is the bit number.

Effective Address field — Specifies the destination location. Only data alterable addressing modes are allowed as shown:

Addressing Mode	Mode	Register	Addressing Mode	Mode	Register
Dn*	000	register number	d(An, Xi)	110	register number
An	—	—	Abs.W	111	000
(An)	010	register number	Abs.L	111	001
(An)+	011	register number	d(PC)	—	—
−(An)	100	register number	d(PC, Xi)	—	—
d(An)	101	register number	Imm	—	—

*Long only; all others are byte only

— Continued —

BSET

Test a Bit and Clear

BSET

Instruction Format (Bit Number Static):

15	14	13	12	11	10	9	8	7	6	5 4 3	2 1 0
0	0	0	0	1	0	0	0	1	1	Effective Address Mode	Register
						bit number					

Instruction Fields (Bit Number Static):

Effective Address field — Specifies the destination location. Only data alterable addressing modes are allowed as shown:

Addressing Mode	Mode	Register	Addressing Mode	Mode	Register
Dn*	000	register number	d(An, Xi)	110	register number
An	—	—	Abs.W	111	000
(An)	010	register number	Abs.L	111	001
(An) +	011	register number	d(PC)	—	—
– (An)	100	register number	d(PC, Xi)	—	—
d(An)	101	register number	Imm	—	—

*Long only; all others are byte only.

bit number field — Specifies the bit number.

BSR

Branch to Subroutine

Operation: PC → − (SP); PC + d → PC

**Assembler
Syntax:** BSR <label>

Attributes: Size = (Byte, Word)

Description: The long word address of the instruction immediately following the BSR in-struction is pushed onto the system stack. Program execution then continues at location (PC) + displacement. Displacement is a twos complement integer which counts the relative distances in bytes. The value in PC is the current instruction location plus two. If the 8-bit displacement in the instruction word is zero, then the 16-bit displacement (word immediately following the instruction) is used.

Condition Codes: Not affected.

Instruction Format:

15	14	13	12	11	10	9	8	7	6	5	4	3	2	1	0
0	1	1	0	0	0	0	1	8-bit Displacement							
16-bit Displacement if 8-bit Displacement = 0															

Instruction Fields:

8-bit Displacement field — Twos complement integer specifying the relative distance (in bytes) between the branch instruction and the next instruction to be executed if the condition is met.

16-bit Displacement field — Allows a larger displacement than 8 bits. Used only if the 8-bit displacement is equal to zero.

Note: A short subroutine branch to the immediately following instruction cannot be done because it would result in a zero offset which forces a word branch instruction definition.

BTST

BTST

Operation: ~(<bit number> OF Destination)→Z

Assembler BTST Dn, <ea>
Syntax: BTST #<data>, <ea>

Attributes: Size = (Byte, Long)

Description: A bit in the destination operand is tested and the state of the specified bit is reflected in the Z condition code. If a data register is the destination, then the bit numbering is modulo 32, allowing bit manipulation on all bits in a data register. If a memory location is the destination, a byte is read from that location, and the bit operation performed using the bit number modulo 8 with zero referring to the least-signifcant bit. The bit number for this operation may be specified in two different ways:

1. Immediate — the bit number is specified in a second word of the instruction.
2. Register — the bit number is contained in a data register specified in the instruction.

Condition Codes:

X	N	Z	V	C
—	—	*	—	—

N   Not affected.
Z   Set if the bit tested is zero. Cleared otherwise.
V   Not affected.
C   Not affected.
X   Not affected.

Instruction Format (Bit Number Dynamic):

15	14	13	12	11	10	9	8	7	6	5	4	3	2	1	0
0	0	0	0	Register			1	0	0	Effective Address Mode | Register					

Instruction Fields (Bit Number Dynamic):

Register field — Specifies the data register whose content is the bit number.

Effective Address field — Specifies the destination location. Only data addressing modes are allowed as shown:

Addressing Mode	Mode	Register	Addressing Mode	Mode	Register
Dn*	000	register number	d(An, Xi)	110	register number
An	—	—	Abs.W	111	000
(An)	010	register number	Abs.L	111	001
(An)+	011	register number	d(PC)	111	010
−(An)	100	register number	d(PC, Xi)	111	011
d(An)	101	register number	Imm	—	—

*Long only; all others are byte only.

— Continued —

BTST

Test a Bit

BTST

Instruction Format (Bit Number Static):

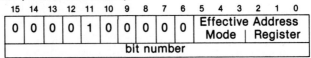

Instruction Fields (Bit Number Static):

Effective Address field — Specifies the destination location. Only data addressing modes are allowed as shown:

Addressing Mode	Mode	Register	Addressing Mode	Mode	Register
Dn*	000	register number	d(An, Xi)	110	register number
An	—	—	Abs.W	111	000
(An)	010	register number	Abs.L	111	001
(An)+	011	register number	d(PC)	111	010
−(An)	100	register number	d(PC, Xi)	111	011
d(An)	101	register number	Imm	—	—

*Long only; all others are byte only.

bit number field — Specifies the bit number.

108

CHK

Check Register Against Bounds

Operation: If Dn<0 or Dn> (<ea>) then TRAP

**Assembler
Syntax:**   CHK <ea>, Dn

Attributes: Size = (Word)

Description: The content of the low order word in the data register specified in the instruction is examined and compared to the upper bound. The upper bound is a twos complement integer. If the register value is less than zero or greater than the upper bound contained in the operand word, then the processor initiates exception processing. The vector number is generated to reference the CHK instruction exception vector.

Condition Codes:

X	N	Z	V	C
—	*	U	U	U

N   Set if Dn<0; cleared if Dn> (<ea>). Undefined otherwise.
Z   Undefined.
V   Undefined.
C   Undefined.
X   Not affected.

Instruction Format:

15	14	13	12	11	10	9	8	7	6	5	4	3	2	1	0
0	1	0	0	Register			1	1	0	Effective Address Mode			Register		

Instruction Fields:

Register field — Specifies the data register whose content is checked.
Effective Address field — Specifies the upper bound operand word. Only data addressing modes are allowed as shown:

Addressing Mode	Mode	Register	Addressing Mode	Mode	Register
Dn	000	register number	d(An, Xi)	110	register number
An	—	—	Abs.W	111	000
(An)	010	register number	Abs.L	111	001
(An) +	011	register number	d(PC)	111	010
− (An)	100	register number	d(PC, Xi)	111	011
d(An)	101	register number	Imm	111	100

CLR

Clear an Operand   # CLR

Operation: 0 → Destination

Assembler Syntax: CLR <ea>

Attributes: Size = (Byte, Word, Long)

Description: The destination is cleared to all zero bits. The size of the operation may be specified to be byte, word, or long.

Condition Codes:

X	N	Z	V	C
—	0	1	0	0

N   Always cleared.
Z   Always set.
V   Always cleared.
C   Always cleared.
X   Not affected.

Instruction Format:

15	14	13	12	11	10	9	8	7	6	5	4	3	2	1	0
0	1	0	0	0	0	1	0	Size		Effective Address Mode | Register					

Instruction Fields:

Size field — Specifies the size of the operation:
00 — byte operation.
01 — word operation.
10 — long operation.

Effective Address field — Specifies the destination location. Only data alterable addressing modes are allowed as shown:

Addressing Mode	Mode	Register	Addressing Mode	Mode	Register
Dn	000	register number	d(An, Xi)	110	register number
An	—	—	Abs.W	111	000
(An)	010	register number	Abs.L	111	001
(An) +	011	register number	d(PC)	—	—
– (An)	100	register number	d(PC, Xi)	—	—
d(An)	101	register number	Imm	—	—

Note: A memory destination is read before it is written to.

CMP   Compare   CMP

Operation: (Destination) – (Source)

Assembler
Syntax: CMP <ea>, Dn

Attributes: Size = (Byte, Word, Long)

Description: Subtract the source operand from the destination operand and set the condition codes according to the result; the destination location is not changed. The size of the operation may be specified to be byte, word, or long.

Condition Codes:

X	N	Z	V	C
—	*	*	*	*

N   Set if the result is negative. Cleared otherwise.
Z   Set if the result is zero. Cleared otherwise.
V   Set if an overflow is generated. Cleared otherwise.
C   Set if a borrow is generated. Cleared otherwise.
X   Not affected.

Instruction Format:

15	14	13	12	11 10 9	8 7 6	5 4 3	2 1 0
1	0	1	1	Register	Op-Mode	Effective Address Mode	Register

Instruction Fields:

Register field — Specifies the destination data register.
Op-Mode field —

Byte	Word	Long	Operation
000	001	010	(<Dn>)–(<ea>)

Effective Address field — Specifies the source operand. All addressing
modes are allowed as shown:

Addressing Mode	Mode	Register	Addressing Mode	Mode	Register
Dn	000	register number	d(An, Xi)	110	register number
An*	001	register number	Abs.W	111	000
(An)	010	register number	Abs.L	111	001
(An)+	011	register number	d(PC)	111	010
–(An)	100	register number	d(PC, Xi)	111	011
d(An)	101	register number	Imm	111	100

*Word and Long only.

Note: CMPA is used when the destination is an address register. CMPI is used
when the source is immediate data. CMPM is used for memory to memory
compares. Most assemblers automatically make this distinction.

CMPA

Compare Address

CMPA

Operation: (Destination) – (Source)

**Assembler
Syntax:** CMPA <ea>, An

Attributes: Size = (Word, Long)

Description: Subtract the source operand from the destination address register and set the condition codes according to the result; the address register is not changed. The size of the operation may be specified to be word or long. Word length source operands are sign extended to 32 bits quantities before the operation is done.

Condition Code:

X	N	Z	V	C
—	*	*	*	*

N   Set if the result is negative. Cleared otherwise.
Z   Set if the result is zero. Cleared otherwise.
V   Set if an overflow is generated. Cleared otherwise.
C   Set if a borrow is generated. Cleared otherwise.
X   Not affected.

Instruction Format:

15	14	13	12	11	10	9	8	7	6	5	4	3	2	1	0
1	0	1	1	Register			Op-Mode			Effective Address					
										Mode			Register		

Instruction Fields:

Register field — Specifies the destination address register.
Op-Mode field — Specifies the size of the operation:
  011 — word operation. The source operand is sign-extended to a long operand and the operation is performed on the address register using all 32 bits.
  111 — long operation.
Effective Address field — Specifies the source operand. All addressing modes are allowed as shown:

Addressing Mode	Mode	Register	Addressing Mode	Mode	Register
Dn	000	register number	d(An, Xi)	110	register number
An	001	register number	Abs.W	111	000
(An)	010	register number	Abs.L	111	001
(An)+	011	register number	d(PC)	111	010
–(An)	100	register number	d(PC, Xi)	111	011
d(An)	101	register number	Imm	111	100

CMPI

Compare Immediate

CMPI

Operation: (Destination) − Immediate Data

**Assembler
Syntax:** CMPI #<data>, <ea>

Attributes: Size = (Byte, Word, Long)

Description: Subtract the immediate data from the destination operand and set the condition codes according to the result; the destination location is not changed. The size of the operation may be specified to be byte, word, or long. The size of the immediate data matches the operation size.

Condition Codes:

X	N	Z	V	C
—	*	*	*	*

N   Set if the result is negative. Cleared otherwise.
Z   Set if the result is zero. Cleared otherwise.
V   Set if an overflow is generated. Cleared otherwise.
C   Set if a borrow is generated. Cleared otherwise.
X   Not affected.

Instruction Format:

15	14	13	12	11	10	9	8	7	6	5	4	3	2	1	0
0	0	0	0	1	1	0	0	Size		Effective Address Mode | Register					
Word Data (16 bits)								Byte Data (8 bits)							
Long Data (32 bits, including previous word)															

Instruction Fields:

Size field — Specifies the size of the operation:
00 — byte operation.
01 — word operation.
10 — long operation.
Effective Address field — Specifies the destination operand. Only data alterable addressing modes are allowed as shown:

Addressing Mode	Mode	Register	Addressing Mode	Mode	Register
Dn	000	register number	d(An, Xi)	110	register number
An	—	—	Abs.W	111	000
(An)	010	register number	Abs.L	111	001
(An)+	011	register number	d(PC)	—	—
−(An)	100	register number	d(PC, Xi)	—	—
d(An)	101	register number	Imm	—	—

Immediate field — (Data immediately following the instruction):
If size = 00, then the data is the low order byte of the immediate word.
If size = 01, then the data is the entire immediate word.
If size = 10, then the data is the next two immediate words.

CMPM   Compare Memory   CMPM

Operation: (Destination) − (Source)

Assembler
Syntax: CMPM (Ay) + , (Ax) +

Attributes: Size = (Byte, Word, Long)

Description: Subtract the source operand from the destination operand, and set the condition codes according to the results; the destination location is not changed. The operands are always addressed with the postincrement addressing mode using the address registers specified in the instruction. The size of the operation may be specified to be byte, word, or long.

Condition Codes:

X	N	Z	V	C
—	*	*	*	*

N   Set if the result is negative. Cleared otherwise.
Z   Set if the result is zero. Cleared otherwise.
V   Set if an overflow is generated. Cleared otherwise.
C   Set if a borrow is generated. Cleared otherwise.
X   Not affected.

Instruction Format:

15	14	13	12	11 10 9	8	7 6	5	4	3	2 1 0
1	0	1	1	Register Rx	1	Size	0	0	1	Register Ry

Instruction Fields:

Register Rx field — (always the destination) Specifies an address register for the postincrement addressing mode.
Size field — Specifies the size of the operation:
00 — byte operation.
01 — word operation.
10 — long operation.
Register Ry field — (always the source) Specifies an address register for the postincrement addressing mode.

DBcc

Test Condition, Decrement, and Branch

DBcc

Operation: If (condition false)
    then Dn − 1 → Dn
  If (Dn ≠ − 1)
    then PC + d → PC
  else PC + 2 → PC (Fall through to next instruction)

**Assembler
Syntax:** DBcc Dn, <label>

Attributes: Size = (Word)

Description: This instruction is a looping primitive of three parameters: a condition, a data register, and a displacement. The instruction first tests the condition to determine if the termination condition for the loop has been met, and if so, no operation is performed. If the termination condition is not true, the low order 16 bits of the counter data register are decremented by one. If the result is − 1, the counter is exhausted and execution continues with the next instruction. If the result is not equal to − 1, execution continues at the location indicated by the current value of PC plus the sign-extended 16-bit displacement. The value in PC is the current instruction location plus two "cc" may specify the following conditions:

CC	carry clear	0100	C		LS	low or same	0011	C + Z
CS	carry set	0101	C		LT	less than	1101	$N \cdot \overline{V} + \overline{N} \cdot V$
EQ	equal	0111	Z		MI	minus	1011	N
F	false	0001	0		NE	not equal	0110	$\overline{Z}$
GE	greater or equal	1100	$N \cdot V + \overline{N} \cdot \overline{V}$		PL	plus	1010	$\overline{N}$
GT	greater than	1110	$N \cdot V \cdot \overline{Z} + \overline{N} \cdot \overline{V} \cdot \overline{Z}$		T	true	0000	1
HI	high	0010	$\overline{C} \cdot \overline{Z}$		VC	overflow clear	1000	$\overline{V}$
LE	less or equal	1111	$Z + \overline{N} \cdot V + N \cdot \overline{V}$		VS	overflow set	1001	V

Condition Codes: Not affected.

Instruction Format:

15	14	13	12	11	10	9	8	7	6	5	4	3	2	1	0
0	1	0	1		Condition			1	1	0	0	1		Register	
Displacement															

Instruction Fields:

Condition field — One of the sixteen conditions discussed in description.
Register field — Specifies the data register which is the counter.
Displacement field — Specifies the distance of the branch (in bytes).

Notes: 1. The terminating condition is like that defined by the UNTIL loop constructs of high-level languages. For example: DBMI can be stated as "decrement and branch until minus."

— Continued —

Notes: (Continued)

2. Most assemblers accept DBRA for DBF for use when no condition is required for termination of a loop.

3. There are two basic ways of entering a loop; at the beginning or by branching to the trailing DBcc instruction. If a loop structure terminated with DBcc is entered at the beginning, the control index count must be one less than the number of loop executions desired. This count is useful for indexed addressing modes and dynamically specified bit operations. However, when entering a loop by branching directly to the trailing DBcc instruction, the control index should equal the loop execution count. In this case, if a zero count occurs, the DBcc instruction will not branch causing complete bypass of the main loop.

DIVS

Signed Divide

DIVS

Operation: (Destination)/(Source) → Destination

**Assembler
Syntax:** DIVS <ea>, Dn

Attributes: Size = (Word)

Description: Divide the destination operand by the source operand and store the result in the destination. The destination operand is a long operand (32 bits) and the source operand is a word operand (16 bits). The operation is performed using signed arithmetic. The result is a 32-bit result such that:

1. The quotient is in the lower word (least significant 16-bits).
2. The remainder is in the upper word (most significant 16-bits).

The sign of the remainder is always the same as the dividend unless the remainder is equal to zero. Two special conditions may arise:

1. Division by zero causes a trap.
2. Overflow may be detected and set before completion of the instruction. If overflow is detected, the condition is flagged but the operands are unaffected.

Condition Codes:

X	N	Z	V	C
—	*	*	*	0

N   Set if the quotient is negative. Cleared otherwise. Undefined if overflow.
Z   Set if the quotient is zero. Cleared otherwise. Undefined if overflow.
V   Set if division overflow is detected. Cleared otherwise.
C   Always cleared.
X   Not affected.

Instruction Format:

15	14	13	12	11 10 9	8	7	6	5 4 3 2 1 0
1	0	0	0	Register	1	1	1	Effective Address Mode | Register

Instruction Fields:

Register field — Specifies any of the eight data registers. This field always specifies the destination operand.

Effective Address field — Specifies the source operand. Only data addressing modes are allowed as shown:

Addressing Mode	Mode	Register	Addressing Mode	Mode	Register
Dn	000	register number	d(An, Xi)	110	register number
An	—	—	Abs.W	111	000
(An)	010	register number	Abs.L	111	001
(An) +	011	register number	d(PC)	111	010
− (An)	100	register number	d(PC, Xi)	111	011
d(An)	101	register number	Imm	111	100

Note: Overflow occurs if the quotient is larger than a 16-bit signed integer.

DIVU

Unsigned Divide

Operation: (Destination)/(Source) → Destination

**Assembler
Syntax:** DIVU <ea>, Dn

Attributes: Size = (Word)

Description: Divide the destination operand by the source operand and store the result in the destination. The destination operand is a long operand (32 bits) and the source operand is a word (16 bit) operand. The operation is performed using unsigned arithmetic. The result is a 32-bit result such that:
1. The quotient is in the lower word (least significnat 16 bits).
2. The remainder is in the upper word (most significant 16 bits).

Two special conditions may arise:
1. Division by zero causes a trap.
2. Overflow may be detected and set before completion of the instruction. If overflow is detected, the condition is flagged but the operands are unaffected.

Condition Codes:

X	N	Z	V	C
—	*	*	*	0

N Set if the most significant bit of the quotient is set. Cleared otherwise. Undefined if overflow.
Z Set if the quotient is zero. Cleared otherwise. Undefined if overflow.
V Set if division overflow is detected. Cleared otherwise.
C Always cleared.
X Not affected.

Instruction Format:

15	14	13	12	11 10 9	8	7	6	5 4 3	2 1 0
1	0	0	0	Register	0	1	1	Effective Address Mode	Register

Instruction Fields:

Register field — specifies any of the eight data registers. This field always specifies the destination operand.

Effective Address field — Specifies the source operand. Only data addressing modes are allowed as shown:

Addressing Mode	Mode	Register	Addressing Mode	Mode	Register
Dn	000	register number	d(An, Xi)	110	register number
An	—	—	Abs.W	111	000
(An)	010	register number	Abs.L	111	001
(An)+	011	register number	d(PC)	111	010
−(An)	100	register number	d(PC, Xi)	111	011
d(An)	101	register number	Imm	111	100

Note: Overflow occurs if the quotient is larger than a 16-bit unsigned integer.

EOR

Exclusive OR Logical

Operation: (Source) ⊕ (Destination) → Destination

**Assembler
Syntax:** EOR Dn, <ea>

Attributes: Size = (Byte, Word, Long)

Description: Exclusive OR the source operand to the destination operand and store the result in the destination location. The size of the operation may be specified to be byte, word, or long. This operation is restricted to data registers as the source operand. The destination operand is specified in the effective address field.

Condition Codes:

X	N	Z	V	C
—	*	*	0	0

N   Set if the most significant bit of the result is set. Cleared otherwise.
Z   Set if the result is zero. Cleared otherwise.
V   Always cleared.
C   Always cleared.
X   Not affected.

Instruction Format:

15	14	13	12	11 10 9	8 7 6	5 4 3	2 1 0
1	0	1	1	Register	Op-Mode	Effective Address Mode	Register

Instruction Fields:

Register field — Specifies any of the eight data registers.
Op-Mode field —

Byte	Word	Long	Operation
100	101	110	(<ea>) ⊕ (<Dx>) → <ea>

Effective Address field — Specifies the destination operand. Only data alterable addressing modes are allowed as shown:

Addressing Mode	Mode	Register	Addressing Mode	Mode	Register
Dn	000	register number	d(An, Xi)	110	register number
An	—	—	Abs.W	111	000
(An)	010	register number	Abs.L	111	001
(An) +	011	register number	d(PC)	—	—
– (An)	100	register number	d(PC, Xi)	—	—
d(An)	101	register number	Imm	—	—

Note: Memory to data register operations are not allowed. EORI is used when the source is immediate data. Most assemblers automatically make this distinction.

EORI

Exclusive OR Immediate

EORI

Operation: Immediate Data ⊕ (Destination) → Destination

**Assembler
Syntax:** EORI #<data>, <ea>

Attributes: Size = (Byte, Word, Long)

Description: Exclusive OR the immediate data to the destination operand and store the result in the destination location. The size of the operation may be specified to be byte, word, or long. The immediate data matches the operation size.

Condition Codes:

X	N	Z	V	C
—	*	*	0	0

N   Set if the most significant bit of the result is set. Cleared otherwise.
Z   Set if the result is zero. Cleared otherwise.
V   Always cleared.
C   Always cleared.
X   Not affected.

Instruction Format:

15	14	13	12	11	10	9	8	7	6	5	4	3	2	1	0
0	0	0	0	1	0	1	0	Size		Effective Address					
										Mode			Register		
Word Data (16 bits)								Byte Data (8 bits)							
Long Data (32 bits, including previous word)															

Instruction Fields:

Size field — Specifies the size of the operation:
   00 — byte operation.
   01 — word operation.
   10 — long operation.

Effective Address field — Specifies the destination operand. Only data alterable addressing modes are allowed as shown:

Addressing Mode	Mode	Register	Addressing Mode	Mode	Register
Dn	000	register number	d(An, Xi)	110	register number
An	—	—	Abs.W	111	000
(An)	010	register number	Abs.L	111	001
(An)+	011	register number	d(PC)	—	—
–(An)	100	register number	d(PC, Xi)	—	—
d(An)	101	register number	Imm	—	—

Immediate field — (Data immediately following the instruction):
   If size = 00, then the data is the low order byte of the immediate word.
   If size = 01, then the data is the entire immediate word.
   If size = 10, then the data is the next two immediate words.

EORI to CCR

EORI Exclusive OR Immediate to Condition Codes **EORI**
to CCR   to CCR

Operation: (Source) ⊕ CCR → CCR

Assembler
Syntax: EORI #xxx, CCR

Attributes: Size = (Byte)

Description: Exclusive OR the immediate operand with the condition codes and store the result in the low-order byte of the status register.

Condition Codes:

X	N	Z	V	C
*	*	*	*	*

N   Changed if bit 3 of immediate operand is one. Unchanged otherwise.
Z   Changed if bit 2 of immediate operand is one. Unchanged otherwise.
V   Changed if bit 1 of immediate operand is one. Unchanged otherwise.
C   Changed if bit 0 of immediate operand is one. Unchanged otherwise.
X   Changed if bit 4 of immediate operand is one. Unchanged otherwise.

Instruction Format:

15	14	13	12	11	10	9	8	7	6	5	4	3	2	1	0
0	0	0	0	1	0	1	0	0	0	1	1	1	1	0	0
0	0	0	0	0	0	0	0	Byte Data (8 bits)							

EORI
to SR

**Exclusive OR Immediate to the Status Register
(Privileged Instruction)**

Operation: If supervisor state
                   then (Source) ⊕ SR → SR
                   else TRAP

**Assembler
Syntax:**   EORI #xxx, SR

Attributes: Size = (Word)

Description: Exclusive OR the immediate operand with the contents of the status
                   register and store the result in the status register. All bits of the status
                   register are affected.

Condition Codes:

```
X  N  Z  V  C
```
*	*	*	*	*

N   Changed if bit 3 of immediate operand is one. Unchanged otherwise.
Z   Changed if bit 2 of immediate operand is one. Unchanged otherwise.
V   Changed if bit 1 of immediate operand is one. Unchanged otherwise.
C   Changed if bit 0 of immediate operand is one. Unchanged otherwise.
X   Changed if bit 4 of immediate operand is one. Unchanged otherwise.

Instruction Format:

15	14	13	12	11	10	9	8	7	6	5	4	3	2	1	0
0	0	0	0	1	0	1	0	0	1	1	1	1	1	0	0
Word Data (16 bits)															

EXG

Exchange Registers

Operation: Rx ↔ Ry

**Assembler
Syntax:** EXG Rx, Ry

Attributes: Size = (Long)

Description: Exchange the contents of two registers. This exchange is always a long (32 bit) operation. Exchange works in three modes:
1. Exchange data registers.
2. Exchange address registers.
3. Exchange a data register and an address register.

Condition Codes: Not affected.

Instruction Format:

15	14	13	12	11 10 9	8	7 6 5 4 3	2 1 0
1	1	0	0	Register Rx	1	Op-Mode	Register Ry

Instruction Fields:

Register Rx field — Specifies either a data register or an address register depending on the mode. If the exchange is between data and address registers, this field always specifies the data register.

Op-Mode field — Specifies whether exchanging:
01000 — data registers.
01001 — address registers.
10001 — data registers and address register.

Register Ry field — Specifies either a data register or an address register depending on the mode. If the exchange is between data and address registers, this field always specifies the address register.

EXT

Sign Extend

Operation: (Destination) Sign-extended → Destination

Assembler
Syntax: EXT Dn

Attributes: Size = (Word, Long)

Description: Extend the sign bit of a data register from a byte to a word or from a word to a long operand depending on the size selected. If the operation is word sized, bit [7] of the designated data register is copied to bits [15:8] of that data register. If the operation is long sized, bit [15] of the designated data register is copied to bits [31:16] of that data register.

Condition Codes:

X	N	Z	V	C
—	*	*	0	0

N   Set if the result is negative. Cleared otherwise.
Z   Set if the result is zero. Cleared otherwise.
V   Always cleared.
C   Always cleared.
X   Not affected.

Instruction Format:

15	14	13	12	11	10	9	8	7	6	5	4	3	2	1	0
0	1	0	0	1	0	0	Op-Mode			0	0	0	Register		

Instruction Fields:

Op-Mode Field — Specifies the size of the sign-extension operation:
010 — Sign-extend low order byte of data register to word.
011 — Sign-extend low order word of data register to long.
Register field — Specifies the data register whose content is to be sign-extended.

ILLEGAL   Illegal Instruction   ILLEGAL

Operation: PC → – (SSP); SR → – (SSP)
               (Illegal Instruction Vector) → PC

Attributes: None

Description: This instruction causes an illegal instruction exception. All other illegal instructions are reserved for future extension of the instruction set.

Condition Codes: Not affected.

Instruction Format:

15	14	13	12	11	10	9	8	7	6	5	4	3	2	1	0
0	1	0	0	1	0	1	0	1	1	1	1	1	1	0	0

JMP

Jump

JMP

Operation: Destination → PC

**Assembler
Syntax:** JMP <ea>

Attributes: Unsized

Description: Program execution continues at the address specified by the instruction. The address is specified by the control addressing modes.

Condition Codes: Not affected.

Instruction Format:

15	14	13	12	11	10	9	8	7	6	5	4	3	2	1	0
0	1	0	0	1	1	1	0	1	1	Effective Address Mode | Register

Instruction Fields:

Effective Address field — Specifies the address of the next instruction. Only control addressing modes are allowed as shown:

Addressing Mode	Mode	Register	Addressing Mode	Mode	Register
Dn	—	—	d(An, Xi)	110	register number
An	—	—	Abs.W	111	000
(An)	010	register number	Abs.L	111	001
(An)+	—	—	d(PC)	111	010
–(An)	—	—	d(PC, Xi)	111	011
d(An)	101	register number	Imm	—	—

126

JSR

Jump to Subroutine

JSR

Operation: PC→ –(SP); Destination→PC

**Assembler
Syntax:** JSR <ea>

Attributes: Unsized

Description: The long word address of the instruction immediately following the JSR instruction is pushed onto the system stack. Program execution then continues at the address specifed in the instruction.

Condition Codes: Not affected.

Instruction Format:

15	14	13	12	11	10	9	8	7	6	5 4 3	2 1 0
0	1	0	0	1	1	1	0	1	0	Effective Address	
										Mode	Register

Instruction Fields:

Effective Address field — Specifies the address of the next instruction. Only control addressing modes are allowed as shown:

Addressing Mode	Mode	Register	Addressing Mode	Mode	Register
Dn	—	—	d(An, Xi)	110	register number
An	—	—	Abs.W	111	000
(An)	010	register number	Abs.L	111	001
(An)+	—	—	d(PC)	111	010
–(An)	—	—	d(PC, Xi)	111	011
d(An)	101	register number	Imm	—	—

LEA

Load Effective Address

LEA

Operation: Destination → An

**Assembler
Syntax:** LEA <ea>, An

Attributes: Size = (Long)

Description: The effective address is loaded into the specified address register. All 32 bits of the address register are affected by this instruction.

Condition Codes: Not affected.

Instruction Format:

15	14	13	12	11	10	9	8	7	6	5	4	3	2	1	0
0	1	0	0	Register			1	1	1	Effective Address Mode			Register		

Instruction Fields:

Register field — Specifies the address register which is to be loaded with the effective address.

Effective Address field — Specifies the address to be loaded into the address register. Only control addressing modes are allowed as shown:

Addressing Mode	Mode	Register	Addressing Mode	Mode	Register
Dn	—	—	d(An, Xi)	110	register number
An	—	—	Abs.W	111	000
(An)	010	register number	Abs.L	111	001
(An)+	—	—	d(PC)	111	010
−(An)	—	—	d(PC, Xi)	111	011
d(An)	101	register number	Imm	—	—

LINK

Link and Allocate

Operation: An → −(SP); SP → An; SP + d → SP

**Assembler
Syntax:** LINK An, #<displacement>

Attributes: Unsized

Description: The current content of the specified address register is pushed onto the stack. After the push, the address register is loaded from the updated stack pointer. Finally, the 16-bit sign-extended displacement is added to the stack pointer. The content of the address register occupies two words on the stack. A negative displacement is specified to allocate stack area.

Condition Codes: Not affected.

Instruction Format:

15	14	13	12	11	10	9	8	7	6	5	4	3	2	1	0
0	1	0	0	1	1	1	0	0	1	0	1	0	Register		
Displacement															

Instruction Fields:

Register field — Specifies the address register through which the link is to be constructed.

Displacement field — Specifies the twos complement integer which is to be added to the stack pointer.

Note: LINK and UNLK can be used to maintain a linked list of local data and parameter areas on the stack for nested subroutine calls.

LSL, LSR Logical Shift LSL, LSR

Operation: (Destination) Shifted by <count> → Destination

Assembler   LSd Dx, Dy
Syntax: LSd #<data>, Dy
             LSd <ea>

Attributes: Size = (Byte, Word, Long)

Description: Shift the bits of the operand in the direction specified. The carry bit
receives the last bit shifted out of the operand. The shift count for the shifting of a register may be specified in two different ways:
1. Immediate — the shift count is specified in the instruction (shift range
   1-8).
2. Register — the shift count is contained in a data register specified in
   the instruction.

The size of the operation may be specified to be byte, word, or long. The
content of memory may be shifted one bit only and the operand size is
restricted to a word.

For LSL, the operand is shifted left; the number of positions shifted is the
shift count. Bits shifted out of the high order bit go to both the carry and the
extend bits; zeroes are shifted into the low order bit.

LSL:

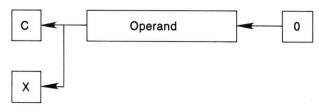

For LSR, the operand is shifted right; the number of positions shifted is the
shift count. Bits shifted out of the low order bit go to both the carry and the
extend bits; zeroes are shifted into the high order bit.

LSR:

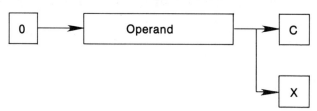

— Continued —

130

LSL, LSR   Logical Shift   LSL, LSR

Condition Codes:

X	N	Z	V	C
*	*	*	0	*

N   Set if the result is negative. Cleared otherwise.
Z   Set if the result is zero. Cleared otherwise.
V   Always cleared.
C   Set according to the last bit shifted out of the operand. Cleared for a shift count of zero.
X   Set according to the last bit shifted out of the operand. Unaffected for a shift count of zero.

Instruction Format (Register Shifts):

15	14	13	12	11	10	9	8	7	6	5	4	3	2	1	0
1	1	1	0	Count/Register			dr	Size		i/r	0	1	Register		

Instruction Fields (Register Shifts):

Count/Register field —
> If i/r = 0, the shift count is specified in this field. The values 0, 1-7 represent a range of 8, 1 to 7 respectively.
> If i/r = 1, the shift count (modulo 64) is contained in the data register specified in this field.

dr field — Specifies the direction of the shift:
> 0 — shift right.
> 1 — shift left.

Size field — Specifies the size of the operation:
> 00 — byte operation.
> 01 — word operation.
> 10 — long operation.

i/r field —
> If i/r = 0, specifies immediate shift count.
> If i/r = 1, specifies register shift count.

Register field — Specifies a data register whose content is to be shifted.

— Continued —

LSL, LSR Logical Shift LSL,LSR

Instruction Format (Memory Shifts):

15	14	13	12	11	10	9	8	7	6	5 4 3	2 1 0
1	1	1	0	0	0	1	dr	1	1	Effective Address Mode	Register

Instruction Fields (Memory Shifts):

dr field — Specifies the direction of the shift:

0 — shift right.

1 — shift left.

Effective Address field — Specifies the operand to be shifted. Only memory alterable addressing modes are allowed as shown:

Addressing Mode	Mode	Register	Addressing Mode	Mode	Register
Dn	—	—	d(An, Xi)	110	register number
An	—	—	Abs.W	111	000
(An)	010	register number	Abs.L	111	001
(An)+	011	register number	d(PC)	—	—
−(An)	100	register number	d(PC, Xi)	—	—
d(An)	101	register number	Imm	—	—

MOVE   Move Data from Source to Destination   MOVE

Operation: (Source) → Destination

**Assembler
Syntax:**   MOVE <ea>, <ea>

Attributes: Size = (Byte, Word, Long)

Description: Move the content of the source to the destination location. The data is examined as it is moved, and the condition codes set accordingly. The size of the operation may be specified to be byte, word, or long.

Condition Codes:

X	N	Z	V	C
—	*	*	0	0

N   Set if the result is negative. Cleared otherwise.
Z   Set if the result is zero. Cleared otherwise.
V   Always cleared.
C   Always cleared.
X   Not affected.

Instruction Format:

15	14	13	12	11	10	9	8	7	6	5	4	3	2	1	0
0	0	Size		Destination Register			Mode			Source Mode			Register		

Instruction Fields:

Size field — Specifies the size of the operand to be moved:
01 — byte operation.
11 — word operation.
10 — long operation.
Destination Effective Address field — Specifies the destination location.
Only data alterable addressing modes are allowed as shown:

Addressing Mode	Mode	Register	Addressing Mode	Mode	Register
Dn	000	register number	d(An, Xi)	110	register number
An	—	—	Abs.W	111	000
(An)	010	register number	Abs.L	111	001
(An)+	011	register number	d(PC)	—	—
−(An)	100	register number	d(PC, Xi)	—	—
d(An)	101	register number	Imm	—	—

— Continued —

MOVE  Move Data from Source to Destination   **MOVE**

Instruction Fields: (Continued)

Source Effective Address field — Specifies the source operand. All addressing modes are allowed as shown:

Addressing Mode	Mode	Register	Addressing Mode	Mode	Register
Dn	000	register number	d(An, Xi)	110	register number
An*	001	register number	Abs.W	111	000
(An)	010	register number	Abs.L	111	001
(An) +	011	register number	d(PC)	111	010
– (An)	100	register number	d(PC, Xi)	111	011
d(An)	101	register number	Imm	111	100

*For byte size operation, address register direct is not allowed.

Notes:
1. MOVEA is used when the destination is an address register. Most assemblers automatically make this distinction.
2. MOVEQ can also be used for certain operations on data registers.

MOVE
to CCR

Move to Condition Codes

MOVE
to CCR

Operation: (Source) → CCR

**Assembler
Syntax:**   MOVE <ea>, CCR

Attributes: Size = (Word)

Description: The content of the source operand is moved to the condition codes. The source operand is a word, but only the low order byte is used to update the condition codes. The upper byte is ignored.

Condition Codes:

X	N	Z	V	C
*	*	*	*	*

N   Set the same as bit 3 of the source operand.
Z   Set the same as bit 2 of the source operand.
V   Set the same as bit 1 of the source operand.
C   Set the same as bit 0 of the source operand.
X   Set the same as bit 4 of the source operand.

Instruction Format:

15	14	13	12	11	10	9	8	7	6	5	4	3	2	1	0
0	1	0	0	0	1	0	0	1	1	Effective Address Mode			Register		

Instruction Fields:

Effective Address field — Specifies the location of the source operand. Only data addressing modes are allowed as shown:

Addressing Mode	Mode	Register	Addressing Mode	Mode	Register
Dn	000	register number	d(An, Xi)	110	register number
An	—	—	Abs.W	111	000
(An)	010	register number	Abs.L	111	001
(An)+	011	register number	d(PC)	111	010
−(An)	100	register number	d(PC, Xi)	111	011
d(An)	101	register number	Imm	111	100

Note: MOVE to CCR is a word operation. AND, OR, and EOR to CCR are byte operations.

MOVE
to SR

Move to the Status Register
(Privileged Instruction)

MOVE
to SR

Operation: If supervisor state
then (Source) → SR
else TRAP

Assembler
Syntax: MOVE <ea>, SR

Attributes: Size = (Word)

Description: The content of the source operand is moved to the status register. The source operand is a word and all bits of the status register are affected.

Condition Codes: Set according to the source operand.

Instruction Format:

15	14	13	12	11	10	9	8	7	6	5	4	3	2	1	0
0	1	0	0	0	1	1	0	1	1	Effective Address Mode / Register					

Instruction Fields:

Effective Address field — Specifies the location of the source operand. Only data addressing modes are allowed as shown:

Addressing Mode	Mode	Register	Addressing Mode	Mode	Register
Dn	000	register number	d(An, Xi)	110	register number
An	—	—	Abs.W	111	000
(An)	010	register number	Abs.L	111	001
(An)+	011	register number	d(PC)	111	010
−(An)	100	register number	d(PC, Xi)	111	011
d(An)	101	register number	Imm	111	100

MOVE from SR

Move from the Status Register

MOVE from SR

Operation: SR → Destination

**Assembler
Syntax:** MOVE SR, <ea>

Attributes: Size = (Word)

Description: The content of the status register is moved to the destination location. The operand size is a word.

Condition Codes: Not affected.

Instruction Format:

15	14	13	12	11	10	9	8	7	6	5	4	3	2	1	0
0	1	0	0	0	0	0	0	1	1						

Effective Address Mode | Register (bits 5–0)

Instruction Fields:

Effective Address field — Specifies the destination location. Only data alterable addressing modes are allowed as shown:

Addressing Mode	Mode	Register	Addressing Mode	Mode	Register
Dn	000	register number	d(An, Xi)	110	register number
An	—	—	Abs.W	111	000
(An)	010	register number	Abs.L	111	001
(An)+	011	register number	d(PC)	—	—
−(An)	100	register number	d(PC, Xi)	—	—
d(An)	101	register number	Imm	—	—

Note: A memory destination is read before it is written to.

MOVE USP

MOVE USP

**Move User Stack Pointer
(Privileged Instruction)**

Operation: If supervisor state
then USP → An;
An → USP
else TRAP

Assembler MOVE USP, An
Syntax: MOVE An, USP

Attributes: Size = (Long)

Description: The contents of the user stack pointer are transferred to or from the specified address register.

Condition Codes: Not affected.

Instruction Format:

15	14	13	12	11	10	9	8	7	6	5	4	3	2	1	0
0	1	0	0	1	1	1	0	0	1	1	0	dr	Register		

Instruction Fields:

dr field — Specifies the direction of transfer:
0 — transfer the address register to the USP.
1 — transfer the USP to the address register.
Register field — Specifies the address register to or from which the user stack pointer is to be transferred.

MOVEA   Move Address   MOVEA

Operation: (Source) → Destination

**Assembler
Syntax:**   MOVEA < ea >, An

Attributes: Size = (Word, Long)

Description: Move the content of the source to the destination address register. The size
of the operation may be specified to be word or long. Word size source
operands are sign extended to 32 bit quantities before the operation is
done.

Condition Codes: Not affected.

Instruction Format:

15	14	13	12	11	10	9	8	7	6	5	4	3	2	1	0
0	0	Size		Destination						Source					
0	0	Size		Register	0	0	1			Mode			Register		

Instruction Fields:

Size field — Specifies the size of the operand to be moved:

11 — Word operation. The source operand is sign-extended to a long
operand and all 32 bits are loaded into the address register.

10 — Long operation.

Destination Register field — Specifies the destination address register.

Source Effective Address field — Specifies the location of the source
operand. All addressing modes are allowed as shown:

Addressing Mode	Mode	Register	Addressing Mode	Mode	Register
Dn	000	register number	d(An, Xi)	110	register number
An	001	register number	Abs.W	111	000
(An)	010	register number	Abs.L	111	001
(An) +	011	register number	d(PC)	111	010
– (An)	100	register number	d(PC, Xi)	111	011
d(An)	101	register number	Imm	111	100

139

MOVEM   Move Multiple Registers   MOVEM

Operation: Registers → Destination
(Source) → Registers

Assembler MOVEM <register list>, <ea>
Syntax: MOVEM <ea>, <register list>

Attributes: Size = (Word, Long)

Description: Selected registers are transferred to or from consecutive memory location starting at the location specified by the effective address. A register is transferred if the bit corresponding to that register is set in the mask field. The instruction selects how much of each register is transferred; either the entire long word can be moved or just the low order word. In the case of a word transfer to the registers, each word is sign-extended to 32 bits (also data registers) and the resulting long word loaded into the associated register.

MOVEM allows three forms of address modes: the control modes, the predecrement mode, or the postincrement mode. If the effective address is in one of the control modes, the registers are transferred starting at the specified address and up through higher addresses. The order of transfer is from data register 0 to data register 7, then from address register 0 to address register 7.

If the effective address is in the predecrement mode, only a register to memory operation is allowed. The registers are stored starting at the specified address minus two and down through lower addresses. The order of storing is from address register 7 to address register 0, then from data register 7 to data register 0. The decremented address register is updated to contain the address of the last word stored.

If the effective address is in the postincrement mode, only a memory to register operation is allowed. The registers are loaded starting at the specified address and up through higher addresses. The order of loading is the same as for the control mode addressing. The incremented address register is updated to contain the address of the last word loaded plus two.

Condition Codes: Not affected.

Instruction Format:

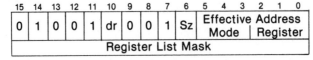

15	14	13	12	11	10	9	8	7	6	5	4	3	2	1	0
0	1	0	0	1	dr	0	0	1	Sz	Effective Address Mode			Register		
Register List Mask															

— Continued —

MOVEM Move Multiple Registers MOVEM

Instruction Fields:

dr field:

Specifies the direction of the transfer:

0 — register to memory

1 — memory to register.

Sz field — Specifies the size of the registers being transferred:

0 — word transfer.

1 — long transfer.

Effective Address field — Specifies the memory address to or from which the registers are to be moved.

For register to memory transfer, only control alterable addressing modes or the predecrement addressing mode are allowed as shown:

Addressing Mode	Mode	Register	Addressing Mode	Mode	Register
Dn	—	—	d(An, Xi)	110	register number
An	—	—	Abs.W	111	000
(An)	010	register number	Abs.L	111	001
(An)+	—	—	d(PC)	—	—
−(An)	100	register number	d(PC, Xi)	—	—
d(An)	101	register number	Imm	—	—

For memory to register transfer, only control addressing modes or the postincrement addressing mode are allowed as shown:

Addressing Mode	Mode	Register	Addressing Mode	Mode	Register
Dn	—	—	d(An, Xi)	110	register number
An	—	—	Abs.W	111	000
(An)	010	register number	Abs.L	111	001
(An)+	011	register number	d(PC)	111	010
−(An)	—	—	d(PC, Xi)	111	011
d(An)	101	register number	Imm	—	—

Register List Mask field — Specifies which registers are to be transferred. The low order bit corresponds to the first register to be transferred; the high bit corresponds to the last register to be transferred. Thus, both for control modes and for the postincrement mode addresses, the mask correspondence is

15	14	13	12	11	10	9	8	7	6	5	4	3	2	1	0
A7	A6	A5	A4	A3	A2	A1	A0	D7	D6	D5	D4	D3	D2	D1	D0

while for the predecrement mode addresses, the mask correspondence is

15	14	13	12	11	10	9	8	7	6	5	4	3	2	1	0
D0	D1	D2	D3	D4	D5	D6	D7	A0	A1	A2	A3	A4	A5	A6	A7

Note: An extra read bus cycle occurs for memory operands. This amounts to a memory word at one address higher than expected being addressed during operation.

MOVEP

Move Peripheral Data

MOVEP

Operation: (Source) → Destination

Assembler MOVEP Dx, d(Ay)
Syntax: MOVEP d(Ay), Dx

Attributes: Size = (Word, Long)

Description: Data is transferred between a data register and alternate bytes of memory, starting at the location specified and incrementing by two. The high order byte of the data register is transferred first and the low order byte is transferred last. The memory address is specified using the address register indirect plus displacement addressing mode. If the address is even, all the transfers are made on the high order half of the data bus; if the address is odd, all the transfers are made on the low order half of the data bus.

Example: Long transfer to/from an even address.

Byte organization in register

31 24	23 16	15 8	7 0
hi-order	mid-upper	mid-lower	low-order

Byte organization in memory (low address at top)

15 14 13 12 11 10 9 8 7 6 5 4 3 2 1 0

hi-order	
mid-upper	
mid-lower	
low-order	

Example: Word transfer to/from an odd address.

Byte organization in register

31 24	23 16	15 8	7 0
		hi-order	low-order

Byte organization in memory (low address at top)

15 14 13 12 11 10 9 8 7 6 5 4 3 2 1 0

	hi-order
	low-order

Condition Codes: Not affected.

— Continued —

MOVEP   Move Peripheral Data   MOVEP

Instruction Format:

15	14	13	12	11 10 9	8 7 6	5	4	3	2 1 0
0	0	0	0	Data Register	Op-Mode	0	0	1	Address Register
Displacement									

Instruction Fields:

Data Register field — Specifies the data register to or from which the data is to be transferred.

Op-Mode field — Specifies the direction and size of the operation:

100 — transfer word from memory to register.

101 — transfer long from memory to register.

110 — transfer word from register to memory.

111 — transfer long from register to memory.

Address Register field — Specifies the address register which is used in the address register indirect plus displacement addressing mode.

Displacement field — Specifies the displacement which is used in calculating the operand address.

MOVEQ

Move Quick

MOVEQ

Operation: Immediate Data → Destination

**Assembler
Syntax:** MOVEQ #<data>, Dn

Attributes: Size = (Long)

Description: Move immediate data to a data register. The data is contained in an 8-bit field within the operation word. The data is sign-extended to a long operand and all 32 bits are transferred to the data register.

Condition Codes:

X	N	Z	V	C
—	*	*	0	0

N   Set if the result is negative. Cleared otherwise.
Z   Set if the result is zero. Cleared otherwise.
V   Always cleared.
C   Always cleared.
X   Not affected.

Instruction Format:

15	14	13	12	11	10	9	8	7	6	5	4	3	2	1	0
0	1	1	1	Register			0	Data							

Instruction Fields:

Register field — Specifies the data register to be loaded.
Data field — 8 bits of data which are sign extended to a long operand.

MULS

Signed Multiply

MULS

Operation: (Source)*(Destination) → Destination

**Assembler
Syntax:** MULS <ea>, Dn

Attributes: Size = (Word)

Description: Multiply two signed 16-bit operands yielding a 32-bit signed result. The operation is performed using signed arithmetic. A register operand is taken from the low order word; the upper word is unused. All 32 bits of the product are saved in the destination data register.

Condition Codes:

X	N	Z	V	C
—	*	*	0	0

N   Set if the result is negative. Cleared otherwise.
Z   Set if the result is zero. Cleared otherwise.
V   Always cleared.
C   Always cleared.
X   Not affected.

Instruction Format:

15	14	13	12	11	10	9	8	7	6	5	4	3	2	1	0
1	1	0	0	Register			1	1	1	Effective Address Mode			Register		

Instruction Fields:

Register field — Specifies one of the data registers. This field always specifies the destination.

Effective Address field — Specifies the source operand. Only data addressing modes are allowed as shown:

Addressing Mode	Mode	Register	Addressing Mode	Mode	Register
Dn	000	register number	d(An, Xi)	110	register number
An	—	—	Abs.W	111	000
(An)	010	register number	Abs.L	111	001
(An)+	011	register number	d(PC)	111	010
−(An)	100	register number	d(PC, Xi)	111	011
d(An)	101	register number	Imm	111	100

MULU

Unsigned Mulitply

Operation: (Source)*(Destination)→Destination

**Assembler
Syntax:** MULU <ea>, Dn

Attributes: Size = (Word)

Description: Multiply two unsigned 16-bit operands yielding a 32-bit unsigned result. The operation is performed using unsigned arithmetic. A register operand is taken from the low order word; the upper word is unused. All 32 bits of the product are saved in the destination data register.

Condition Codes:

X	N	Z	V	C
—	*	*	0	0

N Set if the most significant bit of the result is set. Cleared otherwise.
Z Set if the result is zero. Cleared otherwise.
V Always cleared.
C Always cleared.
X Not affected.

Instruction Format:

15	14	13	12	11 10 9	8	7	6	5 4 3	2 1 0
1	1	0	0	Register	0	1	1	Effective Address Mode	Register

Instruction Fields:

Register field — Specifies one of the data registers. This field always specifies the destination.

Effective Address field — Specifies the source operand. Only data addressing modes are allowed as shown:

Addressing Mode	Mode	Register	Addressing Mode	Mode	Register
Dn	000	register number	d(An, Xi)	110	register number
An	—	—	Abs.W	111	000
(An)	010	register number	Abs.L	111	001
(An) +	011	register number	d(PC)	111	010
− (An)	100	register number	d(PC, Xi)	111	011
d(An)	101	register number	Imm	111	100

146

NBCD

Negate Decimal with Extend

NBCD

Operation: $0 - (Destination)_{10} - X \rightarrow Destination$

**Assembler
Syntax:** NBCD < ea >

Attributes: Size = (Byte)

Description: The operand addressed as the destination and the extend bit are subtracted from zero. The operation is performed using decimal arithmetic. The result is saved in the destination location. This instruction produces the tens complement of the destination if the extend bit is clear, the nines complement if the extend bit is set. This is a byte operation only.

Condition Codes:

X	N	Z	V	C
*	U	*	U	*

N Undefined.
Z Cleared if the result is non-zero. Unchanged otherwise.
V Undefined.
C Set if a borrow (decimal) was generated. Cleared otherwise.
X Set the same as the carry bit.

NOTE
Normally the Z condition code bit is set via programming before the start of an operation. This allows successful tests for zero results upon completion of multiple-precision operations.

Instruction Format:

15	14	13	12	11	10	9	8	7	6	5 4 3	2 1 0
0	1	0	0	1	0	0	0	0	0	Effective Address Mode	Register

Instruction Fields:

Effective Address field — Specifies the destination operand. Only data alterable addressing modes are allowed as shown:

Addressing Mode	Mode	Register	Addressing Mode	Mode	Register
Dn	000	register number	d(An, Xi)	110	register number
An	—	—	Abs.W	111	000
(An)	010	register number	Abs.L	111	001
(An)+	011	register number	d(PC)	—	—
-(An)	100	register number	d(PC, Xi)	—	—
d(An)	101	register number	Imm	—	—

NEG

Negate

NEG

Operation: 0 – (Destination) → Destination

**Assembler
Syntax:**   NEG <ea>

Attributes: Size = (Byte, Word, Long)

Description: The operand addressed as the destination is subtracted from zero. The result is stored in the destination location. The size of the operation may be specified to be byte, word, or long.

Condition Codes:

X	N	Z	V	C
*	*	*	*	*

N   Set if the result is negative. Cleared otherwise.
Z   Set if the result is zero. Cleared otherwise.
V   Set if an overflow is generated. Cleared otherwise.
C   Cleared if the result is zero. Set otherwise.
X   Set the same as the carry bit.

Instruction Format:

15	14	13	12	11	10	9	8	7	6	5 4 3	2 1 0
0	1	0	0	0	1	0	0	Size		Effective Address Mode	Register

Instruction Fields:

Size field — Specifies the size of the operation:
  00 — byte operation.
  01 — word operation.
  10 — long operation.

Effective Address field — Specifies the destination operand. Only data alterable addressing modes are allowed as shown:

Addressing Mode	Mode	Register	Addressing Mode	Mode	Register
Dn	000	register number	d(An, Xi)	110	register number
An	—	—	Abs.W	111	000
(An)	010	register number	Abs.L	111	001
(An)+	011	register number	d(PC)	—	—
–(An)	100	register number	d(PC, Xi)	—	—
d(An)	101	register number	Imm	—	—

NEGX Negate with Extend NEGX

Operation: 0 − (Destination) − X → Destination

**Assembler
Syntax:** NEGX <ea>

Attributes: Size = (Byte, Word, Long)

Description: The operand addressed as the destination and the extend bit are subtracted from zero. The result is stored in the destination location. The size of the operation may be specified to be byte, word, or long.

Condition Codes:

X	N	Z	V	C
*	*	*	*	*

N   Set if the result is negative. Cleared otherwise.
Z   Cleared if the result is non-zero. Unchanged otherwise.
V   Set if an overflow is generated. Cleared otherwise.
C   Set if a borrow is generated. Cleared otherwise.
X   Set the same as the carry bit.

NOTE
Normally the Z condition code bit is set via programming before the start of an operation. This allows successful tests for zero results upon completion of multiple-precision operations.

Instruction Format:

15	14	13	12	11	10	9	8	7	6	5	4	3	2	1	0
0	1	0	0	0	0	0	0	Size		Effective Address Mode			Register		

Instruction Fields:

Size field — Specifies the size of the operation:
  00 — byte operation.
  01 — word operation.
  10 — long operation.
Effective Address field — Specifies the destination operand. Only data alterable addressing modes are allowed as shown:

Addressing Mode	Mode	Register	Addressing Mode	Mode	Register
Dn	000	register number	d(An, Xi)	110	register number
An	—	—	Abs.W	111	000
(An)	010	register number	Abs.L	111	001
(An) +	011	register number	d(PC)	—	—
− (An)	100	register number	d(PC, Xi)	—	—
d(An)	101	register number	Imm	—	—

NOP

NOP

No Operation

NOP

Operation: None

**Assembler
Syntax:**   NOP

Attributes: Unsized

Description: No operation occurs. The processor state, other than the program counter, is unaffected. Execution continues with the instruction following the NOP instruction.

Condition Codes: Not affected.

Instruction Format:

15	14	13	12	11	10	9	8	7	6	5	4	3	2	1	0
0	1	0	0	1	1	1	0	0	1	1	1	0	0	0	1

NOT Logical Complement NOT

Operation: ~(Destination) → Destination

**Assembler
Syntax:** NOT <ea>

Attributes: Size = (Byte, Word, Long)

Description: The ones complement of the destination operand is taken and the result stored in the destination location. The size of the operation may be specified to be byte, word, or long.

Condition Codes:

X	N	Z	V	C
—	*	*	0	0

N Set if the result is negative. Cleared otherwise.
Z Set if the result is zero. Cleared otherwise.
V Always cleared.
C Always cleared.
X Not affected.

Instruction Format:

15	14	13	12	11	10	9	8	7	6	5 4 3	2 1 0
0	1	0	0	0	1	1	0	Size		Effective Address Mode	Register

Instruction Fields:

Size field — Specifies the size of the operation:

00 — byte operation.
01 — word operation.
10 — long operation.

Effective Address field — Specifies the destination operand. Only data alterable addressing modes are allowed as shown:

Addressing Mode	Mode	Register	Addressing Mode	Mode	Register
Dn	000	register number	d(An, Xi)	110	register number
An	—	—	Abs.W	111	000
(An)	010	register number	Abs.L	111	001
(An)+	011	register number	d(PC)	—	—
−(An)	100	register number	d(PC, Xi)	—	—
d(An)	101	register number	Imm	—	—

OR

OR

Operation: (Source) v (Destination) → Destination

Assembler OR <ea>, Dn
Syntax: OR Dn, <ea>

Attributes: Size = (Byte, Word, Long)

Description: Inclusive OR the source operand to the destination operand and store the result in the destination location. The size of the operation may be specified to be byte, word, or long. The contents of an address register may not be used as an operand.

Condition Codes:

X	N	Z	V	C
—	*	*	0	0

N   Set if the most significant bit of the result is set. Cleared otherwise.
Z   Set if the result is zero. Cleared otherwise.
V   Always cleared.
C   Always cleared.
X   Not affected.

Instruction Format:

15	14	13	12	11 10 9	8 7 6	5 4 3	2 1 0
1	0	0	0	Register	Op-Mode	Effective Address Mode	Register

Instruction Fields:

Register field — Specifies any of the eight data registers.
Op-Mode field —

Byte	Word	Long	Operation
000	001	010	(<Dn>) v (<ea>) → <Dn>
100	101	110	(<ea>) v (<Dn>) → <ea>

Effective Address field —

If the location specified is a source operand then only data addressing modes are allowed as shown:

Addressing Mode	Mode	Register	Addressing Mode	Mode	Register
Dn	000	register number	d(An, Xi)	110	register number
An	—	—	Abs.W	111	000
(An)	010	register number	Abs.L	111	001
(An) +	011	register number	d(PC)	111	010
− (An)	100	register number	d(PC, Xi)	111	011
d(An)	101	register number	Imm	111	100

— Continued —

Inclusive OR Logical

Effective Address field (Continued)

If the location specified is a destination operand then only memory alterable addressing modes are allowed as shown:

Addressing Mode	Mode	Register	Addressing Mode	Mode	Register
Dn	—	—	d(An, Xi)	110	register number
An	—	—	Abs.W	111	000
(An)	010	register number	Abs.L	111	001
(An) +	011	register number	d(PC)	—	—
– (An)	100	register number	d(PC, Xi)	—	—
d(An)	101	register number	Imm	—	—

Notes:
1. If the destination is a data register, then it cannot be specified by using the destination <ea> mode, but must use the destination Dn mode instead.
2. ORI is used when the source is immediate data. Most assemblers automatically make this distinction.

ORI

Inclusive OR Immediate

ORI

Operation: Immediate Data v (Destination) → Destination

**Assembler
Syntax:** ORI #<data>, <ea>

Attributes: Size = (Byte, Word, Long)

Description: Inclusive OR the immediate data to the destination operand and store the result in the destination location. The size of the operation may be specified to be byte, word, or long. The size of the immediate data matches the operation size.

Condition Codes:

X	N	Z	V	C
—	*	*	0	0

N   Set if the most significant bit of the result is set. Cleared otherwise.
Z   Set if the result is zero. Cleared otherwise.
V   Always cleared.
C   Always cleared.
X   Not affected.

Instruction Format:

15	14	13	12	11	10	9	8	7	6	5	4	3	2	1	0
0	0	0	0	0	0	0	0	Size		Effective Address Mode | Register					
Word Data (16 bites)								Byte Data (8 bits)							
Long Data (32 bits, including previous word)															

Instruction Fields:

Size field — Specifies the size of the operation:
00 — byte operation.
01 — word operation.
10 — long operation.

Effective Address field — Specifies the destination operand. Only data alterable addressing modes are allowed as shown:

Addressing Mode	Mode	Register	Addressing Mode	Mode	Register
Dn	000	register number	d(An, Xi)	110	register number
An	—	—	Abs.W	111	000
(An)	010	register number	Abs.L	111	001
(An) +	011	register number	d(PC)	—	—
– (An)	100	register number	d(PC, Xi)	—	—
d(An)	101	register number	Imm	—	—

Immediate field — (Data immediately following the instruction):
If size = 00, then the data is the low order byte of the immediate word.
If size = 01, then the data is the entire immediate word.
If size = 10, then the data is the next two immediate words.

154

ORI
to CCR

ORI
to CCR

Operation: (Source) v CCR → CCR

**Assembler
Syntax:** ORI #xxx, CCR

Attributes: Size = (Byte)

Description: Inclusive OR the immediate operand with the condition codes and store the result in the low-order byte of the status register.

Condition Codes:

X	N	Z	V	C
*	*	*	*	*

N   Set if bit 3 of immediate operand is one. Unchanged otherwise.
Z   Set if bit 2 of immediate operand is one. Unchanged otherwise.
V   Set if bit 1 of immediate operand is one. Unchanged otherwise.
C   Set if bit 0 of immediate operand is one. Unchanged otherwise.
X   Set if bit 4 of immediate operand is one. Unchanged otherwise.

Instruction Format:

15	14	13	12	11	10	9	8	7	6	5	4	3	2	1	0
0	0	0	0	0	0	0	0	0	0	1	1	1	1	0	0
0	0	0	0	0	0	0	0	Byte Data (8 bits)							

155

ORI
to SR

ORI
to SR

Operation: If supervisor state
        then (Source) v SR → SR
        else TRAP

Assembler
Syntax: ORI #xxx, SR

Attributes: Size = (Word)

Description: Inclusive OR the immediate operand with the contents of the status register and store the result in the status register. All bits of the status register are affected.

Condition Codes:

X	N	Z	V	C
*	*	*	*	*

N   Set if bit 3 of immediate operand is one. Unchanged otherwise.
Z   Set if bit 2 of immediate operand is one. Unchanged otherwise.
V   Set if bit 1 of immediate operand is one. Unchanged otherwise.
C   Set if bit 0 of immediate operand is one. Unchanged otherwise.
X   Set if bit 4 of immediate operand is one. Unchanged otherwise.

Instruction Format:

15	14	13	12	11	10	9	8	7	6	5	4	3	2	1	0
0	0	0	0	0	0	0	0	0	1	1	1	1	1	0	0
Word Data (16 bits)														

PEA

Push Effective Address

PEA

Operation: Destination → – (SP)

Assembler Syntax: PEA < ea >

Attributes: Size = (Long)

Description: The effective address is computed and pushed onto the stack. A long word address is pushed onto the stack.

Condition Codes: Not affected.

Instruction Format:

15	14	13	12	11	10	9	8	7	6	5 4 3	2 1 0
0	1	0	0	1	0	0	0	0	1	Effective Address Mode	Register

Instruction Fields:

Effective Address field — Specifies the address to be pushed onto the stack. Only control addressing modes are allowed as shown:

Addressing Mode	Mode	Register	Addressing Mode	Mode	Register
Dn	—	—	d(An, Xi)	110	register number
An	—	—	Abs.W	111	000
(An)	010	register number	Abs.L	111	001
(An) +	—	—	d(PC)	111	010
– (An)	—	—	d(PC, Xi)	111	011
d(An)	101	register number	Imm	—	—

RESET

**Reset External Devices
(Privileged Instruction)**

RESET

Operation: If supervisor state
    then Assert RESET Line
    else TRAP

**Assembler
Syntax:**   RESET

Attributes: Unsized

Description: The reset line is asserted causing all external devices to be reset. The processor state, other than the program counter, is unaffected and execution continues with the next instruction.

Condition Codes: Not affected.

Instruction Format:

15	14	13	12	11	10	9	8	7	6	5	4	3	2	1	0
0	1	0	0	1	1	1	0	0	1	1	1	0	0	0	0

ROL
ROR

Rotate (without Extend)

Operation: (Destination) Rotated by < count > → Destination

Assembler ROd Dx, Dy
Syntax: ROd #<data>, Dy
ROd <ea>

Attributes: Size = (Byte, Word, Long)

Description: Rotate the bits of the operand in the direction specified. The extend bit is not included in the rotation. The shift count for the rotation of a register may be specified in two different ways:
1. Immediate — the shift count is specified in the instruction (shift range, 1-8).
2. Register — the shift count is contained in a data register specified in the instruction.
The size of the operation may be specified to be byte, word, or long. The content of memory may be rotated one bit only and the operand size is restricted to a word.

For ROL, the operand is rotated left; the number of positions shifted is the shift count. Bits shifted out of the high order bit go to both the carry bit and back into the low order bit. The extend bit is not modified or used.

ROL:

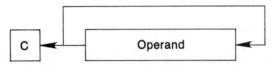

For ROR, the operand is rotated right; the number of position shifted is the shift count. Bits shifted out of the low order bit go to both the carry bit and back into the high order bit. The extend bit is not modified or used.

ROR:

Condition Codes:

X	N	Z	V	C
—	*	*	0	*

N   Set if the most significant bit of the result is set. Cleared otherwise.
Z   Set if the result is zero. Cleared otherwise.
V   Always cleared.
C   Set according to the last bit shfited out of the operand. Cleared for a shift count of zero.
X   Not affected.

— Continued —

ROL
ROR

Rotate (Without Extend)

ROL ROR heading right side

ROL
ROR

Instruction Format (Register Rotate):

15	14	13	12	11 10 9	8	7 6	5	4	3	2 1 0
1	1	1	0	Count/ Register	dr	Size	i/r	1	1	Register

Instruction Fields (Register Rotate):

Count/Register field —
> if i/r = 0, the rotate count is specified in this field. The values 0, 1-7 represent a range of 8, 1 to 7 respectively.
> If i/r = 1, the rotate count (modulo 64) is contained in the data register specified in this field.

dr field — Specifies the direction of the rotate:
> 0 — rotate right.
> 1 — rotate left.

Size field — Specifies the size of the operation:
> 00 — byte operation.
> 01 — word operation.
> 10 — long operation.

i/r field —
> If i/r = 0, specifies immediate rotate count.
> If i/r = 1, specifies register rotate count.

Register field — Specifies a data register whose content is to be rotated.

Instruction Format (Memory Rotate):

15	14	13	12	11	10	9	8	7	6	5 4 3	2 1 0
1	1	1	0	0	1	1	dr	1	1	Effective Address Mode	Register

Instruction Fields (Memory Rotate):

dr field — Specifies the direction of the rotate:
> 0 — rotate right
> 1 — rotate left.

Effective Address field — Specifies the operand to be rotated. Only memory alterable addressing modes are allowed as shown:

Addressing Mode	Mode	Register	Addressing Mode	Mode	Register
Dn	—	—	d(An, Xi)	110	register number
An	—	—	Abs.W	111	000
(An)	010	register number	Abs.L	111	001
(An)+	011	register number	d(PC)	—	—
−(An)	100	register number	d(PC, Xi)	—	—
d(An)	101	register number	Imm	—	—

ROXL
ROXR

Rotate with Extend

Operation: (Destination) Rotated by < count > → Destination

Assembler   ROXd Dx, Dy
Syntax: ROXd #<data>, Dy
  ROXd <ea>

Attributes: Size = (Byte, Word, Long)

Description: Rotate the bits of the destination operand in the direction specified. The extend bit is included in the rotation. The shift count for the rotation of a register may be specified in two different ways:
  1. Immediate — the shift count is specified in the instruction (shift range, 1-8).
  2. Register — the shift count is contained in a data register specified in the instruction.
The size of the operation may be specified to be byte, word, or long. The content of memory may be rotated one bit only and the operand size is restricted to a word.

For ROXL, the operand is rotated left; the number of positions shifted is the shift count. Bits shifted out of the high order bit go to both the carry and extend bits; the previous value of the extend bit is shifted into the low order bit.

ROXL:

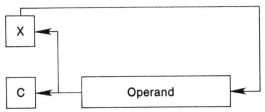

For ROXR, the operand is rotated right; the number of positions shifted is the shift count. Bits shifted out of the low order bit go to both the carry and extend bits; the previous value of the extend bit is shifted into the high order bit.

ROXR:

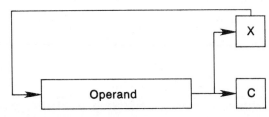

— Continued —

ROXL
ROXR

Rotate with Extend

ROXL
ROXR

Condition Codes:

X	N	Z	V	C
*	*	*	0	*

N   Set if the most significant bit of the result is set. Cleared otherwise.
Z   Set if the result is zero. Cleared otherwise.
V   Always cleared.
C   Set according to the last bit shifted out of the operand. Set to the value of the extend bit for a shift count of zero.
X   Set according to the last bit shifted out of the operand. Unaffected for a shift count of zero.

Instruction Format (Register Rotate):

15	14	13	12	11	10	9	8	7	6	5	4	3	2	1	0
1	1	1	0	Count/Register			dr	Size		i/r	1	0	Register		

Instruction Fields (Register Rotate):

Count/Register field:

     If i/r = 0, the rotate count is specified in this field. The values 0, 1-7 represent range of 8, 1 to 7 respectively.

     If i/r = 1, the rotate count (modulo 64) is contained in the data register specified in this field.

dr field — Specifies the direction of the rotate:

     0 — rotate right.
     1 — rotate left.

Size field — Specifies the size of the operation:

     00 — byte operation.
     01 — word operation.
     10 — long operation.

i/r field —

     If i/r = 0, specifies immediate rotate count.
     If i/r = 1, specifies register rotate count.

Register field — Specifies a data register whose content is to be rotated.

— Continued —

ROXL
ROXR

Rotate with Extend

Instruction Format (Memory Rotate):

15	14	13	12	11	10	9	8	7	6	5 4 3 2 1 0
1	1	1	0	0	1	0	dr	1	1	Effective Address Mode | Register

Instruction Fields (Memory Rotate):

dr field — Specifies the direction of the rotate:

0 — rotate right.

1 — rotate left.

Effective Address field — Specifies the operand to be rotated. Only memory alterable addressing modes are allowed as shown:

Addressing Mode	Mode	Register	Addressing Mode	Mode	Register
Dn	—	—	d(An, Xi)	110	register number
An	—	—	Abs.W	111	000
(An)	010	register number	Abs.L	111	001
(An)+	011	register number	d(PC)	—	—
–(An)	100	register number	d(PC, Xi)	—	—
d(An)	101	register number	Imm	—	—

RTE

**Return from Exception
(Privileged Instruction)**

Operation: If supervisor state
then (SP) + → SR; (SP) + → PC
else TRAP

**Assembler
Syntax:** RTE

Attributes: Unsized

Description: The status register and program counter are pulled from the system stack. The previous status register and program counter are lost. All bits in the status register are affected.

Condition Codes: Set according to the content of the word on the stack.

Instruction Format:

15	14	13	12	11	10	9	8	7	6	5	4	3	2	1	0
0	1	0	0	1	1	1	0	0	1	1	1	0	0	1	1

RTR

Return and Restore Condition Codes

Operation: $(SP) + \rightarrow CC; (SP) + \rightarrow PC$

**Assembler
Syntax:** RTR

Attributes: Unsized

Description: The condition codes and program counter are pulled from the stack. The previous condition codes and program counter are lost. The supervisor portion of the status register is unaffected.

Condition Codes: Set according to the content of the word on the stack.

Instruction Format:

15	14	13	12	11	10	9	8	7	6	5	4	3	2	1	0
0	1	0	0	1	1	1	0	0	1	1	1	0	1	1	1

RTS

Return from Subroutine

RTS

Operation: $(SP) + \rightarrow PC$

Assembler
Syntax: RTS

Attributes: Unsized

Description: The program counter is pulled from the stack. The previous program counter is lost.

Condition Codes: Not affected.

Instruction Format:

15	14	13	12	11	10	9	8	7	6	5	4	3	2	1	0
0	1	0	0	1	1	1	0	0	1	1	1	0	1	0	1

SBCD

Subtract Decimal with Extend

SBCD

Operation: $(Destination)_{10} - (Source)_{10} - X \rightarrow Destination$

Assembler
Syntax:
SBCD Dy, Dx
SBCD $-(Ay)$, $-(Ax)$

Attributes: Size = (Byte)

Description: Subtract the source operand from the destination operand along with the extend bit and store the result in the destination location. The subtraction is performed using binary coded decimal arithmetic. The operands may be addressed in two different ways:

1. Data register to data register: The operands are contained in the data registers specified in the instruction.
2. Memory to memory: The operands are addressed with the predecrement addressing mode using the address registers specified in the instruction.

This operation is a byte operation only.

Condition Codes:

X	N	Z	V	C
*	U	*	U	*

N Undefined.
Z Cleared if the result is non-zero. Unchanged otherwise.
V Undefined.
C Set if a borrow (decimal) is generated. Cleared otherwise.
X Set the same as the carry bit.

NOTE

Normally the Z condition code bit is set via programming before the start of an operation. This allows successful tests for zero results upon completion of multiple-precision operations.

Instruction Format:

15	14	13	12	11	10	9	8	7	6	5	4	3	2	1	0
1	0	0	0	Register Rx			1	0	0	0	0	R/M	Register Ry		

Instruction Fields:

Register Rx field — Specifies the destination register:
If R/M = 0, specifies a data register.
If R/M = 1, specifies an address register for the prececrement addressing mode.
R/M field — Specifies the operand addressing mode:
0 — The operation is data register to data register.
1 — The operation is memory to memory.
Register Ry field — Specifies the source register:
If R/M = 0, specifies a data register.
If R/M = 1, specifies an address register for the predecrement addressing mode.

Scc

Set According to Condition

Scc

Operation: If (Condition True)
then 1's → Destination
else 0's → Destination

**Assembler
Syntax:** Scc <ea>

Attributes: Size = (Byte)

Description: The specified condition code is tested; if the condition is true, the byte specified by the effective address is set to TRUE (all ones), otherwise that byte is set to FALSE (all zeroes). "cc" may specify the following conditions:

CC	carry clear	0100	$\overline{C}$		LS	low or same	0011	$C + Z$
CS	carry set	0101	C		LT	less than	1101	$N \cdot \overline{V} + \overline{N} \cdot V$
EQ	equal	0111	Z		MI	minus	1011	N
F	false	0001	O		NE	not equal	0110	$\overline{Z}$
GE	greater or equal	1100	$N \cdot V + \overline{N} \cdot \overline{V}$		PI	plus	1010	$\overline{N}$
GT	greater than	1110	$N \cdot V \cdot \overline{Z} + \overline{N} \cdot \overline{V} \cdot \overline{Z}$		T	true	0000	1
HI	high	0010	$\overline{C} \cdot \overline{Z}$		VC	overflow clear	1000	$\overline{V}$
LE	less or equal	1111	$Z + N \cdot \overline{V} + \overline{N} \cdot V$		VS	overflow set	1001	V

Condition Codes: Not affected.

Instruction Format:

15	14	13	12	11	10	9	8	7	6	5	4	3	2	1	0
0	1	0	1	Condition				1	1	Effective Address					
										Mode			Register		

Instruction Fields:

Condition field — One of sixteen conditions discussed in description.
Effective Address field — Specifies the location in which the true/false byte is to be stored. Only data alterable addressing modes are allowed as shown:

Addressing Mode	Mode	Register	Addressing Mode	Mode	Register
Dn	000	register number	d(An, Xi)	110	register number
An	—	—	Abs.W	111	000
(An)	010	register number	Abs.L	111	001
(An) +	011	register number	d(PC)	—	—
− (An)	100	register number	d(PC, Xi)	—	—
d(An)	101	register number	Imm	—	—

Notes:
1. A memory destination is read before being written to.
2. An arithmetic one and zero result may be generated by following the Scc instruction with a NEG instruction.

STOP

**Load Status Register and Stop
(Privileged Instruction)**

STOP

Operation: If supervisor state
  then Immediate Data → SR; STOP
  else TRAP

**Assembler
Syntax:** STOP #xxx

Attributes: Unsized

Description: The immediate operand is moved into the entire status register; the program counter is advanced to point to the next instruction and the processor stops fetching and executing instructions. Execution of instructions resumes when a trace, interrupt, or reset exception occurs. A trace exception will occur if the trace state is on when the STOP instruction is executed. If an interrupt request arrives whose priority is higher than the current processor priority, an interrupt exception occurs, otherwise the interrupt request has no effect. If the bit of the immediate data corresponding to the S-bit is off, execution of the instruction will cause a privilege violation. External reset will always initiate reset exception processing.

Condition Codes: Set according to the immediate operand.

Instruction Format:

15	14	13	12	11	10	9	8	7	6	5	4	3	2	1	0
0	1	0	0	1	1	1	0	0	1	1	1	0	0	1	0
Immediate Data															

Instruction Fields:
  Immediate field — Specifies the data to be loaded into the status register.

SUB

SUB

SUB

Subtract Binary

Operation: (Destination) – (Source) → Destination

Assembler   SUB <ea>, Dn
Syntax: SUB Dn, <ea>

Attributes: Size = (Byte, Word, Long)

Description: Subtract the source operand from the destination operand and store the result in the destination. The size of the operation may be specified to be byte, word, or long. The mode of the instruction indicates which operand is the source and which is the destination as well as the operand size.

Condition Codes:

X	N	Z	V	C
*	*	*	*	*

N   Set if the result is negative. Cleared otherwise.
Z   Set if the result is zero. Cleared otherwise.
V   Set if an overflow is generated. Cleared otherwise.
C   Set if a borrow is generated. Cleared otherwise.
X   Set the same as the carry bit.

Instruction Format:

15	14	13	12	11 10 9	8 7 6	5 4 3	2 1 0
1	0	0	1	Register	Op-Mode	Effective Address Mode	Register

Instruction Fields:

Register field — Specifies any of the eight data registers.
Op-Mode field —

Byte	Word	Long	Operation
000	001	010	(<Dn>)–(<ea>)→ <Dn>
100	101	110	(<ea>)–(<Dn>)→ <ea>

Effective Address field — Determines addressing mode:
If the location specified is a source operand, then all addressing modes are allowed as shown:

Addressing Mode	Mode	Register	Addressing Mode	Mode	Register
Dn	000	register number	d(An, Xi)	110	register number
An*	001	register number	Abs.W	111	000
(An)	010	register number	Abs.L	111	001
(An) +	011	register number	d(PC)	111	010
– (An)	100	register number	d(PC, Xi)	111	011
d(An)	101	register number	Imm	111	100

*For byte size operation, address register direct is not allowed.

— Continued —

SUB

SUB

Effective Address field (Continued)

If the location specified is a destination operand, then only alterable memory addressing modes are allowed as shown:

Addressing Mode	Mode	Register	Addressing Mode	Mode	Register
Dn	—	—	d(An, Xi)	110	register number
An	—	—	Abs.W	111	000
(An)	010	register number	Abs.L	111	001
(An)+	011	register number	d(PC)	—	—
−(An)	100	register number	d(PC, Xi)	—	—
d(An)	101	register number	Imm	—	—

Notes:　　1.　If the destination is a data register, then it cannot be specified by using the destination <ea> mode, but must use the destination Dn mode instead.

　　　　　　2.　SUBA is used when the destination is an address register. SUBI and SUBQ are used when the source is immediate data. Most assemblers automatically make this distinction.

SUBA　　　Subtract Address　　　SUBA

Operation: (Destination) − (Source) → Destination

**Assembler
Syntax:** SUBA <ea>, An

Attributes: Size = (Word, Long)

Description: Subtract the source operand from the destination address register and store the result in the address register. The size of the operation may be specified to be word or long. Word size source operands are sign extended to 32 bit quantities before the operation is done.

Condition Codes: Not affected.

Instruction Format:

15	14	13	12	11	10	9	8	7	6	5	4	3	2	1	0
1	0	0	1	\multicolumn{3}{c}{Register}	\multicolumn{3}{c}{Op-Mode}	\multicolumn{6}{c}{Effective Address}

| 1 | 0 | 0 | 1 | Register | Op-Mode | Effective Address Mode \| Register |

Instruction Fields:

Register field — Specifies any of the eight address registers. This is always the destination.

Op-Mode field — Specifies the size of the operation:

011 — Word operation. The source operand is sign-extended to a long operand and the operation is performed on the address register using all 32 bits.

111 — Long operations.

Effective Address field — Specifies the source operand. All addressing modes are allowed as shown:

Addressing Mode	Mode	Register	Addressing Mode	Mode	Register
Dn	000	register number	d(An, Xi)	110	register number
An	001	register number	Abs.W	111	000
(An)	010	register number	Abs.L	111	001
(An)+	011	register number	d(PC)	111	010
−(An)	100	register number	d(PC, Xi)	111	011
d(An)	101	register number	Imm	111	100

SUBI

Subtract Immediate

SUBI

Operation: (Destination) – Immediate Data → Destination

**Assembler
Syntax:** SUBI #<data>, <ea>

Attributes: Size = (Byte, Word, Long)

Description: Subtract the immediate data from the destination operand and store the result in the destination location. The size of the operation may be specified to be byte, word, or long. The size of the immediate data matches the operation size.

Condition Codes:

X	N	Z	V	C
*	*	*	*	*

N   Set if the result is negative. Cleared otherwise.
Z   Set if the result is zero. Cleared otherwise.
V   Set if an overflow is generated. Cleared otherwise.
C   Set if a borrow is generated. Cleared otherwise.
X   Set the same as the carry bit.

Instruction Format:

15	14	13	12	11	10	9	8	7	6	5 4 3	2 1 0
0	0	0	0	0	1	0	0	Size		Effective Address Mode	Register
Word Data (16 bits)								Byte Data (8 bits)			
Long Data (32 bits, including previous word)											

Instruction Fields:

Size field — Specifies the size of the operation.
00 — byte operation.
01 — word operation.
10 — long operation.

Effective Address field — Specifies the destination operand. Only data alterable addressing modes are allowed as shown:

Addressing Mode	Mode	Register	Addressing Mode	Mode	Register
Dn	000	register number	d(An, Xi)	110	register number
An	—	—	Abs.W	111	000
(An)	010	register number	Abs.L	111	001
(An)+	011	register number	d(PC)	—	—
– (An)	100	register number	d(PC, Xi)	—	—
d(An)	101	register number	Imm	—	—

Immediate field — (Data immediately following the instruction)
If size = 00, then the data is the low order byte of the immediate word.
If size = 01, then the data is the entire immediate word.
If size = 10, then the data is the next two immediate words.

173

SUBQ

Subtract Quick

SUBQ

Operation: (Destination) − Immediate Data → Destination

Assembler
Syntax: SUBQ #<data>, <ea>

Attributes: Size = (Byte, Word, Long)

Description: Subtract the immediate data from the destination operand. The data range is from 1-8. The size of the operation may be specified to be byte, word, or long. Word and long operations are also allowed on the address registers and the condition codes are not affected. Word size source operands are sign extended to 32 bit quantities before the operation is done.

Condition Codes:

X	N	Z	V	C
*	*	*	*	*

N   Set if the result is negative. Cleared otherwise.
Z   Set if the result is zero. Cleared otherwise.
V   Set if an overflow is generated. Cleared otherwise.
C   Set if a borrow is generated. Cleared otherwise.
X   Set the same as the carry bit.

The condition codes are not affected if a subtraction from an address register is made.

Instruction Format:

15	14	13	12	11 10 9	8	7 6	5 4 3	2 1 0
0	1	0	1	Data	1	Size	Effective Address Mode	Register

Instruction Fields:

Data field — Three bits of immediate data, 0, 1-7 representing a range of 8, 1 to 7 respectively.

Size field — Specifies the size of the operation:
00 — byte operation.
01 — word operation.
10 — long operation.

Effective Address field — Specifies the destination location. Only alterable addressing modes are allowed as shown:

Addressing Mode	Mode	Register	Addressing Mode	Mode	Register
Dn	000	register number	d(An, Xi)	110	register number
An*	001	register number	Abs.W	111	000
(An)	010	register number	Abs.L	111	001
(An)+	011	register number	d(PC)	—	—
−(An)	100	register number	d(PC, Xi)	—	—
d(An)	101	register number	Imm	—	—

*Word and Long only.

174

SUBX

Subtract with Extend

SUBX

Operation: (Destination) − (Source) − X → Destination

Assembler
Syntax: SUBX Dy, Dx
SUBX − (Ay), − (Ax)

Attributes: Size = (Byte, Word, Long)

Description: Subtract the source operand from the destination operand along with the extend bit and store the result in the destination location. The operands may be addressed in two different ways:
1. Data register to data register: The operands are contained in data registers specified in the instruction.
2. Memory to memory. The operands are contained in memory and addressed with the predecrement addressing mode using the address registers specified in the instruction.
The size of the operation may be specified to be byte, word, or long.

Condition Codes:

X	N	Z	V	C
*	*	*	*	*

N   Set if the result is negative. Cleared otherwise.
Z   Cleared if the result is non-zero. Unchanged otherwise.
V   Set if an overflow is generated. Cleared otherwise.
C   Set if a carry is generated. Cleared otherwise.
X   Set the same as the carry bit.

NOTE

Normally the Z condition code bit is set via programming before the start of an operation. This allows successful tests for zero results upon completion of multiple-precision operations.

Instruction Format:

15	14	13	12	11 10 9	8	7 6 5	4	3	2 1 0
1	0	0	1	Register Rx	1	Size	0 0	R/M	Register Ry

— Continued —

SUBX   Subtract with Extend   SUBX

Instruction Fields:

Register Rx field — Specifies the destination register:

If R/M = 0, specifies a data register.

If R/M = 1, specifies an address register for the predecrement addressing mode.

Size field — Specifies the size of the operation:

00 — byte operation.

01 — word operation.

10 — long operation.

R/M field — Specifies the operand addressing mode:

0 — The operation is data register to data register.

1 — The operation is memory to memory.

Register Ry field — Specifies the source register:

If R/M = 0, specifies a data register.

If R/M = 1, specifies an address register for the predecrement addressing mode.

SWAP

Swap Register Halves

SWAP

Operation: Register [31:16] ↔ Register [15:0]

**Assembler
Syntax:** SWAP Dn

Attributes: Size = (Word)

Description: Exchange the 16-bit halves of a data register.

Condition Codes:

X	N	Z	V	C
—	*	*	0	0

N   Set if the most significant bit of the 32-bit result is set. Cleared otherwise.
Z   Set if the 32-bit result is zero. Cleared otherwise.
V   Always cleared.
C   Always cleared.
X   Not affected.

Instruction Format:

15	14	13	12	11	10	9	8	7	6	5	4	3	2	1	0
0	1	0	0	1	0	0	0	0	1	0	0	0	Register		

Instruction Fields:

Register field — Specifies the data register to swap.

TAS
Test and Set an Operand

TAS

Operation: (Destination) Tested → CC; 1 → bit 7 OF Destination

**Assembler
Syntax:**   TAS <ea>

Attributes: Size = (Byte)

Description: Test and set the byte operand addressed by the effective address field. The current value of the operand is tested and N and Z are set accordingly. The high order bit of the operand is set. The operation is indivisible (using a read-modify-write memory cycle) to allow synchronization of several processors.

Condition Codes:

X	N	Z	V	C
—	*	*	0	0

N   Set if the most significant bit of the operand was set. Cleared otherwise.
Z   Set if the operand was zero. Cleared otherwise.
V   Always cleared.
C   Always cleared.
X   Not affected.

Instruction Format:

15	14	13	12	11	10	9	8	7	6	5 4 3	2 1 0
0	1	0	0	1	0	1	0	1	1	Effective Address Mode	Register

Instruction Fields:

Effective Address field — Specifies the location of the tested operand. Only data alterable addressing modes are allowed as shown:

Addressing Mode	Mode	Register	Addressing Mode	Mode	Register
Dn	000	register number	d(An, Xi)	110	register number
An	—	—	Abs.W	111	000
(An)	010	register number	Abs.L	111	001
(An) +	011	register number	d(PC)	—	—
– (An)	100	register number	d(PC, Xi)	—	—
d(An)	101	register number	Imm	—	—

Note: Bus error retry is inhibited on the read portion of the TAS read-modify-write bus cycle to ensure system integrity. The bus error exception is always taken.

TRAP   Trap   TRAP

Operation: PC→ − (SSP); SR→ − (SSP); (Vector)→PC

Assembler
Syntax: TRAP #<vector>

Attributes: Unsized

Description: The processor initiates exception processing. The vector number is generated to reference the TRAP instruction exception vector specified by the low order four bits of the instruction. Sixteen TRAP instruction vectors are available.

Condition Codes: Not affected.

Instruction Format:

15	14	13	12	11	10	9	8	7	6	5	4	3	2	1	0
0	1	0	0	1	1	1	0	0	1	0	0	Vector			

Instruction Fields:

Vector field — Specifies which trap vector contains the new program counter to be loaded.

TRAPV

Trap on Overflow

TRAPV

Operation: If V then TRAP

**Assembler
Syntax:**   TRAPV

Attributes: Unsized

Description: If the overflow condition is on, the processor initiates exception processing. The vector number is generated to reference the TRAPV exception vector. If the overflow condition is off, no operation is performed and execution continues with the next instruction in sequence.

Condition Codes: Not affected.

Instruction Format:

15	14	13	12	11	10	9	8	7	6	5	4	3	2	1	0
0	1	0	0	1	1	1	0	0	1	1	1	0	1	1	0

TST

Test an Operand

TST

Operation: (Destination) Tested → CC

**Assembler
Syntax:** TST <ea>

Attributes: Size = (Byte, Word, Long)

Description: Compare the operand with zero. No results are saved; however, the condition codes are set according to results of the test. The size of the operation may be specified to be byte, word, or long.

Condition Codes:

X	N	Z	V	C
—	*	*	0	0

N   Set if the operand is negative. Cleared otherwise.
Z   Set if the operand is zero. Cleared otherwise.
V   Always cleared.
C   Always cleared.
X   Not affected.

Instruction Format:

15	14	13	12	11	10	9	8	7	6	5	4	3	2	1	0
0	1	0	0	1	0	1	0	Size		Effective Address Mode			Register		

Instruction Fields:

Size field — Specifies the size of the operation:
00 — byte operation.
01 — word operation.
10 — long operation.

Effective Address field — Specifies the destination operand. Only data alterable addressing modes are allowed as shown:

Addressing Mode	Mode	Register	Addressing Mode	Mode	Register
Dn	000	register number	d(An, Xi)	110	register number
An	—	—	Abs.W	111	000
(An)	010	register number	Abs.L	111	001
(An)+	011	register number	d(PC)	—	—
−(An)	100	register number	d(PC, Xi)	—	—
d(An)	101	register number	Imm	—	—

UNLK

Unlink

UNLK

Operation: An → SP; (SP) + → An

**Assembler
Syntax:** UNLK An

Attributes: Unsized

Description: The stack pointer is loaded from the specified address register. The address register is then loaded with the long word pulled from the top of the stack.

Condition Codes: Not affected.

Instruction Format:

15	14	13	12	11	10	9	8	7	6	5	4	3	2	1	0
0	1	0	0	1	1	1	0	0	1	0	1	1	Register		

Instruction Fields:

Register field — specifies the address register through which the unlinking is to be done.

APPENDIX C
INSTRUCTION FORMAT SUMMARY

C.1 INTRODUCTION

This appendix provides a summary of the first word in each instruction of the instruction set. Table C-1 is an operation code (op-code) map which illustrates how bits 15 through 12 are used to specify the operations. The remaining paragraph groups the instructions according to the op-code map.

Table C-1. Operation Code Map

Bits 15 through 12	Operation	Bits 15 through 12	Operation
0000	Bit Manipulation/MOVEP/Immediate	1000	OR/DIV/SBCD
0001	Move Byte	1001	SUB/SUBX
0010	Move Long	1010	(Unassigned)
0011	Move Word	1011	CMP/EOR
0100	Miscellaneous	1100	AND/MUL/ABCD/EXG
0101	ADDQ/SUBQ/Scc/DBcc	1101	ADD/ADDX
0110	Bcc/BSR	1110	Shift/Rotate
0111	MOVEQ	1111	(Unassigned)

Table C-2. Effective Address Encoding Summary

Addressing Mode	Mode	Register
Data Register Direct	000	register number
Address Register Direct	001	register number
Address Register Indirect	010	register number
Address Register Indirect with Postincrement	011	register number
Address Register Indirect with Predecrement	100	register number
Address Register Indirect with Displacement	101	register number
Address Register Indirect with Index	110	register number
Absolute Short	111	000
Absolute Long	111	001
Program Counter with Displacement	111	010
Program Counter with Index	111	011
Immediate or Status Register	111	100

Table C-3. Conditional Tests

Mnemonic	Condition	Encoding	Test
T	true	0000	1
F	false	0001	0
HI	high	0010	$\overline{C}\cdot\overline{Z}$
LS	low or same	0011	$C+Z$
CC(HS)	carry clear	0100	$\overline{C}$
CS(LO)	carry set	0101	C
NE	not equal	0110	$\overline{Z}$
EQ	equal	0111	Z
VC	overflow clear	1000	$\overline{V}$
VS	overflow set	1001	V
PL	plus	1010	$\overline{N}$
MI	minus	1011	N
GE	greater or equal	1100	$N\cdot V+\overline{N}\cdot\overline{V}$
LT	less than	1101	$N\cdot\overline{V}+\overline{N}\cdot V$
GT	greater than	1110	$N\cdot V\cdot\overline{Z}+\overline{N}\cdot\overline{V}\cdot\overline{Z}$
LE	less or equal	1111	$Z+N\cdot\overline{V}+\overline{N}\cdot V$

C.2 BIT MANIPULATION, MOVE PERIPHERAL, IMMEDIATE INSTRUCTIONS

Dynamic Bit

15	14	13	12	11	10	9	8	7	6	5	4	3	2	1	0
0	0	0	0	Register			1	Type		Effective Address					
										Mode			Register		

Static Bit

15	14	13	12	11	10	9	8	7	6	5	4	3	2	1	0
0	0	0	0	1	0	0	0	Type		Effective Address					
										Mode			Register		

Type field: 00 = TST 10 = CLR
01 = CHG 11 = SET

MOVEP

15	14	13	12	11	10	9	8	7	6	5	4	3	2	1	0
0	0	0	0	Register			Op-Mode			0	0	1	Register		

Op-Mode field: 100 = transfer word from memory to register
101 = transfer long word from memory to register
110 = transfer word from register to memory
111 = transfer long word from register to memory

OR Immediate

15	14	13	12	11	10	9	8	7	6	5	4	3	2	1	0
0	0	0	0	0	0	0	0	Size		Effective Address					
										Mode			Register		

Size field: 00 = byte
01 = word
11 = long word

OR Immediate to CCR

15	14	13	12	11	10	9	8	7	6	5	4	3	2	1	0
0	0	0	0	0	0	0	0	0	0	1	1	1	1	0	0

OR Immediate to SR

15	14	13	12	11	10	9	8	7	6	5	4	3	2	1	0
0	0	0	0	0	0	0	0	0	1	1	1	1	1	0	0

AND Immediate

15	14	13	12	11	10	9	8	7	6	5	4	3	2	1	0
0	0	0	0	0	0	1	0	Size		Effective Address Mode			Register		

*

AND Immediate to CCR

5	14	13	12	11	10	9	8	7	6	5	4	3	2	1	0
0	0	0	0	0	0	1	0	0	0	1	1	1	1	0	0

AND Immediate to SR

15	14	13	12	11	10	9	8	7	6	5	4	3	2	1	0
0	0	0	0	0	0	1	0	0	1	1	1	1	1	0	0

SUB Immediate

15	14	13	12	11	10	9	8	7	6	5	4	3	2	1	0
0	0	0	0	0	1	0	0	Size		Effective Address Mode			Register		

*

ADD Immediate

15	14	13	12	11	10	9	8	7	6	5	4	3	2	1	0
0	0	0	0	0	1	1	0	Size		Effective Address Mode			Register		

*

EOR Immediate

15	14	13	12	11	10	9	8	7	6	5	4	3	2	1	0
0	0	0	0	1	0	1	0	Size		Effective Address Mode			Register		

*

*Size field: 00 = byte
01 = word
11 = long word

185

EOR Immediate to CCR

15	14	13	12	11	10	9	8	7	6	5	4	3	2	1	0
0	0	0	0	1	0	1	0	0	0	1	1	1	1	0	0

EOR Immediate to SR

15	14	13	12	11	10	9	8	7	6	5	4	3	2	1	0
0	0	0	0	1	0	1	0	0	1	1	1	1	1	0	0

CMP Immediate

15	14	13	12	11	10	9	8	7	6	5	4	3	2	1	0
0	0	0	0	1	1	0	0	Size		Effective Address Mode			Register		

Size field: 00 = byte
01 = word
11 = long word

C.3 MOVE BYTE INSTRUCTION

MOVE Byte

15	14	13	12	11	10	9	8	7	6	5	4	3	2	1	1
0	0	0	1	Destination Register			Mode			Source Mode			Register		

Note Register and Mode location

C.4 MOVE LONG INSTRUCTION

MOVE Long

15	14	13	12	11	10	9	8	7	6	5	4	3	2	1	0
0	0	1	0	Destination Register			Mode			Source Mode			Register		

Note Register and Mode location

C.5 MOVE WORD INSTRUCTION

MOVE Word

15	14	13	12	11	10	9	8	7	6	5	4	3	2	1	0
0	0	1	1	Destination Register			Mode			Source Mode			Register		

Note Register and Mode location

C.6 MISCELLANEOUS INSTRUCTIONS

NEGX

15	14	13	12	11	10	9	8	7	6	5	4	3	2	1	0
0	1	0	0	0	0	0	0	Size		Effective Address					
										Mode			Register		

*

MOVE from SR

15	14	13	12	11	10	9	8	7	6	5	4	3	2	1	0
0	1	0	0	0	0	0	0	1	1	Effective Address					
										Mode			Register		

CLR

15	14	13	12	11	10	9	8	7	6	5	4	3	2	1	0
0	1	0	0	0	0	1	0	Size		Effective Address					
										Mode			Register		

*

NEG

15	14	13	12	11	10	9	8	7	6	5	4	3	2	1	0
0	1	0	0	0	1	0	0	Size		Effective Address					
										Mode			Register		

*

MOVE to CCR

15	14	13	12	11	10	9	8	7	6	5	4	3	2	1	0
0	1	0	0	0	1	0	0	1	1	Effective Address					
										Mode			Register		

NOT

15	14	13	12	11	10	9	8	7	6	5	4	3	2	1	0
0	1	0	0	0	1	1	0	Size		Effective Address					
										Mode			Register		

*

MOVE to SR

15	14	13	12	11	10	9	8	7	6	5	4	3	2	1	0
0	1	0	0	0	1	1	0	1	1	Effective Address					
										Mode			Register		

*Size field: 00 = byte
           01 = word
           11 = long word

NBCD

15	14	13	12	11	10	9	8	7	6	5	4	3	2	1	0
0	1	0	0	1	0	0	0	0	0			Effective Address			

15	14	13	12	11	10	9	8	7	6	5	4	3	2	1	0
0	1	0	0	1	0	0	0	0	0	Mode			Register		

PEA

15	14	13	12	11	10	9	8	7	6	5	4	3	2	1	0
0	1	0	0	1	0	0	0	0	1	Effective Address — Mode			Register		

SWAP

15	14	13	12	11	10	9	8	7	6	5	4	3	2	1	0
0	1	0	0	1	0	0	0	0	1	0	0	0	Register		

MOVEM Registers to EA

15	14	13	12	11	10	9	8	7	6	5	4	3	2	1	0
0	1	0	0	1	0	0	0	1	Sz	Effective Address — Mode			Register		

Sz field: 0 = word transfer
1 = long word transfer

EXTW

15	14	13	12	11	10	9	8	7	6	5	4	3	2	1	0
0	1	0	0	1	0	0	0	1	0	0	0	0	Register		

EXTL

15	14	13	12	11	10	9	8	7	6	5	4	3	2	1	0
0	1	0	0	1	0	0	0	1	1	0	0	0	Register		

TST

15	14	13	12	11	10	9	8	7	6	5	4	3	2	1	0
0	1	0	0	1	0	1	0	Size		Effective Address — Mode			Register		

Size field: 00 = byte
01 = word
11 = long word

TAS

15	14	13	12	11	10	9	8	7	6	5	4	3	2	1	0
0	1	0	0	1	0	1	0	1	1	Effective Address Mode			Register		

ILLEGAL

15	14	13	12	11	10	9	8	7	6	5	4	3	2	1	0
0	1	0	0	1	0	1	0	1	1	1	1	1	1	0	0

MOVEM EA to Registers

15	14	13	12	11	10	9	8	7	6	5	4	3	2	1	0
0	1	0	0	1	1	0	0	1	Sz	Effective Address Mode			Register		

Sz field: 0 = word transfer
1 = long word transfer

TRAP

15	14	13	12	11	10	9	8	7	6	5	4	3	2	1	0
0	1	0	0	1	1	1	0	0	1	0	0	Vector			

LINK

15	14	13	12	11	10	9	8	7	6	5	4	3	2	1	0
0	1	0	0	1	1	1	0	0	1	0	1	0	Register		

UNLK

15	14	13	12	11	10	9	8	7	6	5	4	3	2	1	0
0	1	0	0	1	1	1	0	0	1	0	1	1	Register		

MOVE to USP

15	14	13	12	11	10	9	8	7	6	5	4	3	2	1	0
0	1	0	0	1	1	1	0	0	1	1	0	0	Register		

MOVE from USP

15	14	13	12	11	10	9	8	7	6	5	4	3	2	1	0
0	1	0	0	1	1	1	0	0	1	1	0	1	Register		

RESET

15	14	13	12	11	10	9	8	7	6	5	4	3	2	1	0
0	1	0	0	1	1	1	0	0	1	1	1	0	0	0	0

NOP

15	14	13	12	11	10	9	8	7	6	5	4	3	2	1	0
0	1	0	0	1	1	1	0	0	1	1	1	0	0	0	1

STOP

15	14	13	12	11	10	9	8	7	6	5	4	3	2	1	0
0	1	0	0	1	1	1	0	0	1	1	1	0	0	1	0

RTE

15	14	13	12	11	10	9	8	7	6	5	4	3	2	1	0
0	1	0	0	1	1	1	0	0	1	1	1	0	0	1	1

RTS

15	14	13	12	11	10	9	8	7	6	5	4	3	2	1	0
0	1	0	0	1	1	1	0	0	1	1	1	0	1	0	1

TRAPV

15	14	13	12	11	10	9	8	7	6	5	4	3	2	1	0
0	1	0	0	1	1	1	0	0	1	1	1	0	1	1	0

RTR

15	14	13	12	11	10	9	8	7	6	5	4	3	2	1	0
0	1	0	0	1	1	1	0	0	1	1	1	0	1	1	1

JSR

15	14	13	12	11	10	9	8	7	6	5 4 3	2 1 0
0	1	0	0	1	1	1	0	1	0	Effective Address Mode	Register

JMP

15	14	13	12	11	10	9	8	7	6	5 4 3	2 1 0
0	1	0	0	1	1	1	0	1	1	Effective Address Mode	Register

CHK

15	14	13	12	11 10 9	8	7	6	5 4 3	2 1 0
0	1	0	0	Register	1	1	0	Effective Address Mode	Register

LEA

15	14	13	12	11 10 9	8	7	6	5 4 3	2 1 0
0	1	0	0	Register	1	1	1	Effective Address Mode	Register

C.7 ADD QUICK, SUBTRACT QUICK, SET CONDITIONALLY, DECREMENT INSTRUCTIONS

ADDQ

15	14	13	12	11	10	9	8	7	6	5	4	3	2	1	0
0	1	0	1	Data			0	Size		Effective Address					
										Mode			Register		

SUBQ

15	14	13	12	11	10	9	8	7	6	5	4	3	2	1	0
0	1	0	1	Data			1	Size		Effective Address					
										Mode			Register		

Data field: Three bits of immediate data, 0, 1-7, representing a range of: 8, 1-7, respectively.

Size field: 00 = byte
01 = word
10 = long word

Scc

15	14	13	12	11	10	9	8	7	6	5	4	3	2	1	0
0	1	0	1	Condition				1	1	Effective Address					
										Mode			Register		

DBcc

15	14	13	12	11	10	9	8	7	6	5	4	3	2	1	0
0	1	0	1	Condition				1	1	0	0	1	Register		

Condition field: See Table C-3

C.8 BRANCH CONDITIONALLY INSTRUCTION

Bcc

15	14	13	12	11	10	9	8	7	6	5	4	3	2	1	0
0	1	1	0	Condition				8-bit Displacement							

Condition field: See Table C-3

BSR

15	14	13	12	11	10	9	8	7	6	5	4	3	2	1	0
0	1	1	0	0	0	0	1	8-bit Displacement							

8-bit Displacement field: Twos complement integer representing the relative distance in bytes. If 0, 16-bit displacement is in extension word.

C.9 MOVE QUICK INSTRUCTION

MOVEQ

15	14	13	12	11	10	9	8	7	6	5	4	3	2	1	0
0	1	1	1	Register			0	Data*							

*Data is sign extended to a long operand, and all 32 bits are transferred to the data register.

C.10 OR, DIVIDE, SUBTRACT DECIMAL INSTRUCTIONS

OR

15	14	13	12	11	10	9	8	7	6	5	4	3	2	1	0
1	0	0	0	Register			Op-Mode			Effective Address					
										Mode			Register		

Op-Mode field:

	Byte	Word	Long	Operation
	000	001	010	$(<Dn>) \wedge (<ea>) \rightarrow <Dn>$
	100	101	110	$(<ea>) \wedge (<Dn>) \rightarrow <ea>$

DIVU

15	14	13	12	11	10	9	8	7	6	5	4	3	2	1	0
1	0	0	0	Register			0	1	1	Effective Address					
										Mode			Register		

DIVS

15	14	13	12	11	10	9	8	7	6	5	4	3	2	1	0
1	0	0	0	Register			1	1	1	Effective Address					
										Mode			Register		

SBCD

15	14	13	12	11	10	9	8	7	6	5	4	3	2	1	0
1	0	0	0	Destination Register*			1	0	0	0	0	R/M	Source Register*		

R/M field: 0 = register-register
1 = memory-memory

*If R/M = 0, specifies a data register.
If R/M = 1, specifies an address register for the predecrement addressing mode.

C.11 SUBTRACT, SUBTRACT EXTENDED INSTRUCTIONS

SUB

15	14	13	12	11	10	9	8	7	6	5	4	3	2	1	0
1	0	0	1	Register			Op-Mode			Effective Address					
										Mode			Register		

Op-Mode field:

	Byte	Word	Long	Operation
	000	001	010	$(<Dn>) + (<ea>) \rightarrow <Dn>$
	100	101	110	$(<ea>) + (<Dn>) \rightarrow <ea>$

SUBX

15	14	13	12	11	10	9	8	7	6	5	4	3	2	1	0
1	0	0	1	Destination Register*			1	Size		0	0	R/M	Source Register*		

R/M field: 0 = register-register
1 = memory-memory

*If R/M = 0, specifies a data register.
If R/M = 1, specifies an address register for the predecrement addressing mode.

C.12 COMPARE, EXCLUSIVE OR INSTRUCTIONS

CMP

15	14	13	12	11	10	9	8	7	6	5	4	3	2	1	0
1	0	1	1	Register			Op-Mode			Effective Address					
										Mode			Register		

Op-Mode field:
	Byte	Word	Long	Operation
	000	001	010	$(<Dn>)-(<ea>)$

CMPM

15	14	13	12	11	10	9	8	7	6	5	4	3	2	1	0
1	0	1	1	Register			1	Size		0	0	1	Register		

EOR

15	14	13	12	11	10	9	8	7	6	5	4	3	2	1	0
1	0	1	1	Register			1	Size		Effective Address					
										Mode			Register		

Size field: 00 = byte
01 = word
10 = long word

C.13 AND, MULTIPLY, ADD DECIMAL, EXCHANGE INSTRUCTIONS

AND

15	14	13	12	11	10	9	8	7	6	5	4	3	2	1	0
1	1	0	0	Register			Op-Mode			Effective Address					
										Mode			Register		

Op-Mode field:
	Byte	Word	Long	Operation
	000	001	010	$(<Dn>)-(<ea>) \rightarrow <Dn>$
	100	101	110	$(<ea>)-(<Dn>) \rightarrow <ea>$

MULU

15	14	13	12	11	10	9	8	7	6	5	4	3	2	1	0
1	1	0	0	Register			0	1	1	Effective Address					
										Mode			Register		

MULS

15	14	13	12	11	10	9	8	7	6	5	4	3	2	1	0
1	1	0	0	Register			1	1	1	Effective Address					
										Mode			Register		

ABCD

15	14	13	12	11	10	9	8	7	6	5	4	3	2	1	0
1	1	0	0	Destination Register*			1	0	0	0	0	R/M	Source Register*		

R/M field: 0 = register-register
            1 = memory-memory

*If R/M = 0, specifies a data register.
If R/M = 1, specifies an address register for the predecrement addressing mode.

EXGD

15	14	13	12	11	10	9	8	7	6	5	4	3	2	1	0
1	1	0	0	Data Register			1	0	1	0	0	0	Data Register		

EXGA

15	14	13	12	11	10	9	8	7	6	5	4	3	2	1	0
1	1	0	0	Address Register			1	0	1	0	0	1	Address Register		

EXGM

15	14	13	12	11	10	9	8	7	6	5	4	3	2	1	0
1	1	0	0	Data Register			1	1	0	0	0	1	Address Register		

C.14 ADD, ADD EXTENDED INSTRUCTIONS

ADD

15	14	13	12	11	10	9	8	7	6	5	4	3	2	1	0
1	1	0	1	Register			Op-Mode			Effective Address					
										Mode			Register		

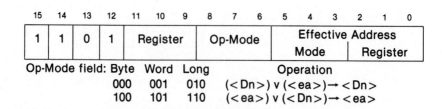

Op-Mode field: Byte Word Long   Operation
              000   001   010   (<Dn>) v (<ea>)→ <Dn>
              100   101   110   (<ea>) v (<Dn>)→ <ea>

ADDX

15	14	13	12	11	10	9	8	7	6	5	4	3	2	1	0
1	1	0	1	Destination Register*			1	Size		0	0	R/M	Source Register*		

R/M field: 0 = register-register
1 = memory-memory

*If R/M = 0, specifies a data register

If R/M = 1, specifies an address register for the predecrement addressing mode.

C.15 SHIFT/ROTATE INSTRUCTIONS

Register

15	14	13	12	11	10	9	8	7	6	5	4	3	2	1	0
1	1	1	0	Count/Register			dr	Size		i/r	Type		Register		

Count/Register field: If i/r field = 0, specifies count
If i/r field = 1, specifies a data register that contains the count.

dr field: 0 = right
1 = left

Size field: 00 = byte
01 = word
11 = long word

i/r field: 0 = immediate count
1 = register count

Type field: 00 = arithmetic shift
01 = logical shift
10 = rotate with extend
11 = rotate

Memory

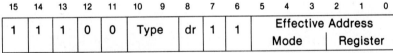

15	14	13	12	11	10	9	8	7	6	5	4	3	2	1	0
1	1	1	0	0	Type		dr	1	1	Effective Address Mode			Register		

Type field: 00 = arithmetic shift
01 = logical shift
10 = rotate with extend
11 = rotate

dr field: 0 = right
1 = left

APPENDIX D
INSTRUCTION EXECUTION TIMES

D.1 INTRODUCTION

This Appendix contains listings of the instruction execution times in terms of external clock (CLK) periods. In this data, it is assumed that both memory read and write cycle times are four clock periods. A longer memory cycle will cause the generation of wait states which must be added to the total instruction time.

The number of bus read and write cycles for each instruction is also included with the timing data. This data is enclosed in parenthesis following the number of clock periods and is shown as: (r/w) where r is the number of read cycles and w is the number of write cycles included in the clock period number. Recalling that either a read or write cycle requires four clock periods, a timing number given as 18(3/1) relates to 12 clock periods for the three read cycles, plus 4 clock periods for the one write cycle, plus 2 cycles required for some internal function of the processor.

NOTE

The number of periods includes instruction fetch and all applicable operand fetches and stores.

D.2 EFFECTIVE ADDRESS OPERAND CALCULATION TIMING

Table D-1 lists the number of clock periods required to compute an instruction's effective address. It includes fetching of any extension words, the address computation, and fetching of the memory operand. The number of bus read and write cycles is shown in parenthesis as (r/w). Note there are no write cycles involved in processing the effective address.

Table D-1. Effective Address Calculation Timing

Addressing Mode		Byte, Word	Long
	Register		
Dn	Data Register Direct	0(0/0)	0(0/0)
An	Address Register Direct	0(0/0)	0(0/0)
	Memory		
An@	Address Register Indirect	4(1/0)	8(2/0)
An@ +	Address Register Indirect with Postincrement	4(1/0)	8(2/0)
An@ –	Address Register Indirect with Predecrement	6(1/0)	10(2/0)
An@(d)	Address Register Indirect with Displacement	8(2/0)	12(3/0)
An@(d, ix)*	Address Register Indirect with Index	10(2/0)	14(3/0)
xxx.W	Absolute Short	8(2/0)	12(3/0)
xxx.L	Absolute Long	12(3/0)	16(4/0)
PC@(d)	Program Counter with Displacement	8(2/0)	12(3/0)
PC@(d, ix)*	Program Counter with Index	10(2/0)	14(3/0)
#xxx	Immediate	4(1/0)	8(2/0)

*The size of the index register (ix) does not affect execution time.

D.3 MOVE INSTRUCTION CLOCK PERIODS

Tables D-2 and D-3 indicate the number of clock periods for the move instruction. This data includes instruction fetch, operand reads, and operand writes. The number of bus read and write cycles is shown in parenthesis as: (r/w).

Table D-2. Move Byte and Word Instruction Clock Periods

Source	Destination								
	Dn	An	An@	An@ +	An@ −	An@(d)	An@(d,ix)*	xxx.W	xxx.L
Dn	4(1/0)	4(1/0)	8(1/1)	8(1/1)	8(1/1)	12(2/1)	14(2/1)	12(2/1)	16(3/1)
An	4(1/0)	4(1/0)	8(1/1)	8(1/1)	8(1/1)	12(2/1)	14(2/1)	12(2/1)	16(3/1)
An@	8(2/0)	8(2/0)	12(2/1)	12(2/1)	12(2/1)	16(3/1)	18(3/1)	16(3/1)	20(4/1)
An@ +	8(2/0)	8(2/0)	12(2/1)	12(2/1)	12(2/1)	16(3/1)	18(3/1)	16(3/1)	20(4/1)
An@ −	10(2/0)	10(2/0)	14(2/1)	14(2/1)	14(2/1)	18(3/1)	20(3/1)	18(3/1)	22(4/1)
An@(d)	12(3/0)	12(3/0)	16(3/1)	16(3/1)	16(3/1)	20(4/1)	22(4/1)	20(4/1)	24(5/1)
An@(d, ix)*	14(3/0)	14(3/0)	18(3/1)	18(3/1)	18(3/1)	22(4/1)	24(4/1)	22(4/1)	26(5/1)
xxx.W	12(3/0)	12(3/0)	16(3/1)	16(3/1)	16(3/1)	20(4/1)	22(4/1)	20(4/1)	24(5/1)
xxx.L	16(4/0)	16(4/0)	20(4/1)	20(4/1)	20(4/1)	24(5/1)	26(5/1)	24(5/1)	28(6/1)
PC@(d)	12(3/0)	12(3/0)	16(3/1)	16(3/1)	16(3/1)	20(4/1)	22(4/1)	20(4/1)	24(5/1)
PC@(d, ix)*	14(3/0)	14(3/0)	18(3/1)	18(3/1)	18(3/1)	22(4/1)	24(4/1)	22(4/1)	26(5/1)
#xxx	8(2/0)	8(2/0)	12(2/1)	12(2/1)	12(2/1)	16(3/1)	18(3/1)	16(3/1)	20(4/1)

The size of the index register (ix) does not affect execution time.

Table D-3. Move Long Instruction Clock Periods

Source	Destination								
	Dn	An	An@	An@ +	An@ −	An@(d)	An@(d,ix)*	xxx.W	xxx.L
Dn	4(1/0)	4(1/0)	12(1/2)	12(1/2)	14(1/2)	16(2/2)	18(2/2)	16(2/2)	20(3/2)
An	4(1/0)	4(1/0)	12(1/2)	12(1/2)	14(1/2)	16(2/2)	18(2/2)	16(2/2)	20(3/2)
An@	12(3/0)	12(3/0)	20(3/2)	20(3/2)	20(3/2)	24(4/2)	26(4/2)	24(4/2)	28(5/2)
An@ +	12(3/0)	12(3/0)	20(3/2)	20(3/2)	20(3/2)	24(4/2)	26(4/2)	24(4/2)	28(5/2)
An@ −	14(3/0)	14(3/0)	22(3/2)	22(3/2)	22(3/2)	26(4/2)	28(4/2)	26(4/2)	30(5/2)
An@(d)	16(4/0)	16(4/0)	24(4/2)	24(4/2)	24(4/2)	28(5/2)	30(5/2)	28(5/2)	32(6/2)
An@(d, ix)*	18(4/0)	18(4/0)	26(4/2)	26(4/2)	26(4/2)	30(5/2)	32(5/2)	30(5/2)	34(6/2)
xxx.W	16(4/0)	16(4/0)	24(4/2)	24(4/2)	24(4/2)	28(5/2)	30(5/2)	28(5/2)	32(6/2)
xxx.L	20(5/0)	20(5/0)	28(5/2)	28(5/2)	28(5/2)	32(6/2)	34(6/2)	32(6/2)	36(7/2)
PC@(d)	16(4/0)	16(4/0)	24(4/2)	24(4/2)	24(4/2)	28(5/2)	30(5/2)	28(5/2)	32(6/2)
PC@(d, ix)*	18(4/0)	18(4/0)	26(4/2)	26(4/2)	26(4/2)	30(5/2)	32(5/2)	30(5/2)	34(6/2)
#xxx	12(3/0)	12(3/0)	20(3/2)	20(3/2)	20(3/2)	24(4/2)	26(4/2)	24(4/2)	28(5/2)

*The size of the index register (ix) does not affect execution time.

D.4 STANDARD INSTRUCTION CLOCK PERIODS

The number of clock periods shown in Table D-4 indicates the time required to perform the operations, store the results, and read the next instruction. The number of bus read and write cycles is shown in parenthesis as: (r/w). The number of clock periods and the number of read and write cycles must be added to those of the effective address calculation where indicated.

In Table D-4, the headings have the following meanings: An = address register operand, Dn = data register operand, ea = an operand specified by an effective address, and M = memory effective address operand.

Table D-4. Standard Instruction Clock Periods

Instruction	Size	op <ea>, An	op <ea>, Dn	op Dn, <M>
ADD	Byte, Word	8(1/0) +	4(1/0) +	8(1/1) +
ADD	Long	6(1/0) + **	6(1/0) + **	12(1/2) +
AND	Byte, Word	—	4(1/0) +	8(1/1) +
AND	Long	—	6(1/0) + **	12(1/2) +
CMP	Byte, Word	6(1/0) +	4(1/0) +	—
CMP	Long	6(1/0) +	6(1/0) +	—
DIVS	—	—	158(1/0) + *	—
DIVU	—	—	140(1/0) + *	—
EOR	Byte, Word	—	4(1/0)***	8(1/1) +
EOR	Long	—	8(1/0)***	12(1/2) +
MULS	—	—	70(1/0) + *	—
MULU	—	—	70(1/0) + *	—
OR	Byte, Word	—	4(1/0) +	8(1/1) +
OR	Long	—	6(1/0) + **	12(1/1) +
SUB	Byte, Word	8(1/0) +	4(1/0) +	8(1/1) +
SUB	Long	6(1/0) + **	6(1/0) + **	12(1/2) +

+ add effective address calculation time

* indicates maximum value

** total of 8 clock periods for instruction if the effective address is register direct

*** only available effective address mode is data register direct

D.5 IMMEDIATE INSTRUCTION CLOCK PERIODS

The number of clock periods shown in Table D-5 includes the time to fetch immediate operands, perform the operations, store the results, and read the next operation. The number of bus read and write cycles is shown in parenthesis as: (r/w). The number of clock periods and the number of read and write cycles must be added to those of the effective address calculation where indicated.

In Table D-5, the headings have the following meanings: # = immediate operand, Dn = data register operand, An = address register operand, and M = memory operand.

Table D-5. Immediate Instruction Clock Periods

Instruction	Size	op #, Dn	op #, An	op #, M
ADDI	Byte, Word	8(2/0)	—	12(2/1) +
	Long	16(3/0)	—	20(3/2) +
ADDQ	Byte, Word	4(1/0)	8(1/0)*	8(1/1) +
	Long	8(1/0)	8(1/0)	12(1/2) +
ANDI	Byte, Word	8(2/0)	—	12(2/1) +
	Long	16(3/0)	—	20(3/2) +
CMPI	Byte, Word	8(2/0)	8(2/0)	8(2/0) +
	Long	14(3/0)	14(3/0)	12(3/0) +
EORI	Byte, Word	8(2/0)	—	12(2/1) +
	Long	16(3/0)	—	20(3/2) +
MOVEQ	Long	4(1/0)	—	—
ORI	Byte, Word	8(2/0)	—	12(2/1) +
	Long	16(3/0)	—	20(3/2) +
SUBI	Byte, Word	8(2/0)	—	12(2/1) +
	Long	16(3/0)	—	20(3/2) +
SUBQ	Byte, Word	4(1/0)	8(1/0)*	8(1/1) +
	Long	8(1/0)	8(1/0)	12(1/2) +

+ add effective address calculation time
*word only

D.6 SINGLE OPERAND INSTRUCTION CLOCK PERIODS

Table D-6 indicates the number of clock periods for the single operand instructions. The number of bus read and write cycles is shown in parenthesis as: (r/w). The number of clock periods and the number of read and write cycles must be added to those of the effective address calculation where indicated.

Table D-6. Single Operand Instruction Clock Periods

Instruction	Size	Register	Memory
CLR	Byte, Word	4(1/0)	8(1/1) +
	Long	6(1/0)	12(1/2) +
NBCD	Byte	6(1/1)	8(1/1) +
NEG	Byte, Word	4(1/0)	8(1/1) +
	Long	6(1/0)	12(1/2) +
NEGX	Byte, Word	4(1/0)	8(1/1) +
	Long	6(1/0)	12(1/2) +
NOT	Byte, Word	4(1/0)	8(1/1) +
	Long	6(1/0)	12(1/2) +
S$_{CC}$	Byte, False	4(1/0)	8(1/1) +
	Byte, True	6(1/0)	8(1/1) +
TAS	Byte	4(1/0)	10(1/1) +
TST	Byte, Word	4(1/0)	4(1/0) +
	Long	4(1/0)	4(1/0) +

+ add effective address calculation time

D.7 SHIFT/ROTATE INSTRUCTION CLOCK PERIODS

Table D-7 indicates the number of clock periods for the shift and rotate instructions. The number of bus read and write cycles is shown in parenthesis as: (r/w). The number of clock periods and the number of read and write cycles must be added to those of the effective address calculation where indicated.

Table D-7. Shift/Rotate Instruction Clock Periods

Instruction	Size	Register	Memory
ASR, ASL	Byte, Word	6 + 2n(1/0)	8(1/1) +
	Long	8 + 2n(1/0)	—
LSR, LSL	Byte, Word	6 + 2n(1/0)	8(1/1) +
	Long	8 + 2n(1/0)	—
ROR, ROL	Byte, Word	6 + 2n(1/0)	8(1/1) +
	Long	8 + 2n(1/0)	—
ROXR, ROXL	Byte, Word	6 + 2n(1/0)	8(1/1) +
	Long	8 + 2n(1/0)	—

+ add effective address calculation time
n is the shift count

D.8 BIT MANIPULATION INSTRUCTION CLOCK PERIODS

Table D-8 indicates the number of clock periods required for the bit manipulation instructions. The number of bus read and write cycles is shown in parenthesis as: (r/w). The number of clock periods and the number of read and write cycles must be added to those of the effective address calculation where indicated.

Table D-8. Bit Manipulation Instruction Clock Periods

Instruction	Size	Dynamic		Static	
		Register	Memory	Register	Memory
BCHG	Byte	—	8(1/1) +	—	12(2/1) +
	Long	8(1/0)*	—	12(2/0)*	—
BCLR	Byte	—	8(1/1) +	—	12(2/1) +
	Long	10(1/0)*	—	14(2/0)*	—
BSET	Byte	—	8(1/1) +	—	12(2/1) +
	Long	8(1/0)*	—	12(2/0)*	—
BTST	Byte	—	4(1/0) +	—	8(2/0) +
	Long	6(1/0)	—	10(2/0)	—

+ add effective address calculation time

* indicates maximum value

D.9 CONDITIONAL INSTRUCTION CLOCK PERIODS

Table D-9 indicates the number of clock periods required for the conditional instructions. The number of bus read and write cycles is indicated in parenthesis as: (r/w). The number of clock periods and the number of read and write cycles must be added to those of the effective address calculation where indicated.

Table D-9. Conditional Instruction Clock Periods

Instruction	Displacement	Trap or Branch Taken	Trap or Branch Not Taken
BCC	Byte	10(2/0)	8(1/0)
	Word	10(2/0)	12(2/0)
BRA	Byte	10(2/0)	—
	Word	10(2/0)	—
BSR	Byte	18(2/2)	—
	Word	18(2/2)	—
DBCC	CC true	—	12(2/0)
	CC false	10(2/0)	14(3/0)
CHK	—	40(5/3) + *	8(1/0) +
TRAP	—	34(4/3)	—
TRAPV	—	34(5/3)	4(1/0)

+ add effective address calculation time

* indicates maximum value

D.10 JMP, JSR, LEA, PEA, MOVEM INSTRUCTION CLOCK PERIODS

Table D-10 indicates the number of clock periods required for the jump, jump to subroutine, load effective address, push effective address, and move multiple register instructions. The number of bus read and write cycles is shown in parenthesis as: (r/w).

TABLE D-10. JMP, JSR, LEA, PEA, MOVEM Instruction Clock Periods

Instr	Size	An@	An@ +	An@ −	An@(d)	An@(d, ix)*	xxx.W	xxx.L	PC@(d)	PC@(d, ix)*
JMP	—	8(2/0)	—	—	10(2/0)	14(2/0)	10(2/0)	12(3/0)	10(2/0)	14(3/0)
JSR	—	16(2/2)	—	—	18(2/2)	22(2/2)	18(2/2)	20(3/2)	18(2/2)	22(2/2)
LEA	—	4(1/0)	—	—	8(2/0)	12(2/0)	8(2/0)	12(3/0)	8(2/0)	12(2/0)
PEA	—	12(1/2)	—	—	16(2/2)	20(2/2)	16(2/2)	20(3/2)	16(2/2)	20(2/2)
MOVEM M → R	Word	12 + 4n (3 + n/0)	12 + 4n (3 + n/0)	—	16 + 4n (4 + n/0)	18 + 4n (4 + n/0)	16 + 4n (4 + n/0)	20 + 4n (5 + n/0)	16 + 4n (4 + n/0)	18 + 4n (4 + n/0)
	Long	12 + 8n (3 + 2n/0)	12 + 8n (3 + 2n/0)	—	16 + 8n (4 + 2n/0)	18 + 8n (4 + 2n/0)	16 + 8n (4 + 2n/0)	20 + 8n (5 + 2n/0)	16 + 8n (4 + 2n/0)	18 + 8n (4 + 2n/0)
MOVEM R → M	Word	8 + 5n (2/n)	—	8 + 5n (2/n)	12 + 5n (3/n)	14 + 5n (3/n)	12 + 5n (3/n)	16 + 5n (4/n)	—	—
	Long	8 + 10n (2/2n)	—	8 + 10n (2/2n)	12 + 10n (3/2n)	14 + 10n (3/2n)	12 + 10n (3/2n)	16 + 10n (4/2n)	—	—

n is the number of registers to move

*the size of the index register (ix) does not affect the instruction's execution time

D.11 MULTI-PRECISION INSTRUCTION CLOCK PERIODS

Table D-11 indicates the number of clock periods for the multi-precision instructions. The number of clock periods includes the time to fetch both operands, perform the operations, store the results, and read the next instructions. The number of read and write cycles is shown in parenthesis as: (r/w).

In Table D-11, the headings have the following meanings: Dn = data register operand and M = memory operand.

Table D-11. Multi-Precision Instruction Clock Periods

Instruction	Size	op Dn, Dn	op M, M
ADDX	Byte, Word	4(1/0)	18(3/1)
	Long	8(1/0)	30(5/2)
CMPM	Byte, Word	—	12(3/0)
	Long	—	20(5/0)
SUBX	Byte, Word	4(1/0)	18(3/1)
	Long	8(1/0)	30(5/2)
ABCD	Byte	6(1/0)	18(3/1)
SBCD	Byte	6(1/0)	18(3/1)

D.12 MISCELLANEOUS INSTRUCTION CLOCK PERIODS

Tables D-12 and D-13 indicate the number of clock periods for the miscellaneous instructions listed. The number of bus read and write cycles is shown in parenthesis as: (r/w). The number of clock periods and the number of read and write cycles must be added to those of the effective address calculation where indicated.

Table D-12. Miscellaneous Instruction Clock Periods

Instruction	Register	Memory	Instruction	Register	Memory
ANDI to CCR	20(3/0)	—	MOVE from USP	4(1/0)	—
ANDI to SR	20(3/0)	—	NOP	4(1/0)	—
EORI to CCR	20(3/0)	—	ORI to CCR	20(3/0)	—
EORI to SR	20(3/0)	—	ORI to SR	20(3/0)	—
EXG	6(1/0)	—	RESET	132(1/0)	—
EXT	4(1/0)	—	RTE	20(5/0)	—
LINK	18(2/2)	—	RTR	20(5/0)	—
MOVE to CCR	12(2/0)	12(2/0)+	RTS	16(4/0)	—
MOVE to SR	12(2/0)	12(2/0)+	STOP	4(0/0)	—
MOVE from SR	6(1/0)	8(1/1)+	SWAP	4(1/0)	—
MOVE to USP	4(1/0)	—	UNLK	12(3/0)	—

+ add effective address calculation time

Table D-13. Move Peripheral Instruction Clock Periods

Instruction	Size	Register → Memory	Memory → Register
MOVEP	Word	16(2/2)	16(4/0)
	Long	24(2/4)	24(6/0)

D.13 EXCEPTION PROCESSING CLOCK PERIODS

Table D-14 indicates the number of clock periods for exception processing. The number of clock periods includes the time for all stacking, the vector fetch, and the fetch of the first instruction of the handler routine. The number of bus read and write cycles is shown in parenthesis as: (r/w).

Table D-14. Exception Processing Clock Periods

Exception	Periods
Address Error	50(4/7)
Bus Error	50(4/7)
Interrupt	44(5/3)[*]
Illegal Instruction	34(4/3)
Privileged Instruction	34(4/3)
Trace	34(4/3)

* The interrupt acknowledge bus cycle is assumed to take four external clock periods

APPENDIX E
PREFETCH

E.1 INTRODUCTION

The MC68000 uses a two-word tightly coupled instruction prefetch mechanism to enhance performance. This mechanism is described in terms of the microcode operations involved. If the execution is defined to begin when the microroutine for that instruction is entered, some features of the prefetch mechanism can be described.

1. When execution of an instruction begins, the operation word and the word following have already been fetched. The operation word is in the instruction decoder.

2. In the case of multiword instructions, as each additional word of the instruction is used internally, a fetch is made to the instruction stream to replace it.

3. The last fetch from the instruction stream is made when the operation word is discarded and decoding is started on the next instruction.

4. If the instruction is a single-word instruction causing a branch, the second word is not used. But because this word is fetched by the previous instruction, it is impossible to avoid this superfluous fetch. In the case of an interrupt or trace exception, both words are not used.

5. The program counter usually points to the last word fetched from the instruction stream.

E.2 INSTRUCTION PREFETCH

The following example illustrates many of the features of instruction prefetch. The contents of memory are assumed to be as illustrated in Figure E-1.

```
            ORG       0                    DEFINE RESTART VECTOR

            DC.L      INISSP               INITIAL SYSTEM STACK POINTER
            DC.L      RESTART              RESTART SYSTEM ENTRY POINT

            ORG       INTVECTOR            DEFINE AN INTERRUPT VECTOR
            DC.L      INTHANDLER           HANDLER ADDRESS FOR THIS VECTOR

            ORG                            SYSTEM RESTART CODE
RESTART:
            NOP                            NO OPERATION EXAMPLE
            BRA.S     LABEL                SHORT BRANCH
            ADD.W     D0,D1                ADD REGISTER TO REGISTER
LABEL:
            SUB.W     DISP(A0),A1          SUBTRACT REGISTER INDIRECT WITH OFFSET
            CMP.W     D2,D3                COMPARE REGISTER TO REGISTER
            SGE.B     D7                   Scc TO REGISTER
            ...
            ...
INTHANDLER:
            MOVE.W    LONGADR1,LONGADR2    MOVE WORD FROM AND TO LONG ADDRESS
            NOP                            NO OPERATION
            SWAP.W                         REGISTER SWAP
```

Figure E-1. Instruction Prefetch Example, Memory Contents

The sequence we shall illustrate consists of the power-up reset, the execution of NOP, BRA, SUB, the taking of an interrupt, and the execution of the MOVE.W xxx.L to yyy.L. The order of operations described within each microroutine is not exact, but is intended for illustrative purpose only.

Microroutine	Operation	Location	Operand
Reset	Read	0	SSP High
	Read	2	SSP Low
	Read	4	PC High
	Read	6	PC Low
	Read	(PC)	NOP
	Read	+(PC)	BRA
	<begin NOP>		
NOP	Read	+(PC)	ADD
	<begin BRA>		
BRA	PC=PC+d		
	Read	(PC)	SUB
	Read	+(PC)	DISP
	<begin SUB>		
SUB	Read	+(PC)	CMP
	Read	DISP(A0)	<src>
	Read	+(PC)	SGE
	<begin CMP>	<take INT>	
INTERRUPT	Write	−(SSP)	PC Low
	Write	−(SSP)	PC High
	Read	<INT ACK>	Vector #
	Write	−(SSP)	SR
	Read	(VR)	PC High
	Read	+(VR)	PC Low
	Read	(PC)	MOVE
	Read	+(PC)	xxx High
	<begin MOVE>		
MOVE	Read	+(PC)	xxx Low
	Read	+(PC)	yyy High
	Read	xxx	<src>
	Read	+(PC)	yyy Low
	Read	+(PC)	NOP
	Write	yyy	<dest>
	Read	+(PC)	SWAP
	<begin NOP>		

Figure E-2. Instruction Prefetch Example

E.3 DATA PREFETCH

Normally the MC68000 prefetches only instructions and not data. However, when the MOVEM instruction is used to move data from memory to registers, the data stream is prefetched in order to optimize performance. As a result, the processor reads one extra word beyond the higher end of the source area. For example, the instruction sequence in Figure E-3 will operate as shown in Figure E-4.

	...		MOVE TWO
	MOVEM.L	A,D0/D1	LONGWORDS
	...		INTO REGISTERS
A	DC.W	1	WORD 1
B	DC.W	2	WORD 2
C	DC.W	3	WORD 3
D	DC.W	4	WORD 4
E	DC.W	5	WORD 5
F	DC.W	6	WORD 6

Assume Effective Address Evaluation is Already Done

Microroutine	Operation	Location	Other Operations
	...		
MOVEM	Read	A	
			Prepare to Fill D0
	Read	B	A → DOH
	Read	C	B → DOL
			Prepare to Fill D1
	Read	D	C → D1H
	Read	E	D → D1L
			Detect Register List Complete

Figure E-3.
MOVEM Example, Memory Contents

Figure E-4.
MOVEM Example, Operation Sequence

APPENDIX F
MC68451 MEMORY MANAGEMENT UNIT

F.1 INTRODUCTION

The MC68451 Memory Management Unit (MMU) provides address translation and protection for the 16 megabyte addressing range of the MC68000 processor. Each bus master (or processor) in the M68000 family provides a function code and an address during each bus cycle. The function code specifies an address space and the address specifies a location within that address space. The function codes distinguish between user and supervisor spaces and, within these, between data and program spaces. This separation of address spaces provides the basis for memory management and protection by the operating system. Provision is also made for other bus masters, such as the MC68450 Direct Access Controller (DMAC), to have separate address spaces for efficient direct memory access. A multitasking operating system is simplified and reliability is enhanced through the use of a memory management unit.

The MC68451 is the basic element of a memory management mechanism in an MC68000-based system. The operating system is responsible for ensuring the proper execution of user tasks in the system environment, and memory management is basic to this responsibility. The memory management mechanism provides the operating system with the capability to allocate, control, and protect the system memory. A block diagram of a memory management mechanism using a single MMU is shown in Figure F-1.

A memory management mechanism implemented with one or more MC68451 MMUs can provide address translation, separation, and write protection for the system memory. The memory management mechanism can be programmed to cause an interrupt when a chosen section of memory is accessed, and can directly translate a logical address into a physical address, making it available to the processor for use by the operating system. Using these features, the memory management mechanism can provide separation and security for user programs and allow the operating system to manage the memory in an efficient fashion for multitasking.

F.2 MEMORY SEGMENTS

The memory management mechanism partitions the logical address space into contiguous pieces called segments. Each segment is a section of the logical address space of a task which is mapped via the memory management mechanism into the physical address space. Each task may have any number of segments. Segments may be defined as user or supervisor, data-only or program-only, or program and data. They may be accessed by only one task or shared between two or more tasks. In addition, any segment can be write protected to ensure system integrity. If an undefined segment is accessed, a FAULT is generated by the MMU and applied to the bus error input of the processor.

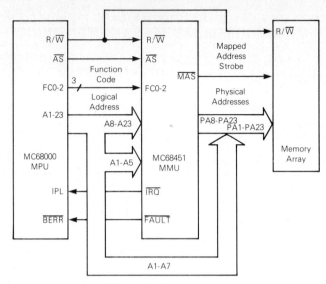

Figure F-1. Memory Management Mechanism Block Diagram

F.3 FUNCTION CODES AND ADDRESS SPACES

Each bus master in the M68000 family provides a function code during each bus cycle to indicate the address space to be used for that cycle. The address bus then specifies a location within this address space for the operation taking place during that bus cycle.

The function codes appear on the FC0-FC2 lines of the MC68000 and divide the memory references into two logical address spaces — the supervisor and the user spaces. Each of these is further divided into program and data spaces. A separate address space is also provided for interrupt acknowledge bus cycles giving a total of five defined function codes.

In addition to the 3-bit function code provided by the MC68000, the MMU also allows a fourth function code line (FC3) which provides for the possibility of another bus master in the system. In this case, FC3 would be tied to bus grant acknowledge input of the MC68000 to enable a second set of eight function codes. This raises the total number of possible function codes to sixteen. If there is only one bus master (the MPU), the FC3 pin of the MMU should be tied low and only eight address spaces used.

F.4 ADDRESS SPACE NUMBERS

To separate the address spaces of different tasks, each address space is given an identifying number. This should not be confused with the address space indicated by the function code. Each function code defines a unique address space and within each of these there can exist a number of different tasks. Each of these tasks needs an address space number (ASN) to distinguish it from the other tasks with which it may share an address space.

The address space numbers are kept in the MMU in a set of registers called the address space table (AST). The AST contains an 8-bit entry for each possible function code (16). Each entry can be assigned an address space number and, during a bus cycle, the function code is used to index into this table to select the cycle address space number. This number is then associatively compared with the address space number in each descriptor to attempt to find a match.

F.5 DESCRIPTORS

Address translation is done using descriptors. A descriptor is a set of six registers (nine bytes) which describes a memory segment and how that segment is to be mapped to the physical addresses. Each descriptor contains base addresses for the logical and physical spaces of each segment. These base addresses are then masked with the logical address masks. The size of the segment is then defined by "don't cares" in the low-order bits of the masks. This method allows segment sizes from a minimum of 256 bytes to a maximum of 16 megabytes in binary increments (i.e., powers of two). This also forces both logical and physical addresses of segment boundaries to lie on a segment size boundary. That is, a segment can only start on an address which is a multiple of 2^k.

The segments can be defined so that they are physically shared between tasks. A functional block diagram of an MC68451 MMU is shown in Figure F-2.

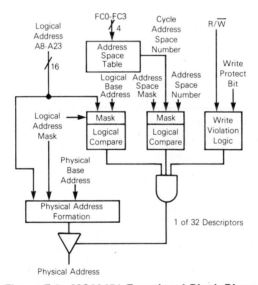

Figure F-2. MC68451 Functional Block Diagram

During normal translation, the MMU translates the logical address provided by the MC68000 to a physical address which is then presented to the memory array. This is accomplished by matching the logical address with the information in the descriptors and then mapping it into the physical address space.

The logical address is composed of address lines A1-A23 as shown in the memory management mechanism block diagram, Figure F-1. The upper 16 bits of this address (A8-A23) are translated by the MMU and mapped into a physical address (PA8-PA23). The lower seven bits of the logical address (A1-A7) bypass the MMU and become the low-order physical address bits (PA1-PA7).

F.6 MMU REGISTER DESCRIPTION

A programmer's model of the MMU is shown in Figure F-3. The MMU register consists of two groups: the descriptors and the system registers. Each of the 32 descriptors is nine bytes long and defines one memory segment.

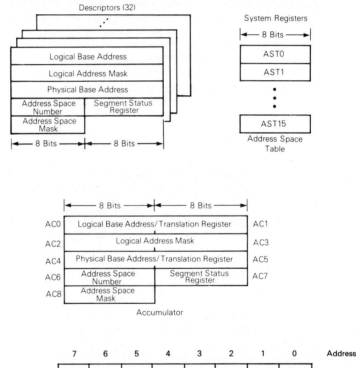

Figure F-3. MC68451 Programmers Model

210

The system registers contain both information local to the MMU and information global to the memory management mechanism. Each bit in the system registers and the segment status registers, except the address space table, is one of four types:

Control   Control bits can be set or cleared by the processor to select MMU options. These are read/write bits.

Status Alterable   Status alterable bits are set or cleared by the MMU to indicate status information. These are also read/write bits.

Status Unalterable Status unalterable bits are set or cleared by the MMU to reflect status information. These bits cannot be written by the processor.

Reserved   Reserved bits are reserved for future expansion. They cannot be written and are zero when read.

The system registers are all directly addressable from the physical address space. Accessing these registers causes certain operations to be performed. The descriptors are not directly addressable, but are accessed using the descriptor pointer and the accumulator.

In the following discussion, a segment access is defined as a successful match occurring on a segment during normal translation.

F.6.1 DESCRIPTORS. Each MMU contains 32 descriptors (0-31), each of which can define one memory segment. A descriptor is loaded by the processor using the accumulator and descriptor pointer with a load descriptor operation. The segment status register (SSR) can be written to indirectly by the processor using the descriptor pointer. Each descriptor consists of the following registers:

Logical Base Address (LBA)   Address Space Number (ASN)

Logical Address Mask (LAM)   Address Space Mask (ASM)

Physical Base Address (PBA)   Segment Status Register (SSR)

F.6.1.1 Logical Base Address (LBA). The logical base address register is a 16-bit register which, together with the logical address mask, defines the logical addressing range of a segment. This is typically the first address in the segment, although it can be any address within the range defined by the logical address mask.

F.6.1.2 Logical Address Mask (LAM). The logical address mask is a 16-bit mask which defines the bit positions in the logical base address register which are to be used for range matching. Ones, in the mask, mark significant bit positions while zeroes indicate "don't care" positions. A range match occurs if, in each bit position in the logical address mask which is set to one, the logical base address register matches the incoming logical address. The matching function is depicted schematically in Figure F-4.

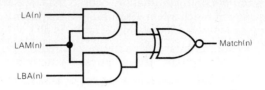

Note: LA(n) Indicates Bit N of Logical Address

Figure F-4. Schematic Representation for Address Matching

F.6.1.3 Physical Base Address (PBA). The physical base address register is a 16-bit register which, together with the logical address mask and the incoming logical address, is used to form the physical address. The logical address is passed through to the physical address in those bit positions of the logical address mask which contain zeroes (the "don't cares") and the physical base address is gated out in those positions which contain ones. A schematic representation of the physical address generation mechanism is shown in Figure F-5.

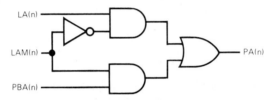

Figure F-5. Schematic Representation of Physical Address Generation

F.6.1.4 Address Space Number (ASN). The address space number is an 8-bit number which, together with the address space mask, is used in detecting a match with the cycle address space number.

F.6.1.5 Address Space Mask (ASM). The address space mask is an 8-bit mask which defines the significant bit positions in the address space number to be used in descriptor matching. As in the logical address mask, the bit positions which are set are used for matching and the bit positions that are clear are "don't cares." A space match occurs if, in the significant bit positions, the cycle address space number matches the address space number. Address space matching is schematically similar to logical address matching as shown in Figure F-4.

F.6.1.6 Segment Status Register (SSR). Each descriptor has an 8-bit segment status register. The segment status register can be written to in two ways: using the load descriptor operation or indirectly using the descriptor pointer in a write status register operation. Each bit is labeled as control or status alterable. Bits 5 and 6 are reserved for future use.

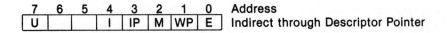

7	6	5	4	3	2	1	0	Address
U			I	IP	M	WP	E	Indirect through Descriptor Pointer

U U (Used) is set by the MMU if the segment was accessed since it was defined. This bit is status alterable.

Set: a)   by a Segment access (successful translation using the segment)
              b)   by an MPU write of "1"

Cleared: a)   Reset (in segment #0 of master)
              b)   MPU write of "0"

I If the I (Interrupt) control bit is set, an interrupt is generated upon accessing the segment.

Set: a)   MPU writes "1"

Cleared: a)   MPU writes "0"
              b)   Reset (segment #0 of master)

IP IP (Interrupt Pending) is set if the "I" bit is set when the segment is accessed. $\overline{IRQout}$ is asserted if an IP bit, in one or more SSRs, is set and IE in the global status register is set. $\overline{IRQout}$ is negated when all the IP bits in all SSRs are clear or IE is cleared. IP is status alterable and should be cleared by the interrupt service routine.

Set: a)   Segment access and "1" is set
              b)   MPU writes "1"

Cleared: a)   MPU writes a "0"
              b)   Reset (in segment #0 of master)
              c)   E bit is a "0"

M The M (Modified) bit is set by the MMU if the segment has been written to since it was defined. The M bit is status alterable.

Set: a)   Successful write to the segment
              b)   MPU writes a "1"

Cleared: a)   MPU writes a "0"
              b)   Reset (segment #0 in master)

WP If the WP (Write Protect) control bit is set, the segment is write protected. A write access to the segment with WP set will cause a write violation.

Set: a)   MPU writes a "1"

Cleared: a)   MPU writes a "0"
              b)   Reset (segment #0 in master)

E E (Enable) is a control bit which, when set, enables the segment to participate in the matching process. E can be cleared (the segment disabled) by a write to the SSR, but a load descriptor operation must be performed to set it.

Set: a)   Load descriptor with AC7, bit #0
              b)   Reset (segment #0 in master)

Cleared: a)   MPU writes a "0"
              b)   Unsuccessful load descriptor operation on this descriptor
              c)   Load descriptor operation with AC7, bit #0 clear

F.6.2 SYSTEM REGISTERS. The system registers consist of:

Address Space Table (AST)	Descriptor Pointer (DP)
Accumulator (AC0-AC8)	Result Descriptor Pointer (RDP)
Global Status Register (GSR)	Interrupt Descriptor Pointer (IDP)
Local Status Register (LSR)	Interrupt Vector Register (IVR)

F.6.2.1 Address Space Table (AST). Each MMU has a local copy of the address space table. This table is organized as sixteen 8-bit, read/write registers located starting at address $00. Each entry is programmed by the operating system with a unique address space number, each of which is associated with a task. During a memory access, the MMU receives a 4-bit function code (FC0-FC3) which is used to index into the address space table to select the cycle address space number. This number is then used to check for a match with the address space number in each of the 32 segment descriptors.

Only the MC68000 microprocessor and the MC68450 direct memory access controller only provide a 3-bit function code. In a system with more than one bus master, the bus grant acknowledge signal from the processor could be inverted and used as the fourth bit, FC3. This would result in the address space table organization shown in Figure F-6.

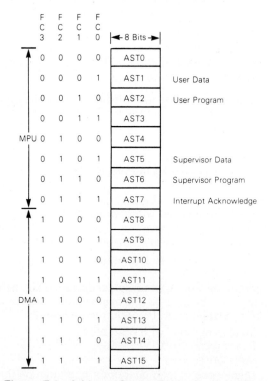

Figure F-6. Address Space Table Organization

F.6.2.2. Accumulator (AC0-AC8). The accumulator (Figure F-3) is used to access the descriptors, perform direct translation, and latch information during a fault. The accumulator consists of nine 8-bit registers. The register assignments for each operation in which it participates is shown in Table F-1.

The contents of the accumulator can be either local or global depending on the preceding operations. The global accumulator for load and global accumulator for translate bits in the local status register (LSR) indicate whether the information in the accumulator is sufficiently global to perform a load descriptor or direct translation operation.

Table F-1. Accumulator Assignments for Operation

Register Assignment	Load/Read Descriptor	Direct Translation	Normal Translation (Fault)
AC0	Logical Base Address (MSB)	Logical Translation Register (MSB)	Logical Address (MSB)
AC1	Logical Base Address (LSB)	Logical Translation Register (LSB)	Logical Address (LSB)
AC2	Logical Address Mask (MSB)		
AC3	Logical Address Mask (LSB)		
AC4	Physical Base Address (MSB)	Physical Translation Register (MSB)	
AC5	Pysical Base Address (LSB)	Physical Translation Register (LSB)	
AC6	Address Space Number	Address Space Number	Cycle Address Space Number
AC7	Segment Status		
AC8	Address Space Mask		

F.6.2.3 Global Status Register (GSR). The global status register is an 8-bit register used to reflect faults and to enable interrupts from an MMU. All MMUs maintain identical information in their global status registers. Bits 1, 2, 3, 4, and 5 are reversed for future use. The organization of the global states register is shown below.

```
         7   6   5   4   3   2   1   0    Address
GSR    | F | DF |   |   |   |   |   | IE |  $2D
```

F   F (Fault) is a status alterable bit that is set by the MMU whenever $\overline{\text{FAULT}}$in is detected. Clearing the F bit automatically clears bits L4-L7 in the local status register.
  Set: a) Write violation detected in this MMU
            b) $\overline{\text{FAULT}}$in detected (write violation in another MMU)
            c) ALLin detected (Undefined Segment Access)
            d) MPU writes a "1"
  Cleared: a) Reset asserted
            b) MPU writes a "0"

DF   DF (Double Fault) is set if a $\overline{\text{FAULT}}$in signal was detected with F set. DF is a status alterable bit.
  Set: a) $\overline{\text{FAULT}}$in detected and F was previously set
            b) MPU writes a "1"
  Cleared: a) Reset
            b) MPU writes a "0"

IE   If IE (Interrupt Enable) is set, the interrupt-request line is enabled. This is a read/write
     control bit.
     Set: a)   MPU writes a "1"
     Cleared: a)   Reset
                 b)   MPU writes a "0"

F.6.2.4 Local Status Register (LSR). The local status register is an 8-bit register which
reflects information local to its MMU. The local status register can be globally written but
the global accumulator for load, global accumulator for translate, and local interrupt
pending bits will not be affected. Bits L4-L7 are cleared if the fault line in the global
status register is cleared. All bits in the local status register are cleared on reset. The
organization of the local status register is shown below.

	7	6	5	4	3	2	1	0	Address
LSR	L7	L6	L5	L4	RW	GAT	GAL	LIP	$2F

RW   RW is a status alterable bit which reflects the state of the R/$\overline{\text{W}}$ pin at the time
     $\overline{\text{FAULT}}$in is asserted.
     Set: a)   MPU writes a "1"
                 b)   Read of segment when F in SSR is set
     Cleared: a)   Reset
                 b)   MPU writes a "0"
                 c)   Write of segment when F in SSR is set

GAT GAT (Global Accumulator for Translate) is set by the MMU if AC0, AC1, and AC6 are
     globally consistent.
     Set: a)   If AC0, AC1, and AC6 are globally consistent (they were last
                      modified as a result of a global write)
     Cleared: a)   Reset
                 b)   If AC0, AC1, and AC6 are not globally consistent

GAL GAL (Global Accumulator for Load) is set if AC0, AC1, AC2, AC3, AC6, and AC8 are
     globally consistent.
     Set: a)   If AC0, AC1, AC2, AC3, AC6, and AC8 are globally consistent
     Cleared: a)   Reset
                 b)   If AC0, AC1, AC2, AC3, AC6, and AC8 are not globally consistent

LIP LIP (Local Interrupt Pending) is set if one or more descriptors have IP set in their seg-
     ment status registers.
     Set: a)   If IP is set in any descriptor
     Cleared: a)   Reset
                 b)   If all IP bits are clear

L4- The status information encoded in L4-L7 reflects the status of the MMU after the last
L7   event (an operation or fault). These bits are encoded and changed as a unit. They are
     cleared whenever the F bit in the GSR is cleared and are alterable by the MPU.

216

L7	L6	L5	L4		
0	0	0	0	NO	The MMU was not the source of the last event.
1	0	0	0	DT	A direct translation was locally successful. A match was found in one of the MMUs descriptors.
1	0	0	1	LD	A load descriptor fault occurred. A previously defined descriptor conflicts with the descriptor being loaded.
1	0	1	0	USA	An undefined segment access was attempted. The logical address was not matched in any descriptor in the MMU.
1	1	0	0	WV	A write violation occurred. A segment defined in this MMU was write protected and a write to that memory segment was attempted. The NVR bit in the RDP will show whether the USA or WV occurred in this MMU.

Set:
    a) Various bits set if DT, LD, USA, or WV occur
    b) MPU writes a "1"

Cleared:
    a) Reset
    b) MPU writes a "0"
    c) When F bit in GSR is cleared
    d) If MMU was not the source of the last event (NO)

F.6.2.5 Descriptor Pointer (DP). The descriptor pointer is an 8-bit read/write pointer register located at address $29. The five low-order bits identify the descriptor to be used in the load descriptor, read segment status (transfer descriptor), and write segment status operations. Bits 5, 6, and 7 are reserved.

The descriptor pointer is initialized to $00 on reset. It can be globally written by the processor. The descriptor pointer is loaded by the memory management mechanism with the number of the descriptor matched in a direct translation operation to allow a subsequent transfer descriptor operation to load the matched descriptor into the accumulator.

F.6.2.6 Result Descriptor Pointer (RDP). The result descriptor pointer is an 8-bit, read-only register that identifies a descriptor involved in the following events: a write violation, a load descriptor failure, or a direct translation success. The result descriptor pointer is loaded from a priority encoder which determines the highest priority descriptor involved. For example, in a load descriptor operation, more than one descriptor currently in the MMU may collide with the descriptor being loaded. Only the number of the highest priority descriptor will be loaded into the result descriptor pointer. Descriptor 0 is considered to be the highest priority and 31 is the lowest.

The bit assignments are shown below. Bits 5 and 6 are reserved. The result descriptor pointer is initialized to $80 on reset.

	7	6	5	4	3	2	1	0	Address
RDP	NVR			R4	R3	R2	R1	R0	$3B

NVR   If no descriptor is selected by the priority encoder when the RDP is loaded, NVR (No Valid Result) is set, otherwise it is cleared. This bit is status unalterable.

     Set: a)   Reset
                b)   No result from WV, LD, or DT
     Cleared: a)   A WV, LD failure of DT success in this MMU

R0-
R4   R0-R4 encode the number of the descriptor selected by the priority encoder

F.6.2.7 Interrupt Descriptor Pointer (IDP). The interrupt descriptor pointer is an 8-bit read-only register that is read to determine which descriptor caused an interrupt. Each time it is read, the interrupt descriptor pointer is loaded from the priority encoder with the highest-priority descriptor which has the interrupt pending bit in its segment status register set. If no descriptor has an interrupt pending bit set, the no valid interrupt bit is set.

The bit assignment is shown below. Bits 5 and 6 are reserved.

	7	6	5	4	3	2	1	0	Address
IDP	NVI			I4	I3	I2	I1	I0	$39

NVI   NVI is set if no descriptor has IP set, otherwise it is cleared.

I0-I4   These bits encode the number of the descriptor selected by the priority encoder.

F.6.2.8 Interrupt Vector Register (IVR). The interrupt vector register is an 8-bit read/write register containing the interrupt vector. Its contents are put on data lines D0-D7 during the interrupt acknowledge operation to provide the processor with a vector number. The interrupt vector register is initialized to $0F (the MC68000 uninitialized-device vector number) on reset.

F.7 MMU OPERATIONS

Table F-2 shows the operations which can be performed. Each operation is initiated by the access of an address given on the register select lines RS1-RS5 and the upper and lower data strobes. The access can be from either the logical or physical address bus. In a multiprocessor system, an external processor could access the memory management mechanism from the physical address bus. If the access is from the logical address bus, an address translation is first performed. If the access is from the physical address bus, the operation state is entered directly from the idle state.

218

Table F-2. Summary of MMU Functions

Function	Summary
Idle	The MMU backs off the bus to prepare for a new access.
Reset	The MMU is pre-emptively initialized.
Normal Translation	The MMU attempts to translate an access from the logical address bus.
Operations	The MMU is accessed from the logical or physical bus.
Write System Registers	An operation to globally write system registers.
Read System Registers	An operation to read the system registers.
Write Segment Status	The SSR of a descriptor can be quickly changed using this operation. The enable bit cannot be set using it, however.
Load Descriptor	With this operation, the contents of the accumulator are loaded into the descriptor pointed to by the descriptor pointer.
Transfer Descriptor	This operation transfers the contents of the selected descriptor into the accumulator.
Direct Translation	An operation to globally translate a logical address for the operating system.
Interrupt Acknowledge	An operation that supplies a vector number to the MPU in response to IACK.

The operation phase is always entered with PAD0-PAD15 in the high-impedance state and either (in the case of an operation following a normal translation) one MMU asserting $\overline{\text{HAD}}$ to hold the physical address, or (in the case of an access from the physical bus) the external processor holding the address. If both chip select and either the upper or lower data strobe is asserted or interrupt acknowledge and interrupt request in are asserted, the MMU asserts $\overline{\text{ED}}$ to enable the data transceivers.

If interrupt acknowledge and interrupt request in are asserted, an interrupt acknowledge operation is performed. If chip select and either the upper or lower data strobe is asserted, the memory management mechanism determines which operation to perform by decoding the register select lines and the read/write line. These signals tell which register is associated with the operation, which operation to perform, and whether the operation is local or global.

After each operation, data transfer acknowledge is asserted to indicate to the processor that the operation is finished. When the processor negates the data strobe, data transfer acknowledge and $\overline{\text{ED}}$ are rescinded and PAD0-PAD15 are placed in the high-impedance state. If address strobe is negated, or had been negated since the last normal translation, the MMU enters the idle state.

After the data transfer acknowledge handshake, if address strobe remains asserted and chip select and either the upper or lower data strobe is asserted, another master operation is performed. If address strobe remains asserted and $\overline{\text{GO}}$in and either the upper or lower data strobe is asserted, another slave operation is performed.

F.7.1 OPERATIONS ADDRESS MAP. Table F-3 shows the operations address map. Each system register has an address at which it can be read or written. In addition, some addresses do not correspond to a register, but rather designate an operation to be performed by reading that location.

The data strobes are logically separate and operations using both are independent. The operation ends when both data strobes are negated.

219

Address Binary RRRRRR SSSSSS 543210	Hex	Operation R	Operation W	Register or Operation
000000	00	L	G	AST 0 (Alternate, FC3 = 0)
000010	02	L	G	AST 1 (User Data)
000100	04	L	G	AST 2 (User Program)
000110	06	L	G	AST 3 (Alternate, FC3 = 0)
001000	08	L	G	AST 4 (Alternate, FC3 = 0)
001010	0A	L	G	AST 5 (Supervisor Data)
001100	0C	L	G	AST 6 (Supervisor Program)
001110	0E	L	G	AST 7 (Interrupt Acknowledge)
010000	10	L	G	AST 8 (Alternate, FC3 = 1)
010010	12	L	G	AST 9 (Alternate, FC3 = 1)
010100	14	L	G	AST 10 (Alternate, FC3 = 1)
010110	16	L	G	AST 11 (Alternate, FC3 = 1)
011000	18	L	G	AST 12 (Alternate, FC3 = 1)
011010	1A	L	G	AST 13 (Alternate, FC3 = 1)
011100	1C	L	G	AST 14 (Alternate, FC3 = 1)
011110	1E	L	G	AST 15 (Alternate, FC3 = 1)
100000	20	L	G	AC0 (LBA/Translation ADDR (MSB))
100001	21	L	G	AC1 (LAB/Translation ADDR (LSB))
100010	22	L	G	AC2 (LAM (MSB))
100011	23	L	G	AC3 (LAM (LSB))
100100	24	L	G	AC4 (PBA/Translated ADDR (MSB))
100101	25	L	G	AC5 (PBA/Translated ADDR (LSB))
100110	26	L	G	AC6 (Address Space Number)
100111	27	I	G	AC7 (Status Register)
101000	28	L	G	AC8 (Address Space Mask)
101001	29	L	G	DP (Descriptor Pointer)
101011	2B	L	G	IVR Interrupt Vector Register
101101	2D	L	G	GSR Global Status
101111	2F	L	G	LSR Local Status
110001	31	L	L	SSR Segment Status and Transfer Descriptor Operation
111001	39	L	LN	IDP Interrupt Description Pointer
111011	3B	L	LN	RDP Result Descriptor Pointer
111101	3D	G	LN	Direct Translation Operation
111111	3F	G	LN	Load Descriptor Operation
(Otherwise)		LN	LN	Null Operation

L: Local   G: Global   N: Null Operation

*RS0 is an internal signal
    If $\overline{UDS} = 0$ and $\overline{LDS} = 1 \rightarrow RS0 = 0$
    If $\overline{UDS} = 1$ and $\overline{LDS} = 0 \rightarrow RS0 = 1$
    If $\overline{UDS} = 0$ and $\overline{LDS} = 0 \rightarrow RS0 = X$
    If $\overline{UDS} = 1$ and $\overline{LDS} = 1 \rightarrow RS0 = X$

Table F-3. Register Operations Address Map

Some addresses are reserved for future expansion. Any access to an unused location will result in a null operation. If the access is a read, the appropriate byte of the data bus is driven high. If the access is a write, no side-effect occurs.

F.7.2 LOCAL OPERATIONS. Some operations, such as reading the status registers, affect only one MMU. These are called local operations. Local operations include:

Interrupt Acknowledge   Transfer Descriptor

Read System Register   Write Segment Status Register

F.7.2.1 Interrupt Acknowledge. The interrupt acknowledge operation is performed if interrupt acknowledge and interrupt request in are asserted at the beginning of the operation phase. During interrupt acknowledge, the contents of the interrupt vector register are placed on data lines D0-D7 to provide the processor with a vector number.

F.7.2.2 Read System Register. Each system register has an address at which it can be read. Each MMU should be chip selected at a different location to access the registers in each. During a processor read of the interrupt descriptor pointer, it is first loaded from the priority encoder and then gated onto data lines D0-D7.

F.7.2.3 Transfer Descriptor. In order to read the contents of a descriptor, it must be transferred into the accumulator and read from there. The descriptor pointer is first written by the processor with the number of the descriptor desired. The transfer descriptor operation is then performed by reading from the segment status register address ($31).

The contents of the selected descriptor is then transferred into the accumulator as shown in Table F-1 and the contents of the segment status register are gated onto data lines D0-D7. The descriptor registers may then be read from the accumulator.

F.7.2.4 Write Segment Status Register. The segment status register of any descriptor can be written using the descriptor pointer as a pointer. Any bit may be written except the enable bit. Enable may be cleared using this operation but it may not be set.

F.7.3 GLOBAL OPERATIONS. A global operation is one which is performed in parallel on all MMUs in the system. Global operations include:

Writes to System Registers

Load Descriptor Operation

Direct Translation

In global operation, one MMU must be the master and the rest must be slaves. The operation begins with chip select and either the upper or lower data strobe asserted on one MMU. The MMU with chip select asserted becomes the master for that operation. The master asserts $\overline{GO}$out and, upon detecting $\overline{GO}$in as true, the other MMUs become slaves in the operation.

If there is only one MMU present in the system, the $\overline{\text{ANY}}$, ALL, and $\overline{\text{GO}}$ pins must be tied to V$_{CC}$ through pull-up resistors. Global operations then become local only.

F.7.3.1 Write System Register. Each system register that can be written to is written globally. This includes: the accumulator, the address space table, the descriptor pointer, the interrupt vector register, and the local and global status registers. The operation is performed by writing to the desired register's address.

The MMU which has chip select asserted becomes the master by asserting $\overline{\text{GO}}$out. The other MMUs detect $\overline{\text{GO}}$in and become slaves. Each MMU transfers the data on the data bus to the selected register. If the write is to a byte of the accumulator, that register is marked as global. If the fault bit in the global status register is clear, local status register bits L4-L7 are also clear.

When the transfer is completed in each MMU, each will assert ALLout. After all MMUs have asserted ALLout, ALLin will be true and, upon detecting ALLin, the master rescinds $\overline{\text{GO}}$.

F.7.3.2 Load Descriptor Operation. Descriptors are loaded by transferring the contents of the accumulator to the descriptor after performing global checks for collisions. A collision exists when two or more enabled descriptors are programmed to translate the same logical address.

To prepare for descriptor loading, the accumulator must be loaded globally with the logical base address, logical address mask, address space number, and address space mask. To make global collision checks, accumulators AC6 and AC8 must have been globally loaded. If they are, the global accumulator for load bit in the local status register of each MMU is set. To initiate the operation, a read from the address $3F is done. If the load is successful, the data bus will be set to $00. If a collision is found, the load is unsuccessful and the data bus is set to $FF.

During the load descriptor operation, the MMU with chip select asserted becomes the master by asserting $\overline{\text{GO}}$out. The other MMUs detect $\overline{\text{GO}}$in and become slaves. The slave MMUs decode the operation from the register select lines, the read/write line, and the data strobes. The descriptor whose number is in the descriptor pointer is disabled (its enable bit is cleared so that it cannot cause a collision).

If the global accumulator for load bit in the global status register of a slave is clear, bits LA4-LA7 in the local status register are encoded to indicate that a load descriptor fault has occurred and $\overline{\text{ANY}}$out is asserted. If global accumulator for load is set, the slave checks the enabled descriptors against its accumulator for collisions. If a conflict is found, the slave asserts $\overline{\text{ANY}}$out and loads its result descriptor pointer with the number of the descriptor which caused the collision. If no collision is detected, bits L4-L7 in the local status register are cleared. When $\overline{\text{GO}}$in is detected, ALLout and $\overline{\text{ANY}}$out are negated and the operation ends.

The master aborts the transfer if there is a local descriptor conflict, the global accumulator for load bit is clear, or if $\overline{\text{ANY}}$in is asserted. If the failure was not local, bits L4-L7 in the local status register are cleared. Otherwise, bits L4-L7 are encoded for a load descriptor fault and $\overline{\text{ANY}}$out is asserted by the master. The master then puts $FF on data lines to indicate a failure to the processor, negates ALLout and $\overline{\text{ANY}}$out, and rescinds $\overline{\text{GO}}$out. When $\overline{\text{ANY}}$in is negated, the operation is terminated.

If there were no local collisions, its global accumulator for load bit was set, and ALLin is asserted, the master completes the transfer and enables the loaded descriptor. It then puts $00 on D0-D7 to indicate success, clears L4-L7, negates ALLout, and rescinds $\overline{\text{GO}}$out.

F.7.3.3 Direct Translations. The memory management mechanism can be used to directly translate the logical address into a physical address and make it available to the processor in the accumulator. The logical address to be translated is globally loaded into accumulator AC0-AC1 and the address space number to be used is loaded into accumulator AC6. Translation is initiated with a read from the address $3D.

If the translation is successful, the descriptor pointer and result descriptor pointer point to the descriptor which performed the translation and the physical address is loaded into accumulator AC4-AC5. The processor reads $00 from the data bus.

If the logical address could not be translated because it was globally undefined, the data bus is set to $FF to indicate the failure.

Using accumulator AC6 to supply the cycle address space number, each MMU attempts to match the logical address contained in accumulator AC0-AC1 with one of its enabled descriptors. Each MMU must have the same information in accumulator AC0, AC1, and AC6. The global accumulator for translate bit in the local status register is set if these registers have each been globally loaded.

If a match is found and global accumulator for translate bit is set, the physical address is formed as in normal translation and put into accumulator AC4-AC5. The result descriptor pointer and descriptor pointer are loaded from the priority encoder and bits L4-L7 in the local status register are encoded to indicate direct translation. The master puts $00 on data lines D0-D7 to signal that the translation was successful and rescinds $\overline{\text{GO}}$ to terminate the operation.

If no match is found, or the global accumulator for translate bit is clear, the MMU asserts ALLout and bits L4-L7 in the local status register are cleared. The master monitors the $\overline{\text{ANY}}$in and ALLin inputs.

If $\overline{\text{ANY}}$in becomes asserted, then another MMU performed the translation. The master puts $00 on data lines D0-D7 to indicate success, negates ALLout, and rescinds $\overline{\text{GO}}$out. It waits until $\overline{\text{ANY}}$in is negated before terminating the operation.

If ALLin becomes asserted, then none of the MMUs performed the translation. The master puts $FF on data lines D0-D7 to indicate failure, negates ALLout, and rescinds $\overline{\text{GO}}$out to terminate the operation. Each slave MMU negates $\overline{\text{ANY}}$out and ALLout when the master MMU rescinds $\overline{\text{GO}}$ at the end of the operation.

F.8 MMU FUNCTIONAL DESCRIPTION

The memory management mechanism is comprised of one or more memory management units. Each MMU is capable of describing thirty-two segments. If more than thirty-two segments are required in the system, more MMUs can be added to increase the number in 32-segment increments.

In order to perform its operations, some of the information in the MMU's registers must be global. That is, it must be duplicated in all the MMUs in the system. For example, the address space table must be global to ensure that the address space numbers are common to all MMUs. To allow this, certain operations are defined as global. Any system register that can be written is written globally. This includes the accumulator, the address space table, the descriptor pointer, the interrupt vector register, the global status register, and the local status register. The result descriptor pointer and the interrupt descriptor pointer are read-only and, therefore, are local and not global.

The $\overline{\text{ANY}}$, ALL, and $\overline{\text{GO}}$ signal lines are used to connect multiple MMUs to form the memory management mechanism. The memory management mechanism uses these input/output signals to communicate information between MMUs and maintain functional unity. The global operation ($\overline{\text{GO}}$) pin is used to establish the master-slave relationship between MMUs for a given operation. The $\overline{\text{ANY}}$ signal is detected as true if any MMU asserts it, allowing MMUs to report conditions that are important in even one device. The ALL signal is detected as true only if all MMUs assert it. It is used to verify that all MMUs in the system have performed some operation or are in the same state. A sample circuit diagram of a two-MMU system is shown in Figure F-7.

During each global operation, one MMU is specified as the master; all others are designated as slaves. The MMU which has its chip select asserted becomes the master by asserting the $\overline{\text{GO}}$out signal. This signals the other MMUs that they are slaves for that operation. Note that all MMUs may be accessed and, therefore, any one may be the master for a given operation.

F.8.1 MMU FUNCTIONAL STATES.

At any time, an MMU may be in one of five states:

Reset

Idle

Normal Translation

Local Operations

Global Operations

In a global operation, an MMU may be a master (if the chip select signal is asserted) or a slave (if $\overline{\text{GO}}$in is asserted). In addition, two actions can occur regardless of the current state:

1. If $\overline{\text{RESET}}$ is asserted, the Reset operation begins. The memory management mechanism will remain in the Reset state until $\overline{\text{RESET}}$ is negated.

2. $\overline{\text{IRQ}}$out is asserted if local interrupt pending bit in the local status register and interrupt enable bit in the global status register are set, otherwise it is placed in the high-impedance state and should be negated with a pullup resistor.

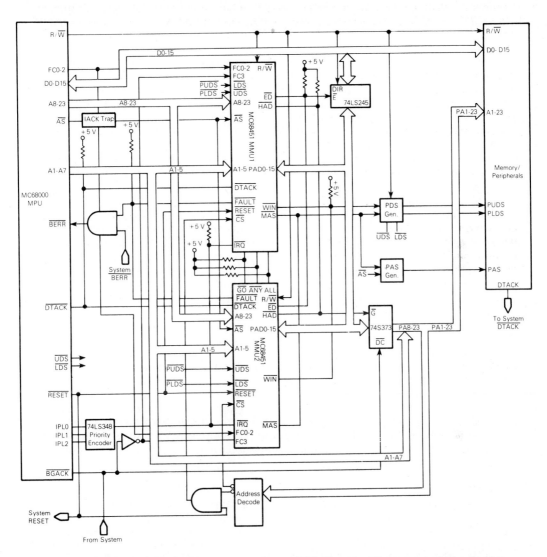

Figure F-7. Sample Circuit Diagram of a Two-MMU Memory Management Mechanism

225

F.8.1.1 Reset State. Asserting RESET will initiate the reset sequence regardless of the state of the MMU. During reset, $\overline{GO}$, data transfer acknowledge, $\overline{ED}$, $\overline{MAS}$, $\overline{HAD}$, and $\overline{WIN}$ signals are rescinded. The physical address port, $\overline{FAULT}$, and $\overline{ANY}$ lines are placed in the high-impedance state. Pullup resistors on the $\overline{FAULT}$ and $\overline{ANY}$ lines keep these signals negated. The ALL pin is driven low to negate it.

The global status register, local status register, descriptor pointer, and the entire address space table are initialized to $00. The result descriptor pointer is initialized to $80 and the interrupt vector register to $0F. All descriptors are disabled by clearing the enable bits in their segment status registers.

In order to allow the address bus to function before the operating system can initialize the memory management mechanism, one MMU is selected to have descriptor #0 initialized so that it maps any logical address unchanged to the physical address bus. The MMU is selected for this by having its chip select line asserted during Reset. This circuit is shown in the diagram in Figure F-7.

Descriptor zero in the selected MMU will have had its logical address mask and address space number cleared to $00, its address space mask set to $FF, and the enable bit set. Because of this, the logical address passes to the physical address bus (via descriptor zero) without alteration. The enable bits of descriptors 1-31 are cleared to zero to disable them and their contents remain uninitialized. If the MMU is not chip selected during reset, the enable bits in all descriptors are cleared and no descriptor is initialized.

F.8.1.2 Idle States. The idle state is used to terminate bus accesses and prepare for new ones. The MMU is "backed-off" the bus; i.e., the data transceivers are placed in the high-impedance state and the address latches are put into the transparent mode. The outputs are driven to the same levels as in reset except that $\overline{HAD}$ is rescinded one-half clock after $\overline{MAS}$ to provide address hold time.

While in the idle state, the MMU uses the function code inputs to index into the address space table to provide the cycle address space number. If address strobe is asserted, a normal translation is performed. If address strobe is negated and chip select, interrupt acknowledge, interrupt request in, $\overline{GO}$, and the data strobes indicate an access from the physical bus, an operation is performed.

F.8.2 NORMAL ADDRESS TRANSLATION. At the start of a bus cycle, the processor presents the logical address, read/write signal, and the function code to the memory management mechanism. The function code is used to index into the address space table to select the cycle address space number. When address strobe is asserted, the normal translation phase begins by sending the cycle address space number, the logical address, and the read/write signal to each descriptor for matching.

NOTE

The function codes must be valid before address strobe is asserted to allow for the table lookup. Current versions of the MC68000 provide this setup time; however, early mask set (R9M, T6E) do not. With these early mask sets, address strobe must be delayed to the MMU.

F.8.2.1 Matching. Matches can occur in two areas: range and space.

A range match occurs if, in each bit position in the logical address mask which is set, the incoming logical address matches the logical base address.

A space match occurs if, in each bit position in the address space mask which is set, the cycle address space number matches the address space number.

F.8.2.2 Translation. An address match occurs if there is a range match and a space match. A write violation occurs if a write is attempted to a write-protected segment. If there is an address match in a descriptor and no write violation, the physical address is formed from the physical base address of that descriptor and the logical address. The logical address is passed through in those bit positions in the logical address mask which are clear (the "don't cares"). In the other bit positions, the physical base address is gated out to the physical address bus.

The used and, if the cycle was a write, the modified bits in the segment status register are set. If the interrupt bit is set, then the interrupt pending bit is set. $\overline{WIN}$ is asserted if the write protect bit is set and the cycle was a read or a read-modify-write. If the cycle was a write, $\overline{MAS}$ is not asserted to prevent the write from modifying data.

After the physical address is stable, $\overline{MAS}$ is asserted to indicate a valid address is on the bus. $\overline{HAD}$ is asserted to hold the address stable on the latches and the PAD0-PAD15 lines are then placed in the high-impedance state. If address strobe is then negated, the cycle has terminated and the MMU returns to the idle state. If address strobe is not negated, the cycle can continue in three ways:

1. Chip select or interrupt acknowledge and interrupt request in are asserted, the MMU will begin an operation as a master.
2. If $\overline{GO}$in is detected by an MMU it will begin a slave operation.
3. If a high-to-low transition is detected on the read/write line, indicating a write, address strobe remains asserted and the matched segment is write protected, a write violation occurs. This would be the result of a read/modify/write bus cycle on a protected segment.

F.8.2.2.1 WRITE VIOLATION. If an address match occurs but the bus cycle was a write to a write protected segment, a write violation occurs. In this case, the result descriptor pointer is loaded from the priority encoder, the fault bit is set in the global status register, and the double fault bit is set if the fault bit was previously set. The state of the read/write line is latched into the read/write bit of the local status register and bits L4-L7 are encoded to indicate write violation. The $\overline{FAULT}$out signal is then asserted for five clock cycles or until address strobe is negated, whichever is greater.

The logical address is latched into AC0 (MSB) and AC1 (LSB) of the accumulator. The cycle address space number is latched into AC6. These registers are marked as non-global with respect to the global accumulator for translate and global accumulator for load bits. If the $\overline{FAULT}$ pin has been connected to the bus error pin on the MC68000, address strobe will be negated as the processor begins the bus error exception processing. When address strobe is negated, the MMU will enter the idle state.

F.8.2.2.2 NO ADDRESS MATCH. If none of the descriptors in a MMU has an address match, that MMU asserts ALLout and monitors $\overline{\text{MAS}}$in, $\overline{\text{FAULT}}$in, and ALLin. There are then three possibilities:

1. The access was successfully translated in another MMU.

2, The access caused a write violation in another MMU.

3. The access was to a globally undefined segment.

F.8.2.3 External Translation. If $\overline{\text{MAS}}$in becomes asserted, the access was successfully translated by another MMU. The MMU negates ALLout and prepares to end the normal translation phase. The cycle can then continue in one of three ways:

1. If address strobe becomes negated, the MMU returns to the idle state.

2. If chip select, or interrupt acknowledge and interrupt request in are asserted, the MMU begins an operation as a master.

3. If $\overline{\text{GO}}$in is detected true, the MMU begins an operation as a slave.

F.8.2.3.1 EXTERNAL WRITE VIOLATION. If the $\overline{\text{FAULT}}$in line is detected true (low), a write violation occurred in another MMU. The detecting MMU then sets the fault bit in the global status register and the double fault bit if the fault bit was already set. Read/write line state is latched into the read/write bit of the local status register and bits L4-L7 are cleared to show that the violation did not take place in this MMU. The cycle can then continue in one of the three ways described in paragraph F.8.2.3.

F.8.2.3.2 UNDEFINED SEGMENT ACCESS. If ALLin is detected true (high), none of the other MMUs in the system obtained a match, indicating the segment is globally undefined. The MMU sets the fault bit in the global status register and the double fault bit if fault bit was set previously. Read/write line state is latched into the read/write bit of the local status register and bits L4-L7 are encoded to show an undefined segment access.

The logical address is latched into the accumulator, AC0 (MSB) and AC1 (LSB) and the cycle address space number is latched into AC6. These registers are marked non-global with respect to the global accumulator for load and global accumulator for translate bits.

All MMUs assert the $\overline{\text{FAULT}}$ line for five clock periods or until address strobe is negated, whichever is longer. To assure the detection of ALLin by all MMUs, ALLout remains asserted for two clock cycles after ALLin is detected true. ALLout is negated before the beginning of the $\overline{\text{FAULT}}$ pulse. When address strobe is negated, the memory management mechanism returns to the idle state.

F.9 SOFTWARE CONSIDERATIONS

F.9.1 SEGMENT MAPPING EXAMPLE. In constructing segments, the size of a given segment is determined by the logical address mask. Although there are no constraints on which bits are significant, one approach is to allow only contiguous, low order zeroes ("don't care"). With this constraint, if there are N zeroes, the size of the segment is

2(8 + N) bytes. Since the seven low-order address lines bypass the MMU, the smallest possible segment is 128 words (256 bytes).

In the logical address space, a segment defined this way extends from the address formed by the logical base address with zeroes in the "don't care" positions in the logical address mask to the address formed by the logical base address with ones in the "don't care" bit positions. In the physical address space, the segment extends from the address formed by the physical base address with zeroes in the "don't care" bit positions in the logical address mask to the address formed with ones in the "don't care" positions.

Figure F-8 shows an example memory map. In this example, the map has been divided between two users and the operating system. The user tasks each have three segments: A, B, and C. The operating system also has three segments: O, V, and R.

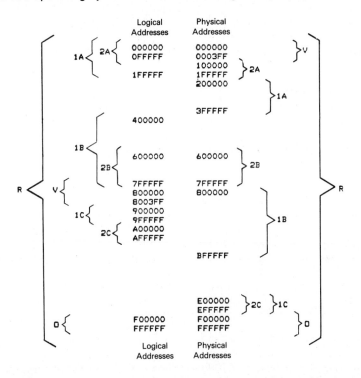

Segment	R	V	O	1A	1B	2C	2A	2B	2C
Logical Base Address (LBA)	0000	8000	F000	0000	7FFF	9000	0000	7FFF	A000
Logical Address Mask (LAM)	0000	FFFC	F000	E000	C000	F000	F000	E000	F000
Physical Base Address (PBA)	0000	0000	F000	2000	BFFF	E000	1000	7FFF	E000
Address Space Number (ASN)	FF	80	80	01	01	01	02	02	02
Address Space Mask (ASM)	FF	80	80	7F	7F	7F	7F	7F	7F

Figure F-8. Address Map Example

Segment R maps the logical addresses unchanged to the physical address space, but only for address space number $00. This segment is automatically generated in descriptor zero in the master MMU on reset. Segments O and V also belong to the operating system and are accessed only by address space numbers with bit 7 set. This is an arbitrary assignment and need not be followed.

Segments 1A, 1B, and 1C belong to user number one, and are accessed by address space numbers $01 and $81. User 1 would be assigned address space number $01 and the operating system would use $81 to access those segments. A parallel situation exists with user 2.

Note that segments 1A and 2A are isolated from each other even though they share the same logical addresses. User 1 is prevented from accessing the same memory as user 2 because his address space number does not match segment 2A. Segments can overlap in physical memory, however, as 1C and 2C do here.

Note the manner in which segments 1B and 2B are defined. Here the logical and physical base addresses are considered to be the top of the segment rather than the bottom. This is useful in describing push-down, pop-up stacks which grow towards low memory. The same segment can be described in the other way also. An alternate descriptor for segment 1B is given below.

Descriptor	1B
Logical Base Address	$4000
Logical Address Mask	$C000
Physical Base Address	$8000
Address Space Number	$01
Address Space Mask	$7F

F.9.2 SEGMENTATION. Since segment sizes must be multiples of two, multiple descriptors can be used to map a segment of non-binary size. For example, a segment of 70K bytes could be constructed using two descriptors: one of 64K bytes and one of 8K bytes, losing 2K bytes to internal fragmentation. A purely binary system would allocate 128K bytes, wasting 62K bytes.

F.9.3 PAGING. If each segment is the same size, a paged system could be implemented. The used and modified bits in the segment status registers allow a variety of placement algorithms and the use of virtual memory.

The memory management mechanism supports virtual processing. The 16 bits of the logical address, the cycle address space number, and the state of the read/write lines are latched during a $\overline{\text{FAULT}}$ to provide enough information for an auxiliary processor to fix a page fault.

F.9.4 INITIALIZATION SOFTWARE. After a reset (power-on or processor initiated), the master MMU (the MMU for which chip select was asserted during reset) will map the logical addresses unchanged into the physical address space using descriptor zero. This will allow the processor to fetch its supervisor stack and program counter (if it was a power-on reset) and begin executing the operating system initialization routine. See the MC68000 Data Sheet for more information.

The operating system would then set up descriptors for itself and system resources (such as the MMU). To enable a descriptor, the operating system loads the descriptor number in the descriptor pointer register, and the logical base address, logical address mask, physical base address, address space number, and address space mask into the accumulator.

The processor then reads from the appropriate physical address to begin the loading operation. The memory management mechanism globally checks for conflicts and loads and enables the descriptor if none are found. As a result of the read, the processor gets a status byte in the low byte of the word. The status will read $00 if the load was successful and $FF if there was a conflict. If a conflict occurred, the result descriptor pointer can be used to find the highest priority conflicting descriptor.

A descriptor can be quickly disabled by writing to its segment status register. The interrupt and write protect bits can be programmed and the used and modified bits can be cleared, but the enable bit can only be set by a load descriptor operation.

Descriptors would then be set up for the user tasks and a task would be selected to execute. Address space table entries AST1 and AST2 would then be loaded with the address space number of the task to be run. These are the address spaces for user data and user program in the MC68000. The program counter and status register to be used by the task are then pushed onto the system stack. The processor then executes an RTE instruction which fetches the status register and program counter off the stack. The status register should have had the supervisor state bit cleared so that the processor will enter the user state and its accesses are then mapped through AST1 and AST2 to start the user task.

To return to the operating system from a user task, a watchdog timer could be used to interrupt the processor. The exception processing caused by this would switch the processor to the supervisor state and the supervisor address spaces would be mapped by the operating systems descriptors.

F.9.5 CONTEXT SWITCHING. Switching the MMU from one user task to the other is very efficient. Suppose two user tasks were present in memory and the processor had returned to the operating system as described above. To switch tasks, the operating system would change AST1 and AST2 to the address space number of the user task which it wished to execute. It would then push the new status register and program counter on the stack and execute an RTE.

Switching between two supervisor tasks is more complex. If AST5 and AST6 are changed while the processor is in the supervisor state, subsequent accesses are immediately mapped through the new address space. A Move Multiple (MOVEM) instruction using the predecrement mode followed by an illegal instruction can be executed to perform the switch. The processor fetches the MOVEM and the illegal instruction, alters AST6 and AST5 (data entry last), then traps through the illegal instruction routine to the new supervisor task. A flag (possibly the illegal instruction opcode) is used to distinguish between normal illegal instructions and attempts to switch tasks in this matter.

Another method is to have a task in the user space perform the switch. The supervisor stack pointer is set up, the processor alerts the status register to put itself in the user state, AST5 and AST6 are changed, and the processor traps to the supervisor task.

NOTES

NOTES

NOTES

NOTES

Leslie
996-4205